THE CRAZY GOLF PRO

MY JOURNEY WITH BIPOLAR DISORDER

DON WALIN

Tellwell Talent
www.tellwell.ca

ISBN
978-0-2288-2086-4 (Hardcover)
978-0-2288-2085-7 (Paperback)
978-0-2288-2087-1 (eBook)

DISCLAIMER

This book is a memoir. It is a work of non-fiction. It is a true story. The characters and events are real. The names of some individuals have been changed to respect their privacy. For the most part I have used real names. I have tried to be as accurate as possible with my memories of the people and events described in this book. It is not my intention to hurt anyone's feelings. I am a very honest person, and my honesty is portrayed throughout my story.

DEDICATION

I dedicate this book to my wife, Elli, the true love of my life.
Also, to my good friend, Jack Thomson, who passed away in January 2020.
And to all of my comrades who are living with mental illness.

TABLE OF CONTENTS

INTRODUCTION

The main premise of my book is about my life playing golf and being a member of the Canadian Professional Golfers' Association (CPGA), my battle with severe mental illness (manic depression/bipolar disorder), my experiences with the spirit world and the ultimate love story. In the end, it's a success story.

Along with bipolar disorder, I also have obsessive-compulsive disorder (OCD) and seasonal affective disorder (SAD). I call this "my mental hat trick." I find it helpful to have a sense of humor about these things, and I hope my book will give some insight into living with three mental illnesses.

I have always been pretty transparent. I'm open and honest. I'm a down-to-earth kind of guy. What you see is what you get. My book is a very honest account of my life story (so far).

I grew up in the small town of Wetaskiwin, Alberta, during the 1970s. I played an immense amount of hockey and golf there. I had a lot of passion for these sports. I started playing golf at age seven.

In 1986, I graduated from the San Diego Golf Academy where I received a diploma in golf operations and management. In 1987, I achieved my childhood dream by becoming a CPGA Golf Professional. In 1993, I accomplished my goal of becoming a head golf professional. I met a lot of people through the great game of golf, which includes some "celebrities." I was fortunate enough to meet and spend some time with some NHL hockey players from the Edmonton Oilers such as Mark Messier, Dave Semenko, Ron Chipperfield and coach Ted Green. Chris Chelios and Mike Mohler are a couple of other NHL players I can add to my list of "name dropping." I met some of these guys during the 1980s when I was living in Edmonton and working at the Windermere Golf & Country Club. It was also the era that Wayne Gretzky and the Edmonton Oilers were in the process of winning five Stanley Cups.

My nickname was "The Rock Star" back in those days. Sex, drugs and rock 'n roll. And drinking. A lot of drinking. Too much. These things were a major part of my lifestyle. My friends and I really did have a lot of fun in those days. I became very honest with myself regarding my drinking and became a self-diagnosed alcoholic. I quit drinking in 1994 and have been a sober alcoholic for twenty-six years now (except for two occasions). I am very candid about my drinking in my story. I ended up in jail on a few occasions because of alcohol-related incidents. Overcoming alcoholism was another obstacle along my life journey.

This book is for anyone who has an interest in manic depression (bipolar disorder). I wrote this for individuals living with this mental illness, as well as their families, friends and loved ones. I have become quite experienced with this mood disorder, and I would like to use my experience to help others. I also explain what it's like for me to have OCD.

When I was first diagnosed in 1989 it was called manic depression. Today, it is more commonly called bipolar disorder. I like the phrase manic depression better because it describes this mental illness more accurately. It is what it says. I interchange these two phrases throughout this book, but they mean the same thing.

Manic depression is a major mood disorder. It is a chemical imbalance in the brain. When imbalanced, people like me experience major highs and lows. During these times, we get into states of mania and depression. The severities of these states differ among individuals. My case was severe.

During the first ten years of my illness (1989-1999), I was hospitalized in psychiatric wards ten times (nine times for manic episodes and once for severe depression). I was almost always committed, which means I was kept there against my will. Sometimes I was kept in a locked ward.

I have written about "spirituality" in this book, however, I'm not trying to convince anyone about what they should or shouldn't believe. All I ask is for you to have an open mind. I am not a religious person and am not affiliated with any type of religion. Because of what I have experienced, I consider myself a "spiritual person."

For the majority of my manic episodes, I thought I was Jesus Christ. During my last manic episode, I thought I was both God and Jesus. At the same time, I always knew that I was still "Don Walin." When manic, I would sense people's spirits/souls coming from within them. Usually, this was a peaceful, loving feeling; it was good, positive energy. I also sensed the spirit of God many times while I was in a state of mania. God also "appeared" to me in/through people. God's energy was profound. It encompassed many traits and qualities. Most of all, I could feel his unconditional love, compassion and understanding. His presence was undeniable to me.

In almost all of my manic states, I sensed the presence of the devil (a.k.a. Lucifer or Satan) in/through people. The devil also "appeared" to me this way five times when I was in a "normal" mood state.

I'm not the only person to think they were Jesus Christ or God when in a state of mania, although this is quite rare. I've come up with my own theory as to why myself and others have experienced this phenomenon. We might not be as crazy as most people would think in this regard.

Psychiatrists diagnosed me as being "delusional" (having false beliefs), "psychotic" (out of touch with reality) and in a "state of psychosis" because of my spiritual experiences. Basically, they would lock me up in a psych ward and give me these incredibly powerful antipsychotic medications such as Thorazine, Haldol, Risperdal or Clozapine. These harsh psych meds had severe side effects, such as muscle tightness. While on Thorazine, I could barely walk at all. I shuffled my feet as if I was 100 years old. They kept me on these horrific psych meds until I wasn't "sensing the spirit world" anymore. My average stay in these psych wards was about five to six weeks. My last one was for about three months.

Psychiatrists are kind of like scientists in that they want "proof" of something in order to believe in it or not. As far as I know, there is no way to prove whether God or the devil exists. In my experience, psychiatrists either wouldn't discuss their spiritual beliefs with me or were very skeptical in this regard. Many psychiatrists simply don't believe God exists at all. (This might apply to the spirit world in general.) If God really does exist and a psychiatrist doesn't believe it, this should be deemed a "false belief," making the psychiatrist delusional!

On the flip side of mania is depression. After every one of my manic episodes, I would suffer from a depressed episode. I would be severely depressed for an average of about eight or nine months. During this time, I thought about committing suicide constantly. Fifty percent of the people with manic depression try to commit suicide at least once. Fifteen percent are successful.

What really sucks is when you get depressed for no good reason. I would say that's the way it was for me at least ninety percent of the time. My depressions were caused by a chemical imbalance in my brain, just like my mania, except with opposite symptoms.

The good news is that people don't have to suffer like I did. In my book, I have a lot of advice for people regarding their mental health. When balanced, people with this illness can do very well and live a normal life.

There is still a lot of stigma towards mental illness, and most of it stems from ignorance. People need to be educated in this regard, and I'm hoping to do my small part by writing this book. Some people think that having a mental illness is a "weakness," that we are weak, feeble people. This, too, is ignorance. These people don't realize the strength and courage it takes to battle through mental illness. They haven't had to climb out of the abyss like we have. They have no idea what we've been through, how difficult it can be and how hard we've had to fight to overcome our demons. Try to walk a mile in our shoes before you judge us. Personally, I had to fight my way through what felt like a tsunami of depressions. It took every ounce of my strength to not even attempt suicide. My manic episodes were extremely difficult as well.

There is a lot of truth in "What doesn't kill you makes you stronger." Overall, my life has been quite a ride. I have put my heart and soul into this book. My life has been an emotional roller coaster, but I have been doing quite well for over twenty years.

The main reason I wrote this book is to give hope and inspiration to as many people as possible. I hope you will find my story informative, educational, inspirational, humorous and most of all, enjoyable!

CHAPTER 1
MY FIRST MANIC EPISODE

Wednesday, June 4, 1989, was the night "it" started. I was three days from turning twenty-five. It was my third year as a member of the Canadian Professional Golfers' Association (CPGA), and I was working in the pro shop at Glen Meadows Golf & Country Club in Sidney, British Columbia, from 2-10 p.m. Everything up to about 8:30 was normal, just another routine day at the golf course. I was alone with the exception of a couple of kids working in the back of the shop, cleaning clubs. This guy walks into the pro shop and says, "Hi, you must be Don." I didn't have a clue who he was. He appeared to be in his early thirties, had sandy blonde hair and these beautiful blue eyes. He was athletically built and very good looking. No, I am not gay in case you might be thinking so.

"YYYYeeesss…" I said curiously.

"Hi, my name is Kelly Murray. You are giving my cousin Shannon Toby golf lessons."

I couldn't believe it! Kelly Murray was a very well-known Canadian Tour player who was especially famous for hitting long drives up to 350 yards! We talked for a few minutes and hit it off immediately. He told me he had just arrived from Vancouver where he had performed in a long drive exhibition. He was playing in the Victoria Open at the prestigious Uplands Golf Club in the morning.

Kelly wanted to hit a few balls on the driving range on the eve of the tournament. I asked him if he would prefer to play a few holes instead, so he decided to do that. I gave him a key to a power cart and off he went by himself to the 10th tee.

"Watch this," I said to the kids in the back shop, "this guy can hit it a mile!"

Kelly did just that. I couldn't see exactly how far that ball went, but the clubhead speed he generated during his swing was amazing.

About an hour later, Kelly walked back into the pro shop and thanked me. It was dark by then. I was in the process of cashing out, then had to vacuum and do the other usual closing procedures. Kelly asked if I wanted to join him for a beer upstairs in the lounge. I told him I would finish closing up and meet him in 15-20 minutes.

We had a few beers in the lounge while he was trying to get hold of a friend who was supposed to caddy for him in the morning. I told him if his buddy wasn't able to caddy, that I could. His tee time was 8:00 a.m., and I didn't have to work until 2:00. Kelly couldn't make contact with his friend, so we agreed that I would caddy for him.

He was going to stay at his aunt's house in Victoria, but after drinking beer for a couple hours I suggested that he just spend the night at my place. I owned a half duplex in Sidney, five minutes from the club, and didn't think it would be a good idea to drive a half hour to Victoria. Kelly accepted my offer.

By this time, we were on a bit of a roll and having a great time! We were back at my place, laughing, telling stories and just really hitting it off and having a lot of fun. We just kept drinking beer and talking, and I guess we lost track of time.

All of a sudden, it was 3:00 a.m.

We were talking about people in the golf industry that we both might know. When I mentioned Doug Lecuyer from Edmonton, a former NHL player for the Chicago Blackhawks in the 1980s and a CPGA Golf Professional, it turned out Kelly knew him. I could be very spontaneous, especially when I was drinking, so I said, "You know Doug? Really? Well, let's call him right now!" With the time difference, it was 4:00 a.m. in Edmonton. Obviously, this was a very inconsiderate time to call someone, but I did a lot of stupid things when I was drunk. Anyway, we both spoke with Doug, and I must say he was a really good sport about it!

At 4:00 a.m., we decided it was best to get some sleep, as he had to tee off in four hours. I set him up in my living room where he would be comfortable.

To the best of my memory, my behavior was normal until something flicked a switch in my brain. Instead of going to my bedroom and getting some sleep like I should have, I grabbed my CPGA appointment book, sat on a chair beside Kelly and wrote like a madman. I was making all these notes, sketches and diagrams. Unfortunately, this book got thrown out somewhere along the way, many years ago. I wish I still had it as this was the very first time I wrote when I was in a manic state.

I finally went upstairs to bed at 5:00 a.m. We both got up at six to get ready, and I mentioned I had stayed up another hour taking notes. He said he knew. He must have thought I was pretty strange. This was almost surely confirmed over the rest of the day!

We hopped in his car and left my place around 6:30 a.m. We stopped at a restaurant for breakfast on the way and arrived at Uplands a half hour before his tee time.

I was so excited! Here I was hanging out with Kelly Murray and caddying for him in a Canadian Tour event. There were professional golfers from all over the world — Jack Nicklaus Jr., Guy Boros, Rick Gibson and other big names were there. At one point, Al Balding, Kelly and I were standing on the practice green talking golf. Al Balding is in the Canadian Sports Hall of Fame and the Canadian Golf Hall of Fame. I had only heard of him, never met him. This conversation with just the three of us was a special moment for me.

I was really into this caddying job and on a natural high. Unbeknownst to me, I was showing symptoms of mental illness for the first time. I didn't have a clue that I was becoming progressively more manic as the day went along.

There was a fair number of spectators, and Kelly was kind of a crowd favorite. I remember him kibitzing and laughing with them. He was trying his best, but we had some fun too. I think he shot 36 or 37 on the front nine.

I thought I would be finished around 12:30 p.m. and have plenty of time to get back to Glen Meadows to start my 2:00 p.m. shift, but it was now looking more like I'd be an hour late if I caddied the whole 18. I went to the pro shop between nines to call my boss, Doug Mahovlic, the head pro at Glen Meadows, and ask him if it was OK. I had worked many overtime hours for him without any overtime pay, but I still knew what his answer was going to be.

"No, you can't!" he said.

"I quit," I said.

This decision was based on several factors. Doug was not exactly my favorite person. It was like walking on eggshells when he was around; I never knew what kind of mood he would be in or what he would say to me. We had a couple of "run-ins" with each other, and I'd had enough. Another factor was that I was becoming more and more manic and beginning to lose my insight and ability to make reasonable, sound and logical judgments and decisions. I had no other job or income. I owned a half duplex with mortgage payments with two roommates to worry about. These things didn't enter my mind at the time.

After my phone call, I caught up with Kelly on the 10th hole. "How did your phone call go?" he asked me.

"No problem at all!" I replied. "I can finish caddying for you and go to work later."

I didn't want to tell him what really happened as I was worried it would throw him off his game.

That day was a lot of fun for me. I didn't know the Uplands Golf Club very well and had only played there a couple of times myself, so was unable to give Kelly much help with "course management" or strategy. He probably knew the course much better than I did. I couldn't help him much with club selection either, as this was the first time I had seen him play and didn't know how far he hit his irons. Mainly, I just carried his bag and helped him read his putts.

The spectators loved watching Kelly launch balls off the tee. It was like John Daly or Tiger Woods cranking the ball 350 yards down the fairway. Kelly was also very creative with his shot making. He seemed to have quite an imagination. Both of these traits are essential if you want to become a good player.

After Thursday's round, we were walking towards the parking lot when we passed by the media station covering the tournament. There was a TV truck there, and Kelly told me to go into the trailer and talk with the crew. Without giving it a second thought, I walked right in there. The crew looked at me and asked if they could help me. I told them Kelly told me to go in there.

"I just wanted to say hello," I said.

They told me I shouldn't be in there, so I apologized and left. I searched for Kelly in the parking lot but couldn't find him. I felt a little dejected and perplexed, but with my mania escalating, it didn't slow me down for long.

Looking back with a healthy mind, it's pretty obvious that Kelly told me to go into that TV truck so he could lose me, and it worked. I don't blame him. I was becoming extremely "entrepreneurial" thinking, coming up with a number of grandiose business ideas and sharing them with Kelly so we could partner up. I had only just become acquainted with him. I'm sure he wasn't thinking I had bipolar disorder and was going into a manic state. No, he probably just thought I was strange.

I said a very quick "Hello" to him a couple of years later at the Alberta Open at the Wolf Creek Golf Course in Ponoka. I don't know if he recognized me or not. I haven't spoken to or seen Kelly since then.

It amazes my wife, Elli, my family and friends at how clearly I can recall my manic episodes. I usually remember things better than they can! My bipolar friends remember their manic episodes with great clarity as well. The only time I get really disoriented and lose my memory is when I am hospitalized in a psychiatric facility and am put on psychiatric medications to stop my mania. Some of these meds are extremely powerful, and I don't remember much of anything after taking them. This was especially true for some of my earliest admissions to psych wards from 1989 to about the mid-1990s. During these earlier admissions, they dispensed immensely powerful psych meds such as Thorazine and Haldol. I hated those drugs! They had terrible side effects. At times, I was so heavily sedated I couldn't walk without assistance. Fortunately, prescription drug treatment is much better these days and there is a wide range of effective options available, many with less severe side effects.

Once I realized Kelly had taken off, I got into a van that was shuttling players, media and tournament officials around town. I had the driver drop me off in downtown Victoria. My destination was Aaron's, a nice restaurant with an outdoor patio facing the inner harbor. I loved going there on a day off, sitting on the patio with a friend, having a few cold beers on a warm, sunny day and enjoying the spectacular view of the harbor along the Pacific Ocean. I loved looking at all kinds of boats, sailboats and amazing yachts drifting in and out and docked at the marina.

Aaron's was owned by Sam Vine at the time, and some of the pro shop staff from Glen Meadows frequented the establishment. Sam always treated us very well with great hospitality, service, food and drinks. It was early afternoon and a table of women were sitting beside me on the patio drinking and carrying on. After a few beers I had a pretty good jag going, so I started socializing with them. By 8:00 p.m., all but one of them had left.

I had participated in some risky sexual behavior ever since I was very young, especially when I was drunk, but "manic promiscuity" can be even worse. It can result in extremely negative, very serious consequences. So, here I am with this woman having joined me at my table. I'm getting pretty loaded and things were good! I was in my glory! The next thing I knew, the two of us were planning to go back to her place. It was pretty obvious that sex was on the menu. Then, I changed the plan. I asked her if she would go home and dress in something "very provocative," and then we would go to a nightclub together. I'm not sure exactly how much of this request was due to my natural "crazy" nature and the fact that I was drunk, or the fact that I was increasingly manic. Probably a combination of the two.

At any rate, she seemed to like this idea and complied without hesitation. She went home by herself and came back wearing a pretty revealing outfit. I definitely had sex on my mind! Throughout the evening, however, I lost interest. We didn't hook up, and I have a vague memory of leaving Aaron's by myself.

I ended up alone at a nightclub called Merlin's in downtown Victoria. I started to feel like I needed to get something healthy into my system, so I ordered four "healthy" drinks from the waitress: a glass of water and three cocktails. A Screwdriver is vodka and orange juice, so I got some fruit. A Caesar has clamato, so that was healthy, and I dusted those off with a Paralyzer — vodka, Kahlua, cola and milk (for a shot of dairy)!

I lined up the drinks in front of me and took a drink of one, then the next and the next. My intentions were good, but obviously a lack of reasoning and insight because of my manic state contributed to these "healthy" choices! The rest of the evening is a blank.

My next memory is in a hotel room Friday morning. I didn't know which hotel, but it turned out to be on the inner harbor. I think I was the first one up that morning (if I had had any sleep at all). There were golf clubs in the room, so I got a putter and some balls and started putting on the carpet in the room. Other people started to get up, and I quickly realized I was in a hotel room with a couple of Canadian Tour players. I had no clue as to how or when I arrived there. It's a little foggy, but I believe one of my roommates was Kevin Leach, the #1 qualifier for the Canadian Tour Spring Qualifying School that was held at Glen Meadows just prior to the Victoria Open. He was an extremely good player and accomplished golfer. I had never met Kevin previous to this encounter. I must have run into him or his roommate at the nightclub and somehow ended up back at their hotel room. I really have no idea how I got there.

I borrowed an extra large, yellow golf shirt with "Southwestern Intercollegiate Invitational - North Ranch C.C." on it from Kevin. I still have it! Kevin wouldn't believe this! Although I haven't worn it for many years, I have kept it all this time as a souvenir of my first manic episode. After breakfast at the hotel restaurant the guys went to the golf course, and I stayed back at the hotel for a while.

At one point, I saw Canadian golf legend Dan Halldorson checking in at the front desk. Dan played on the PGA Tour for several years, as well as the Canadian Tour, and is one of the best golfers that has ever come from Canada. My memory is that he walked into the hotel lobby carrying a nice sized salmon. He must have taken advantage of his Vancouver Island trip by going fishing while he was there for the Victoria Open. I had never met Dan, but some good friends of mine knew Dan quite well from their time in Manitoba together. I thought I would take advantage of this opportunity by introducing myself as a good friend of the McDonalds.

When I am in a manic state, I am the opposite of shy. I usually have no fear and have all the confidence in the world. I feel like there is nothing I can't do. So, I introduced myself. He wasn't very warm or receptive towards me. Granted, he was busy checking in at the time, and I was very manic, so he may have thought that I was just some strange idiot.

That afternoon, I somehow ended up at Gorge Vale Golf Club in Victoria. I was with one other guy, whom I believe was a Canadian Tour player. I don't remember his name, where he was from or any other details other than the two of us ended up playing golf together. That was the first time I played golf when I was manic, and what an experience that was! Everything was done at breakneck speed. I had the power cart pinned the whole time. I played incredibly fast and was generating some pretty serious clubhead speed.

Overall, my golf game that day simulated my state of mind: out of control. At the same time, it was a hell of a lot of fun! I think we only played nine holes.

After we left Gorge Vale, we toured downtown Victoria in his Jeep looking for cocaine, which was the last thing I needed. This must have been his idea because I was never into cocaine. I did try it a few times, but it was never something I would go out looking for. We never found any, which was a good thing.

At about 7:00 p.m. we arrived at The Keg, a restaurant and bar in Victoria. We sat down at a table, and I immediately saw camera flashes going off in the restaurant. I couldn't see who was taking the pictures, but I thought they were taking pictures of me. I was euphoric. All of these flashes for me! I felt like a famous celebrity. Turns out this was my first delusion — a false belief that is a common symptom of mania in a person who has bipolar disorder. My delusions became much more grandiose in subsequent manic episodes. Psychiatrists call these "delusions of grandeur."

The tour player I was with left after a short while. I don't think we ate anything. We just had a couple of drinks. I ended up in The Keg bar by myself, and the place was packed. I was in serious party mode by this time. Around 8:00, I ran into a good friend and co-worker from Glen Meadows, Scott Dickson. Scott was an assistant golf pro and was with his girlfriend, Wendy. I'm not sure if I called Scott to come and join me at The Keg, or if I just ran into them by coincidence. I do know that when I met up with them, I was going a million miles an hour. Scott and Wendy tried their best to slow me down and help me, but by this time it was too late. I was majorly manic, and nothing was going to stop me. My insight, reasoning, common sense and logic were pretty much absent.

They wanted me to go back to Wendy's place. They just wanted me to try and relax, rest and try to get some sleep. Wendy even told me she had some type of medication that would help me sleep. I thought, "Sleep? Forget it!" That was the last thing I wanted to do! When a person is manic, they can go for several days with little or no sleep. I'm pretty sure I ended up at another pub by myself, and I stayed until it closed around 2:30 a.m. Then I walked the downtown streets of Victoria.

I came across a prostitute standing on a street corner and tried to negotiate a deal with her whereby she would come back to Sidney with me and spend the rest of the night. I had never paid for the services of a prostitute in my life, but for some strange reason I felt very lonely and wanted some female company. I wanted her companionship and to have someone to talk with, but I was looking to get laid as well. I didn't have any money on me, so I told her I had the money at home.

She noticed I was wearing a nice diamond ring and asked me if she could see it. I handed it to her, and the next thing I knew she was running away with my ring! I chased her, but she quickly went around the corner and jumped into a taxi. Before I could get there, the taxi drove away. It was almost like they had it planned. I stood on the corner dumbfounded. This ring was from my ex-girlfriend, Linda.

I continued to walk the downtown streets of Victoria until the sun rose on an absolutely gorgeous, clear, blue-skied morning. At about 6 a.m., I was walking down one of the main streets with a lot of stores and businesses on it. There were artists set up and painting and drawing already, so I stopped to look at their work. I came across a restaurant and saw there were quite a few people inside. I went in. I noticed an elderly lady sitting by herself in the back. For some reason, I was drawn to her like a magnet, so I walked to her table. I can't remember what I said to initiate our conversation, but I ended up asking her if I could join her. She welcomed me open-heartedly. She made me feel very comfortable. She had the most beautiful blue eyes. I'm guessing that she may have been in her 70s. For all these years I have remembered this lady's name as "Dorothy Greenwood." For the context of my story, I will apply her name as such.

When I met Dorothy, I was pretty fucked up. I had been missing for two days, and my family and friends had no idea where I was. I had quit my job, and I was losing my mind. After talking with Dorothy for a while, she asked if I wanted to come back to her place to rest. I accepted her offer, and we walked about three blocks to her apartment complex.

Dorothy told me that her husband, Frank, had died a couple of years ago, but "he still came back to visit her" on a pretty regular basis. This didn't scare me, but it certainly got my attention! Anyway, there wasn't a visit from Frank when I was there, which was a good thing considering the state I was in.

I sat on the patio and enjoyed the beautiful morning while Dorothy fixed me something to eat. I was actually feeling euphoric — another symptom of mania. After relaxing and visiting for about two hours, Dorothy asked me if I would like to have a bath. I said, "Sure, that would be nice." She went ahead and prepared my bath water for me. When it was ready, I went into the bathroom, took off my clothes and stepped into the bath. As soon as my body touched the water, I got the shock of my life! I felt this major electric current zip from the top of my head down to my toenails. I was out of that water in a split second. It scared the living shit out of me!

The shock had nothing to do with the temperature of the bath water — it was perfect — but I blamed Dorothy. Somehow, I thought she had caused this — that maybe she was evil or something. I freaked out and started yelling and screaming and swearing at her. I got dressed as fast as I could and wanted to leave as quickly as possible. She calmed me down and made me realize that she wasn't evil or wasn't trying to harm me in any way. I remember her saying, "It felt good though, didn't it?" as if somehow, she knew I would get this shock. It felt more like a mini lightning bolt — not good.

I would have this same experience at least two more times years later while having a shower while manic. These experiences have me thinking there may be a possible logical or scientific explanation or theory as to what would cause them. Every time this happened, the water temperature was perfect, not too hot or too cold. Another symptom of mania is the enhancement of one's senses. Sometimes when a person is manic, they can see, smell, feel, taste and hear better than they could when they are in their "normal state." This enhancement goes far beyond the five physical senses and includes our psychic realm, also known as the sixth sense. When manic, I have had many incredible spiritual encounters, but the psychiatrists are very quick to diagnose them as delusional. These people can be very narrow-minded and not open to discussion on this matter. One of the main reasons I am writing this book is to share my many spiritual encounters, my experiences and my beliefs because of such happenings over many years. I will tell some of these stories and experiences throughout this book.

Back to my "shock theory." The reason I got these shocks is very simple. We are mind, body and soul. Our soul and body contain energy and electricity. Water is a conductor. Mania's main symptom is "increased energy." If the human body's capacity for electrical output increases with a person's increased energy from the mania, would the resulting energy or electricity be substantial enough to cause a shock in the human body when in contact with water? It is possible. If you put a radio or small battery in water, you could get a shock from it. As human beings we have the ability to tap into a much greater source of power if we learn how to do so; we can also generate more energy and power from ourselves.

After Dorothy calmed me down, I sat down at her organ and tried to play a couple of tunes. I tried to play the NHL's theme song they used to play on TV for the hockey games, but I didn't know it. I couldn't play the organ worth a shit, but I was having fun pounding on the keys anyway. Suddenly, Dorothy was telling me to leave her apartment. She seemed pissed off and was talking quite loudly. Before I left, she went into her bedroom and got a pair of sweatpants and a T-shirt that had belonged to Frank. She wanted me to put them on, so I did. Frank must have been a big man. I was a thin and trim 175 lb., and these clothes were way too big for me. Then she got a large green garbage bag and told me to put my golf shirt and slacks that I had been wearing for the last few days into it. I obeyed. She also gave me an old baseball cap of Frank's to wear. We went into the bathroom where she put a bar of soap, some toothpaste and shampoo into the garbage bag. When my bag was ready, Dorothy started yelling at me to leave and to take my bag with me.

I ran out of her apartment, down the stairs and ended up in a grassy park-like area in front of the complex. I stood there, dazed and confused, wearing Frank's giant sweatpants and T-shirt with my garbage bag in hand, thinking "Now what?"

Making a Golf Movie

Then it hit me. Something told me I was in that park to make a movie! The garbage bag was full of "props" for the movie and for TV advertisements! It was about 10:00 a.m. on an absolutely beautiful day for filming. Whatever was telling me to make a movie thought it should be about golf. The moral of the story was that too many people take golf too seriously and, instead, should have some fun on the course.

I was the lead and was supposed to act like the golf professionals on the course as opposed to those who just play for fun. In fact, I was "chosen" to play both roles. I even had a "golf club" — a deflated bicycle tire tube that I had been carrying around with me for the previous few days — in my bag! My physiotherapist had given it to me to do stretching exercises for my bad back. However, I would use this tube as a golf club for my movie.

I waited for a few minutes for the other actors and film crew to arrive. There was no sign of them. I was standing in the park all by myself. I couldn't see another soul anywhere. Then the "something" spoke to me again. Not "spoke" as in audible words that I could actually hear, but more like a telepathic message or communication. Maybe it was my inner voice or conscience. I don't know. Anyway, "the something from somewhere" told me that I would not be seeing the film crew because they would not be visible to me. They would be filming from strategic locations nearby, but for some reason they wouldn't be filming from right out in the open park. I did not question this "information," I just accepted it as I was "told."

When I thought the film crew was ready, I started acting. Wearing Frank's T-shirt and baseball cap as well as his enormous sweatpants, I did my best impression of a novice golfer having the time of his life on the golf course. I would swing the deflated tire tube with a mighty hacker's swing, pretend I knocked the ball down the fairway and then jump up and down with joy, celebrating my good shot and pumping my fist in the air with jubilation! I would then run after my invisible ball. When I got to it, I would take another swing and knock my approach shot onto the green, ten feet from the hole. I would then run up to "the green" and putt my ball into the hole for a birdie three on this par four hole. Again, I would jump up and down and dance around, celebrating my good fortune.

Back on the "tee box" and next up to play was the "golf professional." This fellow takes a much different approach to playing golf. To act this part, I took off Frank's T-shirt and put on the golf shirt that was in my garbage bag. The golf professional's demeanor was much more serious than the amateur. The golf pro I acted out was all business. He wasn't out on the course to have a good time. When he hit a poor shot, he got pissed off and would bang his club into the ground.

I kept alternating back and forth, doing my comparisons between these two different styles of playing golf. I was really having fun with it. Every time I acted the novice golfer, I would put the T-shirt back on, and I would put my ball cap on sideways or backwards. When I was the golf pro, I would change into my golf shirt and put my cap on properly.

My message was to simply relax, have fun on the golf course and not take the game too seriously. Admittedly, my actions — jumping up and down and running around — were a little over the top. There is certain etiquette that all golfers should abide by on the golf course.

PICKED UP BY THE POLICE

I saw a police van parked in front of the park and two police officers were approaching me. I immediately understood that they were actors for my movie, so I thought I would go along with the role.

"Good morning," the one cop said.

"Good morning!" I replied enthusiastically.

"How are you doing today?" he said.

"Great! How are you guys doing?"

"Good. What are you doing here?"

"Making a movie about golf," I said.

"Oh yeah? What's your name?" he asked.

"Don Walin. What are your names?"

"We can't tell you that."

"Why not? I told you my name."

"Have you been drinking, Don?"

"Not since last night."

"Are you on any drugs?"

"No."

"Do you mind if we check you for drugs and weapons, Don?"

"Not at all. Go ahead."

The police (whom I still thought were actors) went ahead and frisked me and found nothing. I answered a bunch more questions, including my address in Sidney, and I told them I was working as an assistant golf professional at Glen Meadows Golf & Country Club up until a few days ago.

"Maybe you want to come with us, Don," said the cop.

"Sure," I said.

I walked with them peacefully and willingly (no handcuffs or anything like that) to their police van. They opened the back door to the van, and I got inside and sat down. I wasn't sure where they were going to take me, but I was thinking that all of this was really cool! I was literally going along for the ride. I was anticipating the next part of the movie but had no idea what it would be.

After ten minutes, the van stopped and the back door opened. I followed the two officers into a building. At first, I had no idea where I was, then I realized I was in a hospital. I don't remember being admitted to the hospital, but I do remember that I was immediately put into a small room by myself. At first, I was okay with this. I was still delusional and thought this was just another scene for my movie. I waited patiently for about fifteen minutes in anticipation for what would happen next.

When they first put me in the room, I thought they wanted to monitor me, study me and use me for research. I thought I was a total genius! The ideas coming into my head were endless, and my mind seemed lightning fast. I didn't know it, but "flight of ideas" and "racing thoughts" are two of mania's symptoms. Most of my ideas were about business and money-making ventures.

I started to become impatient, so I tried to open the door, but it was locked! I began to call out politely, "Hello? Can someone please open this door and let me out?" After no response, I kept pleasantly repeating this for several minutes. I was starting to get really pissed off, and I was no longer thinking I was in a movie. The longer I was left in that room, the angrier I became until I was totally ballistic! I was yelling at the top of my voice that I was going to sue the hospital, doctors and nurses, and that I had the best lawyers in the world. I cursed them with every swear word in the book — loudly. My "manic grandiosity" had me saying things like, "You don't know who you're fucking with, you cocksuckers! I'm one of the smartest and richest men in the world!" I ranted and raged incessantly for what seemed to be a very long time. I was like a raging bull. I was so pissed off!

The door finally opened, and I tried to leave but there were five men there — two of them were very large (probably security guards for the hospital). I was willing to cooperate until I saw one of them holding a large needle. I became paranoid and thought they were there to harm or even kill me. "Paranoid delusions" are another symptom of mania. I did not understand that at least one of these men (perhaps the one that was holding the needle) was a doctor, psychiatrist or maybe a psychiatric nurse, whose intention was to help me. They said the needle would help me, but because of my state of mind I did not trust any of them. I refused to take the needle and would not comply with their terms. Suddenly, two men grabbed a hold of me, and I was injected with the monster sized needle. When they were finished, they left the room. I was again alone and locked up in this small room. I felt so alone, scared and frightened. I didn't know what was happening to me.

The drugs kicked in immediately, and I felt the effects of the heavy sedatives very quickly. I tried to fight them off, but they took a very strong hold over my mind and body. That's the last thing I remember for three days.

CHAPTER 2
MANIC DEPRESSION

I subsequently learned they must have given me Haldol, Thorazine or some similar antipsychotic medication that also acts as a tranquilizer to be administered when someone who is bipolar and in a manic state needs help slowing down. The next thing I remember, three days later, is walking around the Eric Martin Pavilion (the psychiatric ward) at the Royal Jubilee Hospital with my brother, Jim. I was so drugged up, I required Jim's assistance to walk. The psych nurse said I slept for the first three days after my admission. I must have needed the rest as I had very little or no sleep for three days prior to being hospitalized. I was probably awake just enough to have something to eat and for the nurses to give me my medication.

Jim flew from Edmonton and was the first family member to get there. A couple of days later, my mom and brothers, Doug and Gary, arrived. They had made the seventeen-hour drive from Edmonton in my mom's motor home. It was their first time in a psychiatric ward as well, and we discovered I was severely mentally ill.

Scott and Wendy came to visit me as well. Out of all the people I knew when I lived in Sidney and worked at Glen Meadows Golf & Country Club, they were the only ones from that area who I remember coming to see me. I really appreciated that they did this. There was a pool table on the premises, so the three of us decided to have a game. When it was my turn to shoot, I could barely make contact with the cue ball because I was so drugged up. We still had some good laughs, and I really enjoyed their visit.

Dave Lambert, my best friend who I met in high school in Calgary, came to see me. Dave took time off from work and put a lot of time, effort and expense into making the trip. When he heard from my mom about the predicament I was in, he put everything on hold and came to support me. He stayed for about a week, visiting with my family and me. This is what I call a good friend. Dave and I remain very good friends and have known each other for forty years. Our friendship has endured the test of time.

The psychiatrist treating me informed us I had "manic depression." That was in 1989. We now call this "bipolar disorder" — it's exactly the same illness. We had never heard of it and were totally unfamiliar with its causes, symptoms and treatments. These were uncharted waters for us, and we learned a lot about this illness as we went along day by day. I ended up spending six weeks in the Eric Martin Pavilion. We had no clue what we were in for. The next ten years were like a roller coaster ride from hell.

After I was released from the psych ward, my mom, brothers and I went back to my place in Sidney. Having just spent six weeks heavily sedated on extremely powerful psychiatric medications, I was no longer manic. However, I think I was in denial as to what I had just been through and that I actually had manic depression. My family was also in denial as it came out of the blue. It all happened so fast and was a shock for all of us. The denial may have meant we didn't take the illness seriously enough at first.

FROM THE PSYCH WARD TO JAIL

Within the first week of being back home, I was already doing something I shouldn't have been doing: drinking! It wasn't a good idea to be consuming alcohol because I was still taking psychiatric medications. Bad mix. One night after I had been drinking for a few hours, I called a girl who lived in Sidney. We had only met once before, but I knew she was really good looking (the main qualification for a date back in those younger years). We decided to see a movie in Victoria. The only smart thing I did that night was to get her to pick me up in her car because I'd had too much to drink to be driving. I didn't even make it to the movie theatre. When we got to the entrance of the theatre, I started to feel really sick. I sat down on the pavement outside the theatre near the sidewalk. I felt like I was going to get sick to my stomach. That's the last thing I remember from that night.

When I woke up, I was in a jail cell at about 6:00 a.m. the next morning. I felt like shit. I found out that the police had picked me up the night before and put me in the "drunk tank" for being drunk and disorderly in public. It was kind of a scary feeling that I had absolutely no memory of it. The combination of alcohol and psychiatric medications made me very sick and put me in a drunken stupor. It was probably lucky that the police picked me up and put me somewhere safe because I was in no condition to look after myself.

They let me out of jail as soon as I woke up, and I wasn't charged with anything. When I got outside, I realized I was in downtown Victoria. I had to get back home. What happened to the girl I was with the night before? I'm not sure, but I think she just left me when I got so sick outside the movie theatre. If she would have stayed with me and made sure I was going to be OK, perhaps she could have given me a ride home. I would rather have woken up in my own bed than a jail cell! Maybe she didn't take me home because she worried that I might get sick in her car. I can only guess.

I walked a couple of blocks from the police station to a pay phone. It was 6:30 a.m., and I still wasn't thinking very clearly. I called her and asked if she would pick me up and give me a ride home. She said "no." I thought she might be pissed off at me for calling her so early in the morning, but she didn't seem angry. Our first and only date wasn't exactly an enjoyable experience. I don't remember my date's name, but I know I never called or saw her again. A taxi would have cost a lot of money that I didn't have after my manic spending spree, so I decided to take a city bus home, which was only about $2.

It took a couple of days of sobriety for my head to clear. This last episode was bad enough, and I was also still trying to get my head straight. Everything had happened so suddenly. My world got turned upside down quickly.

CHAPTER 3
GROWING UP

St. Albert is located just a little north of Edmonton. When our family lived there in the 1960s and early 1970s, it was a fairly small town. Over time, it has blossomed to become a pretty large city.

My earliest memories are of playing hockey. I loved it. I couldn't get enough of it! I started skating when I was four years old. I have vague memories of hitting golf balls around in the backyard of our house around the same age, but it would be a few more years before I really got into playing golf.

There was an outdoor rink beside the school where I went to grades 1 and 2. I played a ton of hockey there. I was crazy about the sport. When it was freezing cold (like -20°C), we still went there. My feet would be absolutely frozen! We would go into the shack for a few minutes to try and warm up a bit, then go straight back onto the ice. Often, we would have to shovel the snow off the ice before we could play, but that was a small price to pay considering how much fun we had!

I started playing on a hockey team at five. I was in "Atom" and played center for the team. My grandma liked to tell me a little story about when she used to watch me play hockey on my first team. "You would win the faceoff, get the puck and skate through all of their players, then score on their goalie!" she would say. "Then, you would race back to center ice as fast as you could, all ready for another faceoff. You would get the puck, stickhandle your way through their team and score another goal! You did this many times! I loved to watch you play." Spoken by a proud grandma.

There were two reasons why I skated as fast as I could back to center ice for another faceoff after scoring a goal. For one thing, I was obviously very eager. The other reason is because our games at that time only lasted for one hour. I was trying to score as many goals as I could during this relatively short period of time.

We played lots of street hockey in front of our house and used a tennis ball instead of a puck. This was also a lot of fun. I loved watching NHL hockey on TV, especially when the Montreal Canadiens and Boston Bruins were playing. They were my two favorite teams at the time.

The school I went to for Grade 1 and Grade 2 was Sir Alexander Mackenzie. We called it "SAM." I walked to school, as it wasn't far from our house in the neighborhood of Braeside. I was a pretty good student and earned good marks in my first two years of education.

My main interest was hockey, but I was also getting an inkling for the opposite sex. Other boys my age would say silly things like "girls have fleas" and they just weren't interested, but I was intrigued by the ladies. I was curious. Maybe my Gemini was coming out already. I liked some of my older brothers' girlfriends who were a lot more physically "developed" than the girls my age. What a way for a seven-year-old kid to be thinking! Fortunately, I wasn't infatuated or obsessed at such a young age; that waited until I was a teenager.

In 1971, our family moved to Wetaskiwin, Alberta, a small city about forty-five minutes southeast of Edmonton.

WETASKIWIN, ALBERTA

In 1971, the population of Wetaskiwin was only about 7,000. This small city has done some growing over the years and is now about 12,700. In large part, it is a farming community.

My dad purchased a ten acre parcel of land right across the road from the Wetaskiwin Golf Club. He had a "Facto" home built, which looked like a regular house, on top of a hill. The property was mainly all sand and dirt, and my dad worked very hard to get it looking really nice. He landscaped our property and grew grass and trees. Our front yard was huge, about five acres. Dad enjoyed cutting the grass on his "ride-m-mower."

A forest of trees that went downhill a ways before bottoming out was behind the house. This large area was the other five acres of our land. Our acreage was about 2½ miles northwest of town — only a five-minute drive. The road to the golf course clubhouse went right by our place.

This is where I grew up and lived with my dad (Dale) and mom (Muriel). I am the youngest of five boys. Doug is the oldest, followed by Jim, Rick and Gary (the twins), then me. My dad was a pilot for Imperial Oil/Esso and flew out of the Edmonton International Airport, mainly up to the Northwest Territories and the Arctic.

Our only neighbors were the Green family, who lived about a half mile to the east of us. Stan and Ursula were the parents, and they had three daughters. Monica was the oldest, then there was Carol and Andrea who were twins and were one year older than me. Both of our families had twins!

About a quarter mile to the west was a region called "Peace Hills." Apparently, the First Nations people smoked their "peace pipes" there a long time ago. I did find a really cool First Nations arrowhead in that area one time.

From grades 3 to 9, I went to Clear Vista School in Wetaskiwin. The school was right in town but many of my classmates and I lived in the country on farms or acreages. The country bus picked me up on the road at the end of our long downhill driveway. It was very common for me to run down our driveway to catch the bus in time. Over the winter months, I had several wipeouts while doing this.

I was a pretty good student and earned good grades. I was quite popular and had a lot of friends. My favorite class in school was phys ed., and I loved playing floor hockey. I liked playing football, baseball, basketball, volleyball and other sports, but floor hockey was the ultimate! (We didn't play golf in elementary or junior high school.)

My grades dropped a bit from elementary to junior high, but I was still passing all of my courses and doing pretty well at Clear Vista. Wetaskiwin was the perfect place to grow up. In larger cities, it's pretty common for kids to hang out at malls, experiment with drugs and to get in trouble. In our small town, my friends and I didn't do these things. Besides school, my main activities were sports. Golf and hockey were by far my favorites. I played golf for six months a year and hockey for the other six. I worked in the pro shop at the Wetaskiwin Golf Club from when I was nine years old to the age of fifteen. I also worked on the golf course itself, cutting the fairways and working on the grounds crew. I worked after school, on the weekends and during the summer holidays.

During the winter months, we loved snowmobiling. Dad bought a regular Skidoo and two Arctic Cats. There was a ton of snow when we lived there in the 1970s, a lot more than there is now. It was awesome for snowmobiling, and we did a lot of it. It was so much fun! We also towed each other behind our snowmobiles on tire tubes, which was a blast.

My friends and I did a lot of tobogganing at Peace Hills. There were two good runs there. One was long and winding, and the other one was quite steep and had a jump at the bottom. We called this one "Suicide Hill." We also went tubing there.

There was a large pond behind our property, and when frozen over we played a lot of hockey there. Sometimes there were a bunch of us, and sometimes I played by myself. The only thing we had to do was keep the snow cleared off the ice. This was a minor inconvenience that enabled us to have countless hours of fun.

In the summer months, we played football and baseball in our huge front yard and drove our motorbike (a Honda 90). Sometimes, I used our yard as my own condensed version of a driving range, hitting golf balls from one end to the other.

I loved all these things, but the greatest of all was living right across the road from the golf course! From our house, it took me less than ten minutes to get on the course and start playing.

THE WETASKIWIN GOLF CLUB - MY START IN GOLF

I started playing golf when I was seven and fell in love with the game immediately. My first set of clubs was a right-handed seven-piece starter set. Ironically, the name of these clubs was Spalding Future Pro.

When we first moved to Wetaskiwin, our house overlooked the 2nd hole (a par 5) at the time. Years later the layout of the course was altered. I practiced putting on the 2nd green until it got too dark to see. I would see the outside light on our house flash on and off several times, and hear my mom calling me to come home. "Donald! Donald! Time to come home now!" This happened on a regular basis.

During the years we lived there, it was a 9-hole (par 35) course. Shortly after we arrived, a new (and much needed) clubhouse was built on the hill across from Peace Hills. It was a lot larger and was a monumental improvement over the old clubhouse. The new location of the new clubhouse altered the layout and design of the course somewhat. The first hole became a short par 4. It was approximately 330 yards long and was downhill from an elevated tee box. When I was fifteen, I could drive the green, especially if the wind was behind me.

I had some confidence in my golf game during that era and could hit the ball pretty far. There was a balcony on the upper level of the clubhouse where people watched golfers tee off on #1. I liked to show off a bit back then, so I always hoped there would be a lot of spectators watching me smash my drive and attempt to drive the green. The bigger the crowd, the better! A lot of members and locals knew me and knew I was a pretty good player. They liked to watch me hit the ball. It was the same thing coming up the 9th hole. I hoped there were a lot of people watching, and I always tried to play my best in front of them.

It was the only course in Wetaskiwin. After we moved away, an additional 9 holes was built, making it an 18-hole golf course. Years later, another 18-hole course opened in the region.

During my years as a junior golfer, I played as much as I could throughout the golf season, and it took up most of my time. In July and August, I averaged at least 36 holes a day. Countless times I played 45-54 holes in a day, and I even played 63 holes a few times. Playing 63 holes means playing that 9-hole golf course seven times. But that's what my buddies and I did. We just kept going around those 9 holes. And around and around and around! Obviously, I got to know this course very well.

When I wasn't playing, I was on the driving range. I probably hit three hundred range balls a day. That's a conservative estimate. I'm sure there were many days when I hit five hundred balls. I loved hitting golf balls, and I never got tired of it! I developed calluses on my hands from hitting so many balls. I liked to be creative on the range and use my imagination. Eventually, I learned to hit all types of shots. I could intentionally hit draws, hooks, fades, slices, knockdowns and punch shots. At the same time, I worked on trying to hit the ball dead straight.

I practiced a lot on the golf course as well. Later in the evenings when there were no more golfers playing the first few holes, I would go to a vacant hole and practice. I practiced my drives and my approach shots to the green. Then I worked on my short game. I loved to practice in general but spending time on my short game was always my favorite aspect. I would get so engrossed that I would completely lose track of time. It was so much fun! As a result of all the time and effort I put into it, I became very good at chipping, pitching and putting.

There weren't very many sand traps on the course, so I didn't get much experience with playing out of the bunkers. This lack of experience carried on to my adult playing years, and I was never a competent bunker player. It was the weakest part of my game. If you have the right technique and the confidence, a sand shot from a greenside bunker is pretty easy. If you don't, hitting your ball out of a sand trap can produce a lot of anxiety and leave you with little or no confidence in executing the shot. The result is usually a poor sand shot. Higher handicap golfers really struggle with this issue and so did I.

On the weekends and during the summer holidays, I had the same routine. I arrived at the golf course very early in the morning and played golf most of the day. I also worked in the pro shop on a regular basis. My shifts were usually short, about 2-4 hours at a time. The golf course wasn't very busy back then, so I worked on my own, starting when I was only nine. I was paid $4.00/hour, which was the minimum wage then. In the evenings, I played more golf or practiced for a couple of hours. I never went home until it was dark.

I didn't take golf lessons when I was a junior golfer. I learned the golf swing and basic fundamentals, then developed my game from there. Having solid basic fundamentals (grip, alignment, stance, posture and ball position in the stance) is extremely important for all levels. Even the best golfers in the world work on these basics on a regular basis.

I was more of a "feel" player and my swing came pretty naturally to me. As long as I was practicing and playing a lot I usually did OK. When I was young, I didn't even really think about my golf swing; it was automatic. I would visualize a good shot, swing/execute, done. I kept it simple!

When I was nineteen, I learned about the mechanics of the golf swing and began to experiment. Looking back, this was the beginning of the end as far as my natural golf swing was concerned. I simply lost it and never got it back. I always played my best when I wasn't thinking about my swing out on the course. If you want to work on your swing, do it at the driving range. My game didn't improve much (if any), from when I was a junior golfer to when I was a CPGA pro. As I got older, I became too technical and didn't practice or play nearly as much as I did as a junior. Because of this, I lost my natural swing, and my ability to be a "feel player" was severely diminished.

Eventually, I learned a great deal about the golf swing. I understood the proper swing mechanics and the physics involved. The most important thing I learned was the five Ball Flight Laws. This knowledge was essential for me when I started teaching.

HIGHLIGHTS AS A JUNIOR GOLFER 1973-1982

I started playing competitive golf at nine. From 1973-1979, I played in junior golf tournaments in Red Deer, Lacombe, Innisfail, Camrose, Ponoka, Leduc and Edmonton. For the most part, my mom drove me to all of these places. I was incredibly lucky to have her support and devotion and couldn't have done it without her.

1974

I won my age category (10 and under) at the Camrose Junior Open.

1976

By age twelve, I had a 7 handicap. I was shooting in the 70s (for 18 holes) pretty consistently. When I was twelve, I shot a 36 on the 9-hole Wetaskiwin course. I had a two-foot putt on the 9th green for a par (5) and an overall score of even par 35, but I was so nervous I missed it. I hardly ever missed a putt from that close! Even at that young age, I was learning about how psychological this game could be. I did get a small write-up in the local paper for my achievement. By this age, I was a pretty good ball striker and had a very good short game. I had a lot of confidence on and around the greens.

1979

At age fifteen, I had a 3 handicap. I blew a 6 shot lead and ended up tied for third place at the Pepsi Juvenile Golf Championship at the Riverside Golf Club in Edmonton. This was a big tournament for golfers aged fifteen and younger. The best junior golfers of this age group from central and northern Alberta played in this event that I should have won.

I played well on the front nine, shooting a 1 under par 35. I bogeyed the 9th hole, which is an easy par 5, so I felt like I should have had a 34 on the front. A bogey on #9 was disappointing, but I was still pleased with my front nine score. I didn't know it, but I was leading the tournament!

I thought if I played fairly well on the back nine, I might be in contention to win! An 18-hole score in the low- to mid-70s would have a good chance of winning, so my goal was to shoot between 36-39 on the back nine, which would have given me a 71-74. Thinking about this put too much pressure on me. I became nervous and started to play very poorly. The back nine was a disaster. After the first four holes, I had a couple of pars and two bogeys. I was only 1 over par after 13 holes. Once again, I didn't realize I was leading by about 5 shots at this point.

The 14th hole was a very short (110 yards) par 3. I used my wedge, and it should have been a relatively easy hole to make a par on. Instead, I hit an errant tee shot to the right of the green, and my ball ended up amongst some trees. It took me 3 shots to get my ball on the green, then I three-putted for a triple bogey 6. I was shocked and thought my chances of winning were over. On holes 15-17, I made two pars and a bogey.

Standing at the 18th tee box, I was 6 over par on the back nine and 5 over par for the round. I really thought I had blown my chances for a victory. What I didn't find out until later was that I still had a two shot lead! My nearest competitors had already finished. It was all up to me. The 18th hole was a relatively easy par 4. To win, I just had to make a par or a bogey. A double bogey would get me into a playoff for the title. Not knowing this, I thought playing this final hole was just a formality for me.

My drive was in the fairway. I hit my second shot just over the green and into a bunker. While I was preparing to hit my third shot, a cameraman from the *Edmonton Journal* (the local newspaper) was positioning himself very close and taking pictures of me. He made me very nervous, and I lost my focus and concentration. On my sand shot, I skulled my ball, sending it over the green and about 30 yards back down the 18th fairway. This was quite embarrassing, especially because it happened with the cameraman right beside me. There was also a small gallery of people watching our group finish the 18th hole.

It was obvious to me that the cameraman (and perhaps other onlookers) thought I might still be leading or in contention to win. As it turned out, they knew more than I did. When I came to #18, there were two guys tied for the lead. They shot 79. I had mixed feelings when the photographer became part of the scenario. My first thought was that I might still have a chance to win. Why else would he be taking pictures of me? All of a sudden, I had some hope again.

My fourth shot was a short pitch from about 30 yards. Normally, I would have hit this fairly close to the hole and would have a good chance to one-putt for a bogey 5. Had I been able to do it on this day, I would be victorious. Two-putting for a double bogey 6 would have given me a 79, and I would have been in a playoff with two other guys to decide the winner. I ended up pitching my fourth shot on the green and three-putting for a triple bogey 7! I shot 80 and didn't even get into the playoff. I ended up tied for third place, which was a colossal fuck-up!

Two really bad holes on the back nine killed me. I didn't even have any penalty strokes (no lost balls, no out of bounds, no balls in the water, etc.) with the two triple bogeys. At the worst, I should have double bogeyed #14 and #18. Had this happened, I would have shot 78 and won outright. Two bogeys on these holes and I shoot 76. In the end, Clay Handon from the Edmonton Country Club won in a playoff over Billy Nichols from Jasper. Clay shot 41-38=79. I shot 35-45=80.

The next day, there was an article in the *Edmonton Journal* about the tournament. Part of it said "Wetaskiwin's Don Walin probably had the best chance to win the tournament outright. The 15 year old made the turn in one-under-par 35 with a bogey on #9, but triple bogeyed the 110 yard, par three 14th and the par four 18th. He missed the playoff by a single shot and tied for third with an 80."

The Cold Lake Men's Open was held at the Air Force Base golf course in Cold Lake, Alberta. Despite being underage, I was allowed to play against a full field of 150 golfers. A group of about ten of us from Wetaskiwin made the drive up to northern Alberta for a weekend of golf and fun. I was by far the youngest one, however, I was used to playing golf and socializing with adults by this time.

After 36 holes, I was tied for first place in the first flight. I ended up in a playoff against a man who was about thirty-five years old. We tied the first hole. On the second hole (par 4), my opponent had about an eight-foot putt for a double bogey 6. I had a six-foot putt for a par. I had him beat. My ball was right in front of his, so I put a ball marker (a coin) on its spot. My marker was still right on his putting line, so I moved it over a couple of inches to the right so it wouldn't interfere with his putt. This is proper golf etiquette. After I did this for him, he made his putt. It was a double bogey 6 for him.

I missed my 6-footer for par, then tapped my ball in the hole for a bogey 5. I won! There was quite a large gallery watching our playoff. The people cheered loudly for me. They seemed really happy that I won my flight. My fellow Wetaskiwinites gave me the loudest applause. Having their support felt great. I was thrilled!

Immediately after I tapped my ball into the hole for my "victory," my opponent came straight over to me. I thought he was going to shake my hand and congratulate me, which was the normal protocol in this situation. But, as I was soon to find out, this guy wasn't exactly your normal golfer. Golf is a gentleman's game and a game of sportsmanship, two qualities this guy did not possess. Instead of shaking my hand and congratulating me, he said, "You didn't move your ball marker back to its original position before you attempted your putt for par. That's a two-stroke penalty, so you made a 7 on the hole. I made a 6. I win." I was shocked and totally dejected. Defeat snatched out of the jaws of victory — a tough way to lose.

I did forget to move my marker back to its original spot on the green, which is a two-shot penalty. However, it's an honest mistake that sometimes happens to golfers. It's not an attempt to cheat or gain an advantage. We simply forget to move our ball marker (and ball) back to its original position before we hit our next putt. Ensuring your opponent receives a two-shot penalty in this situation is a really low blow. I know that if I saw one of my opponents do this, I would remind them to move their marker back before this penalty was invoked, and they would appreciate this courtesy. I have seen PGA Tour players remind each other to put their ball markers back in the proper place, and these guys are playing for millions of dollars! It's a game of honor. We weren't playing for money. We were amateurs playing for prizes. For winning first place, he won a TV. For finishing in second, I won a Polaroid camera.

The guys from Wetaskiwin were ready to kill this guy! They wanted to tar and feather him at least. A couple of people said they were disappointed that this thirty-five-year-old man did this to a fifteen-year-old boy. As far as I was concerned, I played in a "Men's" open golf tournament, and I wanted to be treated as a man. Looking on the bright side, I learned a lesson. I have never forgotten to replace my ball marker since that infamous day in Cold Lake, Alberta.

The Leduc Junior Open was held at the local golf course. I played terrible on the front nine — shooting a 43 — but made a charge on the back nine. Starting on the 10th hole, I went par, eagle, birdie, par, birdie. I was 4 under par after the first 5 holes. One of the guys in my group was a member at this golf course and told me that I was tied for the course record for the back nine. Once this was in my head, I became very nervous.

The main reason I had such a good start on the back nine was because I had a hot putter. It was on fire! I sank about a forty-foot putt on #11 for my eagle and made putts from over thirty feet for my birdies on #12 and #14. It was unbelievable! My putter went cold once I became nervous. I three-putted #16 for a bogey and three-putted #18 for a double bogey. It was another bad finish for me. I still shot 1 under par on the back nine, but my overall score of 43-35=78 wasn't good enough to win.

1980-1982

The Wetaskiwin Men's Open was the tournament I wanted to win the most because it was my home track where I grew up learning to play, and my dream was to win in front of my hometown people. Because I was playing some pretty good golf, the tournament committee decided to allow me to play in the Men's Open when I was only sixteen — a real thrill for me! For a small town, it was a pretty big tournament. People from all over Alberta came to play in it. It was always full, with a field of about 150 contestants. It was a two-day event, 36 holes, held over the weekend. It attracted some pretty good players.

I ended up playing in the Open three times. I was in the "Championship Flight" each time, playing against the best golfers in the field. It was good experience for me. I did OK but not great in the first two Opens. I forget what I shot, but I know that I wasn't in contention for the title.

When I was eighteen and in my third Open, I came second. I was disappointed that I didn't win, but at the same time, I was pleased because I had played pretty good golf over the two days. In the final round, Randy Hill from Edmonton, a scratch golfer (0 handicap), was in the last group with me and two other guys. It turned into an 18-hole battle between Randy and I. Randy had won this tournament before. He was about seven years older than me and was likely the best amateur in central and northern Alberta. He could really play, and I enjoyed watching him. Randy had a ton of talent. I hung in there with him right to the end. I shot a 75 and a 73 for a 36-hole total of 148. He beat me by two or three shots, but I didn't mind. He was simply a better golfer than me. It just felt good to give him a bit of a challenge that day.

These were some highlights of the golf tournaments I played in when I was a junior golfer, but I usually played in at least three or four each season.

HOCKEY

When the golf season was over, my other addiction took over: hockey. I started playing in the Wetaskiwin "mighty-mites" league when I was eight. Almost immediately, they advanced me into the "mites" league, which was for kids nine to ten years old. I guess they thought I was skilled enough to play in a division where the other boys were a little older. I wasn't a prodigy or a superstar — not even close. I was just a young boy who had a little bit of talent for the game. I started playing both hockey and golf earlier than the average kid, which is the main reason I was more advanced compared to kids my age. With hockey, this difference was the most noticeable from when I was between six and twelve years old. After that, it seemed like the other kids got a lot better. I continued to play pretty good hockey, but as I got a little older, I didn't dominate the game like I was previously able to do on occasion.

I played "mites," "peewee" and "bantam" in Wetaskiwin. I was the captain of the teams I played on in mites and peewee and an assistant captain in bantam. I have no idea of how many goals and assists I scored, but I was my most successful in mites and peewee for scoring points.

In bantam, I played on the Provincial B traveling team, which was made up of the best bantam players in the Wetaskiwin region. We played against teams from Camrose, Ponoka, Drayton Valley, Leduc and Sherwood Park. We also played in tournaments and exhibition games in other parts of Alberta like Red Deer, Lacombe, Innisfail, Viking, Vegreville, Fort Saskatchewan and Edmonton. Our team took a bus to all our games. We had a lot of fun joking around and laughing on these trips. I enjoyed the camaraderie of being on a hockey team.

In south/central Alberta, we went to the extremely small town of Viking to play their bantam team. I was really looking forward to this game because we were going to be playing against Rich and Ron Sutter (twin brothers) of the famous Sutter family. Four of their older brothers were playing in the NHL (Darryl, Duane, Brent and Brian). This in itself was incredible. There was talk about whether the twins would also make it to the big league, which probably put a lot of pressure on them. I don't remember who won the game, but I wasn't very impressed with the Sutter twins. I just didn't see anything very special about how they played. I thought they were both good players, but not great. In fairness to them, I only saw them play that one time. Several years later, both Rich and Ron made it to the NHL and, like their older brothers, had pretty successful careers. Having six of seven brothers play in the NHL is absolutely amazing! Those Sutters are quite a crew, and they're from Viking, Alberta!

One time, I was playing golf with Jeff Williamson at the Wetaskiwin course. We joined up with a guy on the 6th green who was playing by himself. It turned out that this guy was Jeff's cousin, Lindy Ruff. When Jeff introduced me to Lindy, I knew who he was right away. At the time (in the mid- to late-1970s), Lindy was playing in the NHL for the Buffalo Sabres. He was from the nearby small town of Ponoka. Jeff and I played the last few holes with Lindy. Being a hockey nut, this was quite exciting for me! I was only about twelve years old then. I remember that Lindy was a "southpaw" (a left-handed golfer). He went on to have a very lengthy and successful career with the Buffalo Sabres organization. He was a player for them for many years, then became their head coach and then the general manager.

During the 1970s, the Edmonton Oilers were in the WHA, which was when I first became an Oilers fan. In this era, their games were broadcast on Edmonton's CFRN AM radio station. Rod Phillips was the play-by-play announcer for their games. Rod was awesome! He got so excited when he was calling the play that it made it more exciting for the listener. Between the ages of ten and fourteen, I liked to predict the outcome of the Oilers' games. Before each game, I wrote out my own "game summary" that included who I thought would score goals and get assists. I also wrote the time of each goal for each period. I have always been somewhat of a statistics guy, and this is how I got my start.

Wayne Gretzky became a member of the Oilers during the 1978-1979 season when he was only eighteen years old. I became an instant fan and still am forty years later. When they were still in the WHA, he played with B.J. (Blair) MacDonald and Brett Callighen. They called it the GMC line. Those three guys got a lot of points when they played together.

Another Oiler who I really liked was Ron Chipperfield, one of their better players. As a part of my life's destiny, I met Ron several years later when I was working at the Windermere Golf & Country Club in Edmonton. We played golf there together a couple of times.

No scouts came to watch me play — I wasn't "NHL material." Not even close. As it turned out, I didn't even play junior hockey, but I did have some talent. I was a fairly fast skater and could stickhandle and shoot the puck pretty decently. I was a pretty good playmaker and liked to create offensive opportunities. My worst attribute — by far — was that I played with my head down too much, especially when I had possession of the puck. I was an easy target and took a lot of big hits because of this. I don't know how I got into this bad habit. Maybe it was because I had spent so much time "trying to keep my head down" for my golf game. I would have been much more effective and avoided a lot of hits if I used my peripheral vision more when I had the puck. Hockey is a "heads up" game, but I wasn't taught this extremely important aspect.

After the Zamboni had finished flooding the ice, I always wanted to be one of the first guys out there. There was nothing like freshly-flooded ice! I would race around the rink really fast for a while, skating forwards and backwards. I couldn't wait to get a puck on my stick. When I did, I was in heaven. During practices and the warmup sessions before games, I loved stickhandling, passing the puck around with my teammates and shooting. Playing in games was the ultimate because I was so passionate for this great game.

STARTED DRINKING MUCH TOO YOUNG

I was very involved in sports, but I also started drinking alcohol at the age of nine. How stupid is that? It was crazy. I guess I didn't know any better. I was just a kid growing up in an environment where I was surrounded by heavy drinking. My parents both drank, but my dad consumed a lot more than my mom. My dad was a good man. He treated my mom well and was pretty good to us kids. He was a pilot, was smart and worked hard. He was well liked by many people and had several friends. Unfortunately, he had a weakness for alcohol. Most days he would have a couple of drinks (rum & Coke) and that would be it — pretty harmless. But about once a week he would get really drunk. Sometimes, he would go on a two-day bender. He would get drunk one night, then wake up the next morning and start drinking again. Usually, he started these mornings with a "red eye" — beer and clamato or tomato juice. He never got drunk when he had to fly the next day.

Mom and Dad's friends came over a lot. They would sit at the kitchen table and drink for hours and hours. Mostly, they had fun. There was always a lot of laughter. My dad could be very funny after he had a few drinks to loosen him up a bit, and his friends had a good sense of humor as well. I enjoyed being around them when they were having a good time, but I disliked it when Dad had too much.

I spent a lot of time at the golf course clubhouse, which was another drinking environment. I was constantly exposed to this kind of social interaction between people. It seemed fun to me.

My four older brothers and their friends all drank, and I wanted to try it too. When there were several people at our house drinking, it was easy for me to take a beer or two from their supply without being noticed. Often, a good friend of mine who was a year older would join me. We usually just drank one beer each, but that was enough to catch quite a buzz at such a young age.

When I was in Grade 6 (eleven years old), I wanted to make a few bucks, but I turned an entrepreneurial endeavor into something extremely foolish. I was going to sell beers to my classmates. I had been able to stockpile about eight beers, and I put them in my duffle bag and wrapped towels around them so no one could hear them clanking together. I put my bag by the front door to take to school with me. Just as I was getting ready to leave, my plan backfired. Somehow Rick and Gary found out and told my mom. Of course, I got into trouble. Luckily, my dad wasn't home, and he never found out.

By the time the twins were fifteen, they were drinking on a regular basis. They were a bad influence on me. Each year I got older I drank more. In my early teens, I drank almost every weekend with my friends. At that age, my friends and I drank beer while golfing at the Wetaskiwin course. I played a lot with Ron Norman, who was five years older than me. At eighteen, he was old enough to buy alcohol. Ron and I (along with some other friends) would fill up our golf bags with cold beer and drink them during our round. It was a lot of fun. The good thing was we weren't getting into trouble or doing any harm to anyone. In hindsight, it's very clear that I was much too young to be drinking.

One time in my mid-teens, my friends and I were drinking beer in the back alley behind the A&W in Wetaskiwin. All of a sudden, this RCMP paddy wagon comes racing up to us with their lights on. My friends took off running, but I thought I would play it cool and act nonchalant. I tossed my beer into some nearby hedges, which I thought the cops didn't see. My strategy didn't work. They must have seen us drinking our beers. They put me into the back of the paddy wagon by myself and kept me there for about twenty minutes. It seemed like an eternity. They were trying to scare me, and it worked. When they opened the door and told me I could leave, I could barely move. My legs were frozen stiff with fear! I had to shuffle my feet in order to get out of the paddy wagon. I wasn't charged with anything, and the police didn't notify my parents, so I got off lucky in the end.

When it came to drinking, my dad didn't set a good example for us boys. Eventually, it became a huge part of all of our lives, and this was accepted within our family. Over the years, alcohol abuse caused a tremendous amount of turmoil and fighting amongst us brothers. This stress was likely one of the contributing factors to my mental illness.

I became somewhat girl crazy at fourteen. Carli Merrick and Cathy Fonteyne had most of my attention. Carli was my first girlfriend and the first girl I fell in love with. She was thirteen and absolutely beautiful. She had long brunette hair, the most beautiful brown eyes that twinkled and a fairly dark complexion; she got very tanned in the summer months. She also had the figure of an eighteen-year-old. Carli was really friendly and had a great sense of humor, and she was also very smart. She was very popular and had a lot of friends. Carli was very talented and quite athletic as well. She was into ballet and enjoyed playing various sports. She spent a lot of time swimming at the local pool. She was a unique and extremely special person. My feelings for her were very powerful, and I always enjoyed spending time with her. I loved her.

One day, I brought Carli over to my grandma's house because I wanted them to meet. (There have only been two girls/women I have done this with.) As I anticipated, they hit it off right away, and the three of us had a great visit. I knew I had my grandma's approval towards this girl who I felt so strongly about, but there was another connection between them. Carli's last name was "Merrick" and Grandma's maiden name was also "Merrick." I was thinking that this was all meant to be! We didn't go beyond kissing, but it was magical!

CHAPTER 4
1979-1982
HIGH SCHOOL YEARS

Everything was going pretty well when two things happened that really upset me. The first thing was that Carli's parents sent her to a private girl's school in Victoria — 3000km away. I was shocked and didn't know why they did this.

The second thing was that my dad was transferred to Calgary, and I was forced to move there, but I didn't want to leave Wetaskiwin. I put up quite a fight, but in the end I had no choice. We moved there in the summer of 1979, and I started high school (Grade 10) that fall.

Because of our new situation, Carli and I were unable to continue with our relationship. We stayed in touch and wrote letters on a regular basis, and we still really cared for one another. As she was no longer my "official" girlfriend, my focus shifted to someone else: Cathy Fonteyne. Cathy's dad, Val Fonteyne, used to play NHL hockey with Gordie Howe on the Detroit Red Wings in the 1960s. I played golf with her brother Dean, whom I really liked. I had liked Cathy for quite a long time, and she was not easy to convince. It took me a long time before she would go out with me. She was into figure skating, so I watched her a few times; she was pretty good.

Cathy was my girlfriend for a very short time because my move to Calgary put an end to our relationship. We wrote letters for a while, and I saw her a couple of times when I went to Wetaskiwin, but we just lived too far apart to make it work. Cathy and I weren't together long enough to make things serious between us. The good thing is that neither one of us had to suffer from a broken heart when our relationship ended.

As much as I liked Cathy, my feelings were still stronger for Carli. When things ended between Cathy and I, my focus shifted back to Carli. I was hoping that somehow we could get back together again. About two weeks after I received her last letter from Victoria, I had the worst phone call of my life. One of Carli's best friends from Wetaskiwin called to tell me that Carli had been killed in a car accident near Wetaskiwin the previous day. I could hardly believe it. I was shocked. I thought, "Could this really be true? Carli's dead?" Unfortunately, it was true. I was totally devastated.

She had just turned fourteen — way too young to die. It was the first major loss of my life, and I became very depressed for the first time. I went to Wetaskiwin for her funeral. Carli's death was extremely difficult for me.

LORD BEAVERBROOK HIGH SCHOOL

Moving from the small town of Wetaskiwin to the big city of Calgary was overwhelming at first. I started attending Lord Beaverbrook High School, which had about 2300 students from grades 10-12. Clear Vista School in Wetaskiwin had about six hundred students for grades 1-9!

I can be introverted and extroverted. In Grade 10, I was mostly introverted. It took time for me to get used to this large school and being surrounded by these other students whom I didn't know. Even though I'd been on a hockey team since I was five, I didn't even play during the 1979-1980 season. I didn't have the confidence to get involved with a team in the big city for the first year there.

My dad put a pool table in the basement of our new home, so instead of playing hockey, I played pool. A lot of pool. Usually by myself. I spent countless hours practicing. Like most things, if you put enough time and effort into it, you will likely get good at it. Over time, I became a pretty good player. My dad was pretty good at the game, too, but he hardly ever came downstairs to play. I loved it when he did!

The good thing was that I didn't drink a lot during Grade 10, I just played pool. Eventually, I became friends with Neill and Steve from my school. Neill was French and had just moved to Calgary from Montreal, Quebec. He was a decent guy. Steve was a bit of a rock head and was more Neill's friend than mine. Neill was eighteen, which meant he was old enough to buy beer for us. Another good thing was that Neill and Steve weren't big drinkers. As a result, I didn't drink a lot when we were together. We would each have a few beers but didn't get too carried away.

My new friends introduced me to marijuana, a.k.a pot or weed. We didn't even smoke cigarettes in Wetaskiwin, let alone pot! I thought people who smoked pot were "druggies" or "heads." When it came to pot, I was naïve. We smoked it, and I discovered it was harmless. Mainly, it made me feel very relaxed and gave me the munchies. Since I enjoyed smoking pot, I was willing to try the next drug I was introduced to: hash. I liked it as well, so I discovered getting stoned wasn't so bad after all.

WILLOW PARK GOLF & COUNTRY CLUB

Dad bought a membership at Willow Park Golf & Country Club in southeast Calgary mainly so I could play on a regular basis. He seldom played there himself. This was a private golf course and was ranked amongst the best courses in the city. Willow Park wasn't a long golf course, but it was very challenging. The fairways were very narrow, and there were a lot of trees. I hit my 3 iron off the tee on a lot of the holes to give myself a better chance of hitting the fairways, and usually only had a short iron to reach the green on my second shot. The tee boxes, fairways and greens were immaculate. It was a beautiful golf course, kept in superb condition by the superintendent and his grounds crew. I was putting well during that era — I loved those greens. I was a member throughout high school, and I played a lot of golf there. I may have finished third or fourth in the junior club championship one of those years, and I maintained a 3-4 handicap. During Grade 10, I played on the Lord Beaverbrook High School golf team with three others. We competed in a few events against other Calgary high school teams at different courses.

I've had a lot of different jobs in my life. One of my most enjoyable was during high school in Calgary. When I was in Grade 10, I was hired to be the groundskeeper at a rather large townhouse complex in the community I lived in, which was called Midnapore. Mainly, I cut the grass and kept it watered. I watered the trees and kept the grounds nice and clean. My favorite part of the job was using a "ride-m-mower" to cut the grass in the large courtyard in the middle of the complex. The tenants' front yards were pretty small, so I used a push mower to cut their lawns. It turned out to be a year-round job because in the winter months, I shoveled snow off the driveways. This physical work helped keep me in pretty good shape. I worked there the whole time I was in high school and during the summer holidays.

I rode my bike ten minutes to work the first summer, but it didn't take me long to save $3,000 and buy my first car — a 1976 Chevrolet Malibu Classic Olympic Edition. This was my new mode of transportation to go to work and school. Before this, I took the school bus.

Working at golf courses, I would interact with up to two hundred people a day, which I loved. My job as groundskeeper was the complete opposite in this regard. I worked alone and didn't really speak with anyone while I worked. I really enjoyed the solitude. These jobs put me in two totally different working environments, and I loved them both! It must be the Gemini in me.

I had to be very responsible to have the groundskeeping job because I was the only one working there. Essentially, I was my own boss. I scheduled my own work hours and had to be very disciplined. I worked for Equity Capital Corporation, and I only saw my boss, Ivan, every two weeks when he brought my pay check and inspected the grounds. I always had my work done, and the complex looked good, so he was always happy with me. This arrangement worked perfectly for me. The minimum wage at the time was about $4.50/hour but I was getting $6.50/hour and averaging about twenty-five hours per week. As a high school student, I was making approximately $650 per month (probably a little less during the winter). I wasn't getting rich, but I was still pleased. It wasn't bad for the early 1980s. Another bonus was that I was still able to play a lot of golf.

DAVE LAMBERT

At the beginning of Grade 11, I was standing in front of our house waiting for the school bus when this guy I had never seen before walked up and waited there with me. It turned out he was new to the neighborhood and was also starting Grade 11 at Beaverbrook. His name was Dave Lambert, and we hit it off immediately.

Dave, his parents and younger brother, Alec, had recently moved to Calgary from Drayton Valley, Alberta, which is about ninety minutes southwest of Edmonton. They lived just across the street from us, and their house backed onto Fish Creek Park. Our house overlooked the park, so it was only a two-minute walk for us to get to each other's home. We were both sixteen when we met, and our birthdays are only one month apart. Dave and I rode the school bus together for the first part of that school year, but as soon as I got my car, I drove it to school. Dave rode with me or drove his dad's truck, so we didn't have to ride the school bus anymore!

We had a lot in common. For starters, we both loved sports and were both very competitive. We soon realized we must have played against each other in bantam hockey because the teams we played for (Wetaskiwin and Drayton Valley) were in the same league. We both played golf, but I had the edge there. Dave was good at racquet sports. He kicked my ass in squash, racquet ball, tennis and badminton.

Midnapore had a lake called, appropriately, Lake Midnapore. The city stocked it with five thousand rainbow trout each year, and we often took a boat out fishing. During the winter months, we would sometimes go ice fishing. We would usually turn this into a competition to see who would catch the biggest and/or the most fish. There were all kinds of things to do at Lake Midnapore. Dave and I would throw a football around or play catch with a frisbee. We would shoot baskets on the basketball court. There was even a sandy beach where we could relax and suntan. And, of course, we would check out the girls in their bikinis! In the winter, they kept a section of the ice cleared off so people could skate and play hockey, which Dave and I enjoyed doing as well. We were lucky to have these things to do in our community. It was a great place for a couple of high school boys.

Our pool table converted into a ping-pong table, so Dave and I spent a lot of time playing these games as well. I was a little better at pool than Dave, and we were evenly matched at ping-pong. We almost always made this a competition and often had a bet on the line.

Dave and I became best buddies within a short period of time while my friendship with Neill and Steve dissipated. Like most high schools, Beaverbrook was kind of cliquey. Dave and I didn't want to get involved with any of these groups of people, so we just hung out together and did our own thing. In time, we became friends with Randy Grayson and Darren Strand. They were the same age as Dave and me and were also into sports. Randy and Darren were both very athletic. Randy was 6'2" and 255 pounds in Grade 11. He played hockey, lacrosse and football. He went on to play professional football in the Canadian Football League (CFL) with the Toronto Argonauts and the Calgary Stampeders.

After taking a year off from hockey, I got back into it. Darren, Dave and I played together on a juvenile "B" team in Calgary. It was fun to be teammates with my friends.

It wasn't just all about sports in high school! We had other interests. Namely, we liked to party, and we had a vested interest in girls. Dave introduced me to ouzo, a very strong Greek liqueur that has a licorice flavor to it. We drank it with Coke or in shots. Ouzo produced a distinct buzz.

Randy and Darren loved to get stoned, and we smoked a lot of pot and hash. My favorite was black hash, which we would often hot knife for an instant and very powerful buzz. We also took magic mushrooms several times and would laugh uncontrollably. It was a lot of fun! I tried cocaine a few times, but I never used other drugs like acid, LSD or heroin. Being underage, my friends and I couldn't go to the bars, but we went to a lot of really good house parties.

As for girls, we were normal high school guys in that we were interested in them and pursued some of them. There were two girls in particular at Beaverbrook whom I really liked. They both had boyfriends, but that didn't stop me from trying. In the end, all my time and effort to win these girls over was to no avail. They thought I was a nice guy, but they faithfully and loyally stuck to their boyfriends. I was quite disappointed, but I admired them for their loyalty. As things turned out, neither Dave nor I had a girlfriend in high school. In such a large school there were a lot of possibilities, but we were very picky when it came to "girlfriend material." We just didn't find the right one for us at that time of our lives.

Dave's dad, Ralph, was a very successful businessman. He was involved with the oil industry and was based out of Drayton Valley, which was an "oil town." Mr. Lambert was a self-made multimillionaire. He retired in his late 40s and moved to Calgary. When I first met him in 1980, he had a net worth of ten million. Mr. Lambert and I developed a really good relationship. He was extremely intelligent and had a great sense of humor. We got along well, and we laughed a lot when we were together. He was just starting to learn how to play golf when we met, so I helped him a bit with this. Over the next several years, we played some golf together. He was funnier than hell to play with. I liked Mrs. Lambert, Bernice, as well, and we also got along. Dave's parents were good people. I became very close to Dave and his mom and dad. They felt like family to me.

Dave and I did some traveling together when we were in our early 20s. We spent some time in Tucson and Phoenix, Las Vegas and Mazatlán, Mexico, to name a few places. We always had a great time on our trips. The main reason we became such good friends was because we had a lot in common. We had similar interests, thought a lot alike and usually shared the same viewpoint on matters. Despite this, our lives ended up going down two very different paths.

Dave has been extremely fortunate. For one thing, he had a very good relationship with his parents. His father was a good dad, but he was also like a friend and mentor for Dave. Dave had a lot of respect for his dad and learned a lot from him. This applied to business matters and life in general. Dave's dad also helped him and his younger brother, Alec, financially to get their business started in the beginning. They started out with Dalta Rentals Inc., which rented and leased frac tanks to oil companies. They started out with ten tanks. After several years, they changed the name to DC Energy. Their business grew dramatically over the years, and they ended up owning 1,500 tanks. They also owned several large trucks. Their rather small staff in the beginning grew to 250 employees, and the corporation grew to be worth multi-millions of dollars. After working very hard for close to thirty years, Dave and Alec sold DC Energy in 2009, and Dave semi-retired very comfortably at age forty-five. Since then, he has been busy with his business, Aspen Creek Investments, an investment company primarily focusing on real estate investments. He travels a lot for business and for pleasure. He still keeps very busy. Dave has been lucky to have had good mental and physical health throughout his life.

For a large part of my life, I was very entrepreneurial. I had my own dreams and aspirations. If I would have had the fortune of good health, I would have had some success financially. Having mental illnesses changed all of that.

The most important thing as far as I'm concerned is that Dave is a great friend. After knowing each other for forty years, we are still the best of buddies. As much as Dave and I have in common, when it comes to money and lifestyle, our differences are astronomical. Because my CPP Lifetime Disability only pays me $8,400/year and Elli, my wife, earns about $35,000/year, it's obvious why our lifestyles are at two different ends of the spectrum.

More than anything else, I wish I could work, especially as a golf professional. I loved my profession and worked very hard to get to where I was. My last four jobs triggered manic episodes, which resulted in me having to be hospitalized in psychiatric wards. Accepting the fact that I could no longer work was extremely difficult for me. I'm not the kind of guy to sit on my ass and collect a measly $700/month on a CPP Lifetime Disability Pension if I am able to work and make a lot more money instead. Plus, I hate the fact that my wife has to work while I stay at home. If anything, I wish it was the other way around.

My Dad

When I was in Grade 11, my dad bought me a 1980 Oldsmobile Omega. It was a nice car. It was white with a red trim and had red velvet seats. This is a good example of my dad's generosity and shows how good he could be to me. The first thing I did was install a Clarion cassette stereo system that had a booster/equalizer and great speakers. It had excellent sound and was extremely loud! The only problem was those velvet seats. Before long, there were a bunch of little "hash burn" holes in them. I ended up driving that car for five years. It was a good vehicle and a great party car for my buddies and me.

My dad also bought a twenty-nine-foot Californian Wellcraft yacht that year. He kept it at the Sidney Marina on Vancouver Island. It wasn't overly luxurious or fancy, but it was really nice, and it slept at least six people. My dad wasn't rich, we were maybe an upper middle-class family at best, but he loved to have some toys. When it was really cold and snowy in Calgary during the winter months, my dad would sometimes spontaneously decide — often after a few rum & Cokes — to go to the island for a few days with my mom. The flight from Calgary to Victoria only took one hour, and the marina was a twenty-minute drive from there. Compared to Calgary, the weather is a lot warmer on Vancouver Island during the winter, and generally there is no snow. If it was warm enough, my parents would stay on the yacht. Otherwise, they usually stayed at the Cedarwood Motel in Sidney. I went with them once in a while.

The summer months were awesome for spending time on my parent's yacht. My dad navigated us through the Gulf Islands and the San Juan Islands. He took us to places like Salt Spring Island, Roche Harbor, Bedwell Harbour, Friday Harbor and Mayne Island, to name a few. Cruising the open waters of the Pacific Ocean on a very warm, sunny day on a yacht is a tremendous experience. There is a lot of breathtaking scenery, and we often saw dolphins and seals. Once in awhile we would see a whale.

After cruising for several hours, my dad would pull into a marina at one of the islands where we would stay for the night. We would BBQ a steak or something for dinner and have a few cold beers. Sometimes we would check out the island itself to see what was there. It wasn't uncommon for us to find a pub or two along the way. I always found the marinas we stayed at very interesting because I encountered people with their boats and yachts from all over the world. I really enjoyed walking up and down the docks checking out all the different watercraft. There was always quite a variety, including sailboats and commercial fishing vessels. I saw many luxurious yachts valued at well over a million dollars and met a lot of nice people on these excursions.

My Uncle Vince and Aunt Marg Billsten lived on Mayne Island for several years. Uncle Vince was a house builder and built many really nice homes there over the years. They had a beautiful home overlooking the ocean, and I loved going to their place.

My dad was able to unwind and relax for a while when he spent time on his yacht. When he was transferred to Calgary, Imperial Oil/Esso made him manager of human resources, a very stressful job that he hated. For one, he had to wear a suit and tie to work. My dad was a pilot, and he liked flying airplanes, so I don't know why they gave him this office job. I just know it made him very unhappy and caused him a great amount of stress.

In June of 1982, I graduated from Grade 12 at Lord Beaverbrook. I am the only one of the five boys in our family to become a high school graduate.

CHAPTER 5
1983-1984
THE WINDERMERE GOLF
& COUNTRY CLUB

In 1983, my dad was transferred to Edmonton. He was back flying again, which made him happy. Esso had a "King Air," which was an executive jet he flew some of the big wigs around in. Then Esso bought a 737. This new plane was different from the Electra he had flown for so many years, and it had a lot of new computerized gadgets he was unfamiliar with. He basically had to go back to school at age fifty to learn to fly it. Part of his training was going to Vancouver to train on a simulator. All of this was difficult for him, but he managed to do what he needed to. Once again, these were very stressful times for him.

Dad bought a house in south Edmonton in the community of Blue Quill. We put our pool table in the basement, and it was used a great deal over the following years.

In the spring of 1983, my dad bought a membership at the Windermere Golf & Country Club, a private golf course about twenty minutes southwest on the outskirts of Edmonton. I ended up working there and playing a lot of golf there over the next two years. My dad seldom played golf, but I loved it when he did. Sometimes after he played he went to the lounge for a couple of beers. He was well liked by the staff and could be a lot of fun when he was in "relax mode."

MY DAD DIED

On a Sunday in early November of 1983, my mom and dad drove to Wetaskiwin to visit my grandma. I had breakfast with them that morning and everything was OK. Around 5:00 p.m., I was at home by myself when the phone rang. It was my mom. She said Dad had had a heart attack and was in the Wetaskiwin Hospital. The early prognosis was that he might not be able to fly again, but he should survive.

This was a shock and totally came out of the blue. Pilots had to have a full medical exam every six months, and he had just had one a few months previous. A couple of hours later, my mom called me back. She said the update was that my dad's heart attack was more serious than the doctors had originally thought. He had actually suffered a major heart attack, and they were going to transfer him to the Royal Alexandra Hospital in Edmonton. This was scary. I couldn't believe what was happening.

The next morning, Doug, Jim, Gary and I went to the hospital (we weren't able to get in touch with Rick). My mom was there along with my dad's sister and her husband, Auntie Leone and Uncle Keith. Dad was in the ICU, and my poor mom was a complete wreck. I went into his room where he was hooked up to these tubes and machines. It was a shocking sight. I didn't know if he was aware of my presence or not. I knew he might not survive. It was an incredibly difficult experience for me. I had never told my dad that I loved him before, so I made sure I did at that moment. "I love you, Dad" turned out to be the last words I ever spoke to him.

Shortly after this, Jim and I were standing together in the hallway when a nurse basically asked our permission to disconnect our dad's life support mechanism. Jim and I just looked at each other. Before either of us could say anything, another nurse walked up and said Dad had died. He was only fifty-one — far too young to die. I was only nineteen. It was November 8, 1983.

Being a pilot is a very stressful job, and the stress my dad had gone through the previous three years had a lot to do with his heart attack. Plus, raising five Walin boys must have been extremely stressful for him. Too much. His heart couldn't handle any more of it.

As soon as we moved to Edmonton in the winter of '82, I got a full-time job at the Mid-Niter Drug Store on 23rd Avenue. It was a 9-5, Monday-to-Friday job with the weekends and holidays off. I enjoyed this regular working schedule, and it turned out to be the only job I'd ever have with "regular" working hours. The Mid-Niter was half grocery store and half drugstore. I mainly worked on the grocery side of the store. My main duty was pricing the items and stocking the shelves, coolers and freezers. I also worked the cash register. I was only getting paid minimum wage ($5/hour), but I liked my job and the fact that it was only a five-minute walk to work. Karen Hall was the manager, the head pharmacist and my boss. Looking back, she was the nicest boss I've ever had. She treated me well, and she was just a good, down-to-earth person. I ended up working there for about 1½ years.

In the spring of 1983, Jim and I started playing golf at the Windermere Golf & Country Club on a regular basis. During the week, we had a tee time booked for approximately 6 p.m. every evening. I worked at the Mid-Niter until 5, went home for a quick dinner and went straight to the course to get 18 holes in just before dark. Jim and I had both been on the wagon for a few months — no drinking at all. For the first couple of months of the golf season, we played our game of golf and went straight home.

One night after we finished playing, one of the assistant pros, Mike Harrington, asked us if we wanted to go to the lounge for a beer. We looked at each other and thought, why not? After a few beers at the clubhouse, we went to a lounge called David's in south Edmonton. Some of the Windermere staff were there too. We were on a roll now!

Mike came with Jim and me, and we lit a joint as soon as we got in my car. From the back seat Mike said, "You guys smoke lefties too?" ("lefties" was his term for a joint). He was getting his first taste of these "angel" Walin boys. When Jim and I were on the wagon, we liked to get stoned once in a while. From what I know, Jim didn't smoke a lot of dope in his life. I was a different story. We had a blast at David's, but we fell off the wagon in a big way! We really liked the Windermere staff that was there with us. And we met David Vaughn, the owner of the establishment. We liked him too. It turned into quite a party. We stayed there until 7:00 a.m. the next morning! When you enter David's, the lounge is on the right and the restaurant is on the left. I saw people coming in for breakfast while we were still in the lounge drinking! It was quite a start to our new friendships at the Windermere Golf & Country Club. After partying all night and getting no sleep at all, I went to work at the Mid-Niter that next morning. It was a very rough day to say the least. I paid the price for my stupidity.

Shortly after this escapade, Bill Carrington, the head pro at Windermere, hired me as the back shop manager, which was basically a fancy name for a club cleaner. Along with a few other guys, my job was cleaning the members' clubs and taking their clubs in and out of the golf bag storage area. It wasn't a glamorous job by any means, but at least I liked my work environment. I was working at a golf course, and I liked the fact that I worked outside.

During the golf season, I worked part-time at the Mid-Niter and part-time at Windermere where I usually worked the close shift. In the winter months, I went back to full-time at the Mid-Niter. I didn't like cleaning golf clubs for $5/hour as a job, but the other staff members I worked with at Windermere made it a lot easier to tolerate. Bill was OK to work for, but I didn't have a lot of contact with him. He just let me do my job, which worked well with me. I had a lot more contact with his assistant pros Darrell McDonald, Mike Harrington, Howard Vickers and Don Sorenson. I got along with these guys really well. Before long, Darrell, Mike and I became the best of buddies. They were great to work with, and outside of work we hung around together all the time. The other staff who worked upstairs in the lounge/restaurant were also great co-workers. There was Angela Babb, Cheryl Burke and Lori Griffiths to name a few. Connie was the bar manager. We all got along great. I also had a lot of fun partying with these people on many occasions.

To me, Windermere seemed like a private golf course without the private course atmosphere. Many of the members were wealthy, but most of them weren't arrogant or snobby. Some of them were in the oil industry. These guys drank a lot and liked to play cards for a lot of money. Most of the members and their guests were very friendly. A lot of them were real characters. Because of the other staff members and the members themselves, I had the most fun I ever had working at a golf course.

Mike Harrington and I became the dynamic duo. Double trouble. We both liked to drink, and drink we did. A lot. I had just turned nineteen, and Mike was twenty-two. We went to the bar at least five nights a week, which is where we spent our pay checks for about two years. When Mike and I drank, we usually ended up getting absolutely hammered! Once we started, we didn't know when to stop or didn't have the self-control to. Both of us lost our memory on a regular basis when we were drinking. We just laughed about this at the time. Looking back, I don't think it's funny because it's a symptom of alcoholism. Despite this, we had an incredible amount of fun. I do remember that.

When sober, Mike was a pretty quiet guy. He wasn't very talkative or personable. He may have been a bit shy. An amazing transformation took place after he had some beers in him. He would become very talkative and turn into one of the most hilarious people I have ever met! It was guaranteed to happen every time he had several beers, and he was a lot of fun to drink with because of this.

One of our favorite nightclubs in south Edmonton was Barry T's, owned by Barry Tomalty. We went there a lot. Once Mike and I had a few beers in us we were there for the duration. Our friend, Darrell, was wiser than us. He didn't go to the bars nearly as often as my other friends and I, and when he did go, he would have one or two beers then switch to Coke. He was always the first one to leave the bar — usually by midnight or earlier. Darrell didn't have the propensity to drink like the rest of us. Many of us were alcoholics and Darrell wasn't, but he still liked to join us and have fun. He was one of the most personable people I have ever met, and he had a fantastic sense of humor.

Darrell was also very serious about golf. During that era, he was ranked among the top three CPGA assistant pros in central and northern Alberta. Including head pros, Darrell may have been in the top five in this region. I didn't play much golf with Darrell. On occasions that I did, I usually didn't enjoy it because he had a nasty temper on the golf course. If things weren't going his way, he would become irate. His temperament was much better if he was playing well.

Golf is an incredibly difficult game, and the more advanced a golfer gets, the more it becomes a mental game because it's easy to get frustrated or angry when playing this sport. A person must learn how to manage their emotions on the golf course. If they don't, they'll get the best of you. Getting angry will work against you. I know what it's like to lose it, throw clubs, etc. I was quite young when I did this and never did after I became a pro at twenty-two.

At one point, Darrell went to Florida to take lessons from Jimmy Ballard, one of the most prominent golf instructors in the United States. Jimmy was working with Hal Sutton then, who was one of the best players on the PGA Tour. After working with Jimmy, Darrell made some significant changes to his swing. He was working on these changes at the driving range at Windermere, and I was interested in this development. Back then, I didn't know much about the golf swing. I was a fairly good player, mostly because I played and practiced so much, but I had only had a few golf lessons, and I hadn't really studied the mechanics of the swing much. With some help from Darrell, I tried to incorporate some of Jimmy Ballard's teaching methods into my own swing. Some of his techniques seemed very complicated and unusual to me. While Darrell was making these complicated changes to his own swing, I just tried a couple of the more basic methods with mine.

Prior to this, I always tried to keep my head as still as possible during my swing, and I turned my hips on my backswing and my follow through. Jimmy Ballard's method was to move your head laterally in a significant manner during the swing, and to move your hips laterally (as opposed to "turning" them). Under Darrell's guidance, I made these two changes, but this "swaying" motion really fucked up my swing. Ever since then, I had this unwanted motion in my golf swing, and I wasn't able to get my natural swing back!

To make matters worse, I tried to make a major change with my putting technique around the same time. This was also a new method that Darrell was trying. He was a good putter and good player — he was a pro — so I was somewhat influenced by him. I was nineteen and had been a pretty good putter using the KISS method (Keep It Simple, Stupid). This worked the best for me because I didn't get too caught up in the mechanics of the stroke. Once I read my putt and was aligned correctly over the ball, I just made a "straight back and straight through" stroke. I just had to concentrate on the line and speed of my putt. Read it. Aim it. Hit it. Pretty simple. I don't know if this new method Darrell was trying was another Ballard technique, but I was to make an "inside, to square, to inside" stroke. It resembled the motion of a gate opening and closing, back and forth. After trying this new technique for a while, it wasn't working for me, and I tried to go back to my old style. To make a long story short, I was never able to get my old style back and putting became a nightmare. I don't blame Darrell for any of this, I just wish I hadn't started to fuck around with my swing and my putting stroke in the first place.

I know a hell of a lot more about the golf swing and putting now than I did then. The changes I was trying to make don't even make any sense to me now! If I only knew then what I know now.

Darrell played a lot of golf, practiced a lot and played in several professional tournaments. He took the game very seriously. Mike was a different story. He seldom played, I never saw him practice, and I don't recall him playing in any tournaments or events. On the rare occasions I played with him, he would hit a couple of poor shots then quit after two or three holes. I don't think I ever played a full 9 holes with him, let alone 18. He was a poor sport.

PLAYING GOLF WITH THE EDMONTON OILERS

Ron Chipperfield and Ted Green played golf at Windermere on occasion. Ron ("Chipper") played with the Oilers when they were still in the WHA and was one of their best players. Ted played for the Boston Bruins back in the 1960s and 1970s and went on to become a coach of the Oilers.

Both Ron and Ted were good golfers too. Ron had a 2 or 3 handicap and Ted was about a 6. They were nice enough to ask me to play with them at Windermere a couple of times. They were real gentlemen, and I really enjoyed playing golf with them.

One time, some of the members of the Oilers played in a tournament at Windermere. Someone was kind enough to ask me to play in it, and I was more than pleased to accept their offer. I played really well that day. It was a Texas Scramble format, so we didn't keep our individual scores, but we did use a lot of my shots. I was hitting my driver extremely well all day. Most of my drives were 280-290 yards long and in the fairway. I think I would have shot close to even par if it would have been a normal round of golf.

It was a fun day on the course as well. Most of us had a few beers and were pretty relaxed. There were a lot of times over the years when I would play better after a few beers, but if I drank too much, I would lose my coordination and play like shit. Somehow, when I played in this tournament, I had quite a few beers and still managed to keep it together.

After we finished playing, we had dinner and the prize ceremony at the clubhouse (and a few more beers). "Cowboy" Bill Flett, a well-known pro hockey player with the former Calgary Cowboys of the WHA was sitting next to me. It was exciting for me to be there, socializing with him and the others. We decided to have a "horserace," which is usually an individual event, but they decided to make it a team event. Two teams were selected with about fifteen players on each team. The "entry fee" was $20 per player, and the winning team would split the pot of $600. Only one problem: all I had was $20, and this was my beer money, so I couldn't afford to enter the horserace.

Very embarrassingly, I mentioned this to Cowboy Flett. He said, "Don't worry, I've got you covered." I really appreciated his kindness and generosity.

Gary Lecuyer was made captain of one team, and I was the captain of the other team. We started the horserace on the first hole. By the time we got to the second green it was too dark to continue, so we decided to have a putting contest to decide the winner. We started from about thirty feet away. It was so dark that we couldn't see the hole, so someone used a lighter to show everyone where it was. The other team went first, and no one made it. Our team wasn't having any luck either. It came down to our last player who sunk this thirty-foot putt in the dark with only a Bic lighter to guide him. It was unbelievable! Our team was ecstatic! With my share of the $600 our team had won, I was able to pay back Cowboy Flett, and I had a little more beer money for the night. Bonus. All in all, it was a great day for me. I really enjoyed it.

In the fall of 1983, I went to Waterton Lakes Golf Course in Waterton National Park to play in their pro-am with Darrell and a couple of other pros from the Edmonton area. It's beautiful in the Waterton Lakes region. When we arrived, there was snow on the golf course, and we thought we weren't going to be able to play. Then someone had a good idea. They put the sprinklers on all over the course, and it melted the snow off the fairways and greens. Luckily, the weather was warm enough to make this work. It was quite cool and extremely windy, but we managed to get all of our golf in. In the end, I was second-lowest amateur, one or two shots behind the low amateur of the tournament.

In 1984, I played in the Labatt's Pro-Am at the Derrick Golf & Winter Club, a private club in south Edmonton. It was cold and raining. The tournament committee were thinking about canceling the event, but they decided we could play. The pro on our team was Greg Pidlaski, the head pro at the Leduc Golf & Country Club, at the time. My 4 handicap was the lowest amateur on our team. I didn't hit the ball well the first few holes because I was nervous and thought I wasn't swinging well. Greg told me to "Just keep swinging the way you are. You will be fine." He was right. After those first few holes, I settled down and started to hit it better. Then our group came to some "beer holes." I ended up drinking about four beers during the rest of my round, which helped me relax even more and play better. All of the golfers finished the day with a nice dinner at the Derrick. Unfortunately, our team didn't finish in the prizes.

WAYNE GRETZKY & DAVE SEMENKO

I was lucky enough to live in Edmonton during the 1980s, an extremely exciting time for hockey. It was during this era that the Edmonton Oilers built their dynasty and won five Stanley Cups! They were led by Wayne Gretzky and Mark Messier. Other superstars on their team were Hall of Famers Paul Coffey, Jari Kurri, Glenn Anderson and goalie Grant Fuhr to name a few. Wayne was my favorite hockey player and was likely the best to ever play the game. He holds countless records, many of which are so incredible that they won't be beaten. I loved to watch him play because he was a hockey genius. He outsmarted all of the other players, especially the opposition. He always seemed to be two to three steps ahead of the play.

One time, my friends and I were at David's, the lounge I mentioned earlier. On my way to the washroom, David Vaughn (the owner) said, "Hi Donny." He was sitting at a table with some other men. As I was saying, "Hi David, how are you doing?" I saw that Wayne Gretzky was one of the four men sitting there, right in front of me. I thought to myself, "Holy shit, that's Wayne Gretzky!" I was kind of awestruck and dumbfounded. The Great One was only a few feet from me. I only talked with David for a few seconds before rejoining my friends at our table. I told my buddies about my Gretzky encounter right away.

Wayne was having a beer and talking with these guys, so there was no way I was going to ask him for his autograph or bother him in any way. I had an idea of the demands and pressure put on him by his fans (and the general public) for such things, and I thought "Leave the poor guy alone and give him some space to enjoy himself without being hounded!" I tried to do my small part in having this kind of courtesy and respect for Wayne. Besides, I'm not an autograph guy anyway. I have never asked a professional athlete or celebrity for their autograph. If I really like someone who is a celebrity, I want to meet them and get to know them. I would like to be able to sit down and talk with them for a couple of hours. For me, this would include people such as Wayne, Michael J. Fox, Ellen DeGeneres and Oprah.

The Oilers had a few "enforcers" — Dave Semenko, Marty McSorley and Kevin McClelland — who were some of the toughest and best fighters in the NHL. Semenko was like a bodyguard for Gretzky. If someone gave Wayne a cheap shot or got too aggressive with him, they would have to deal with Dave. Often, Dave's mere presence on the ice was enough to give Wayne more room to weave his magic. I've seen him fight many times, and he was one of the best there ever was. He would get this look in his eyes like he was going to kill you. It was scary!

In 1989, Dave Semenko published his own book (with Larry Tucker) titled *Looking Out for Number One.* "Number One," of course, is Wayne Gretzky. It was interesting. Semenko's nickname was "Sammy," and he was also a regular at David's. His girlfriend, Marvette, was a waitress in the lounge. She was Hawaiian or Polynesian and really good looking. She had beautiful darker skin. She was a very good waitress and very outgoing and friendly with the customers. Sammy always sat at the bar in the same spot, usually by himself. He seemed like a quiet guy to me. He would just sit there minding his own business. Once in a while, I would see him talking to someone beside him. He drank beer and smoked cigarettes. I never saw him get drunk. He always appeared to be sober and in total control of himself. Marvette seemed to like my buddies and I. She treated us well and liked to joke around with us. She thought I was cute and would sometimes give me a kiss on the cheek. I would pray to God that Sammy wasn't watching whenever she did this. Luckily, for me, I survived these incidents.

Many years later (after I had quit drinking), I went to David's one time. I was sitting at the bar right beside Semenko. He was drinking beer, and I was drinking O'Doul's, a non-alcoholic beer. He asked me what I was drinking, so I told him and briefly explained my drinking status. He seemed interested in what I was saying. I had heard a rumor that Sammy liked to have a good time and ended up drinking a little too much, too often. I was under the impression that he was thinking about quitting. Having done this myself, I was very familiar with this scenario. I don't know if he ended up quitting or not, but it felt good to at least "plant the seed" with him that day.

I ran into Sammy at Extra Foods in West Kelowna many years later, around 2009. I literally almost collided with him going down one of the aisles. I introduced myself and told him that I knew him a little bit from David's lounge in Edmonton twenty-five years ago. I knew he didn't remember me partly because I looked completely different. Still, he was very friendly. When I said, "It's good to see you Dave!" he said, "It's good to see you too, man!" Dave told me he was scouting for the Oilers. At about 6'3" and 200 pounds, he still looked like he was in really good shape. He had come out to Kelowna for a summer vacation. He told me he was with Clark Gillies (ex-NY Islander) and Ron Flockhart (ex-Philadelphia Flyer). I asked Dave if he was still seeing Marvette. He said he wasn't and that she had moved to Calgary with her family. Our conversation was short but nice. Afterward, I wished I had thought of asking him if he was still drinking or not. If not, I wanted to remind him that I was the guy who introduced him to O'Doul's in the first place all those many years ago.

THE ROCK STAR

My friends and I also had nicknames. Darrell McDonald (Mac), Mike Harrington (Miles) and Bruce Eastcott (The Beast) to name a few. Mac nicknamed me "The Rock Star," which turned into Rock Star, The Rock and simply Rock. This was an affectionate way for Darrell to describe me and my lifestyle during that era. It was all about sex, drugs and rock n' roll. And a lot of drinking. Oh yeah, and a lot of golf too.

I became The Rock Star when I worked with Darrell and Mike at the Windermere Golf & Country Club in 1983 and 1984. A lot of other pros started calling me this and the name stuck. I liked it, but could you imagine being a real Rock Star? What a life that would be! I played a lot of party golf with Rick Wills and Larry Kroft those two years I was at Windermere. Rick was a big guy (about 6'2" and 240 pounds), and he could hit the ball over three hundred yards. Both he and Larry were low handicap players. They were fun to play with and were always very generous sharing their party treats — namely pot and hash joints. Our power carts always had a good supply of beer, whiskey and Coke on board as well. Despite this, we usually kept our composure on the golf course. We didn't get totally hammered out there. And we were usually still able to play some respectable golf. Rick and Larry did this every time they played, which was about five days a week.

When I worked at the Mid-Niter Drug Store, part of my job was to stock the freezers with ice cream and other frozen goods. When I was hung over, which was often, I spent a lot of time in those big freezers. It seemed to help a bit.

My buddies and I started drinking at David's in the afternoon one winter day. By 8:00 p.m., I was well oiled. Gary Meyers, the head pro at the Belvedere Golf & Country Club in Sherwood Park (a private course on the outskirts of Edmonton), showed up. I wasn't a close friend of Gary's, but we had met many times and always got along well. He had a great sense of humor. Gary either didn't drink or drank very little because he appeared to be sober every time I saw him. After hanging out with us, he was going to a Greek restaurant called Yanny's to meet up with some of the Edmonton Oilers players. Somehow, I talked him into taking me with him.

At Yanny's, the only thing I remember is that someone passed a bottle of ouzo to me, which I took a drink from, then passed it to someone else. We sat at a long table. There were a lot of guys there. I think Mark Messier was there, but I'm not certain. I don't know which other Oilers were there because I was too drunk to remember. The only other thing I remember is Gary dropping me off at home at the end of the night.

After the 1983 golf season, Bill Carrington said he wanted me to come back and work for him again in 1984. He told me he would try to get me working in the pro shop a bit, and that he would give me a raise in pay, so I accepted his offer. After about 2½ months into the season, nothing had changed. I was still cleaning golf clubs, I wasn't working in the pro shop, and Bill didn't give me a raise. By the age of nine, I was working in the pro shop at the Wetaskiwin Golf Club. Eleven years later, I was working as a club cleaner.

I felt like I was going backwards in the golf industry. I was very unhappy and discouraged, so I quit. When I went into Bill's office to give him my two weeks' notice, I became quite emotional and was trying hard not to cry. While this was extremely difficult for me, Bill just got pissed off. He should have handled this situation much better.

Soon after, one of the staff members at Windermere told me about the San Diego Golf Academy. Apparently, someone they knew went to the two-year golf school and enjoyed it. I was a little reluctant, but I looked into it further, and the next thing I knew, my mom, Jim, Gary and I drove to San Diego, California, to check it out in person. It was also a vacation for the four of us.

I decided to apply and was accepted. One of the major deciding factors was that I qualified for a lot of financial assistance from student loans and grants. This type of schooling wasn't available anywhere in Canada, so I received a lot of money from both the provincial and federal governments of Canada that paid for my tuition, books and some of my living expenses. The best part was that I didn't have to pay any of the grant money back.

My two year party in Edmonton was over and I was heading for Southern California.

CHAPTER 6
1985-1986
THE SAN DIEGO GOLF ACADEMY

The San Diego Golf Academy (SDGA) is a world-renowned golf institution. In 1985, it was the only one of its kind in the world. It was a four semester program (twenty months in total), and I started classes in January 1985. In August 1986, I graduated with a diploma in Golf Operations and Management. Having this diploma helps graduates get a solid start in their careers in the vast golf industry. My focus was on becoming a golf professional and specializing on teaching golf. The SDGA also helped with job placement for graduates. Many graduates got jobs at some of the finest golf courses around. Some became general managers or club professionals, others were sales representatives for golf companies.

The SDGA is located in Rancho Santa Fe, California (where PGA Tour sensation Phil Mickelson lives), about thirty minutes north of San Diego. The Whispering Palms Golf Course, a 27-hole facility (South course, North course and East course), is located on the site along with five classrooms. We played most of our golf at this course.

There were about thirty students per class, and we took the courses with the same classmates for all four semesters. At any given time, there were about 120 students there from all over the world. When I was there, there were students from thirteen different countries including China, Japan, Malaysia, Australia, Brazil, Switzerland, Mexico and other faraway places. There were students from all over the United States and from right across Canada. Six of us in my class — Trevor Maywood, Lance Dzaman, Glen McCarger, Ross Hutton, Bari Smith and me — formed a special Canadian bond because we all came from the Great White North.

I loved all the different accents, and even the Americans had different accents from the various regions they were from. The New York and Boston accents were quite strong, and then there was the slow southern drawl from people who came from places like Texas. After awhile, I had a good idea where someone was from just by listening to them talk.

Another variety was the ages of the students. They were between 18-65 years of age, with the average around thirty. At twenty, I was one of the younger ones.

In the very beginning, a nineteen-year-old Japanese student named Kosuke Takahashi took a liking to me right away. He spoke very little English, and it was difficult for him to communicate. Despite the language barrier, we got along well. Over time, his English improved, and we became pretty good friends.

Perhaps the nicest guy I met and became good friends with was Jack Geopfrich from South Bend, Indiana. He was smart and had a great sense of humor. Like me, he liked to have a few beers, so we had a lot of good times together. One of the things I enjoyed the most about being a student at the SDGA was meeting and becoming friends with people from all over the globe.

The SDGA had some great instructors. A.J. Bonar, a former club professional from Ohio, Dean Reinmuth, who had played on the European Tour, and Don Witt, who had played on the PGA Tour, were the three pros. With my top priorities being learning the golf swing and teaching, I learned the most from A.J. and Dean.

By far, the most important thing I learned was the five "Ball Flight Laws," which A.J. taught. This helped my game and my teaching more than anything else.

THE FIVE "BALL FLIGHT LAWS"

1. Angle of attack
2. Center hit
3. Path
4. Face
5. Speed

One day, Dean told our class, "I'm teaching this left-handed amateur named Phil Mickelson. I want you guys to remember his name because he's going to become a great player on the PGA Tour." I don't think Dean was his instructor for very long, but his statement proved to be prophetic. Mickelson went on to become one of the best golfers in the history of the game. He has won a large number of PGA Tour events, including several majors, and is still one of the top players in the world as I am writing this book. Phil is also one of my favorite players not only for his golfing abilities, but that he seems to be a nice guy and has a perpetual smile on his face. I like that.

Some of the courses we took were: Golf Shop Management, Teaching Golf, Rules of Golf, Club Repair, Turf Grass Management, Food and Beverage Management, Attitude and Motivation, Language and Communication, Small Business Management, Accounting, and a computer course. There were several other courses we took as well but everything was designed to teach us about the golf industry. My favorite course was Teaching Golf. It always had my full attention and was where my heart was the most. I learned a lot from A.J., a very good instructor. Dean taught a class that focused on the golf swing itself. Unlike A.J., his teaching method was quite technical and somewhat complicated. I enjoyed his class as well, and I consistently finished near the top of our class on Dean's exams.

Students practiced at the Surf & Turf Driving Range in nearby Del Mar. In the third semester, we started teaching golf lessons to the public at this facility. It was our first formal teaching experience, and I loved it right away!

Academically, I did well at SDGA with an overall average of 3.3 (4.0 is straight As). My worst class was the computer course, which was my only D. I hated it! For some reason, I just didn't understand it, and I felt like a complete idiot.

Part of our curriculum for all four semesters was mandatory golf tournaments. Every week on Monday or Tuesday we competed against other SDGA students. We could win small amounts of cash (around $200 or less), it was great experience for competitive golf, and there were some pretty good players there. It usually took a score of 68-71 to win. Joe Novis, Robert Noel and Russ Wright from my class won some of these events and consistently finished in the top three places. I was always excited to play, and I always tried my best. I wanted to win one of these tournaments so much but, unfortunately, I wasn't able to. If I was putting well, I think I could have won a couple of times, but it wasn't meant to be.

Whispering Palms wasn't a long golf course. The fairways were narrow and the rough was long, so it was challenging in that respect. It was very important to hit your drives in the fairways. During my first year, I was hitting my driver terribly! I drove my ball in the rough a lot. As a consequence, I would often hit a 3 wood or a long iron off the tee, which gave me a better chance to keep my ball on the fairway. It was a busy golf course, and we didn't usually play until the afternoons, so the greens had a lot of spike mark damage on them. This didn't help the putting situation.

Between my driver problems and poor putting, my handicap went from 4 to 6, which is the highest it was for many years. By this time, I knew more than ever about the golf swing, but my handicap went up! I was extremely frustrated. Even though I liked A.J.'s teaching method better, it was Dean who helped me fix my driver problems. After I took a couple of lessons from him, I was able to straighten out my driver and started hitting the fairways. What a relief!

Shortly after, I started hitting my irons the best I've ever hit them in my life. From 150 yards, I was hitting my ball within 15-20 feet from the hole on average. Much of the time, I was hitting it less than ten feet from the hole and stuck it within a few feet countless times. I was even more accurate from inside 150 yards. My short irons were deadly. My mid irons and long irons were very good too. From 150-220 yards away, I was swinging the club extremely well. I was hitting a lot of greens in regulation and was getting a lot of really good looks at birdies. I had a lot of confidence with an iron in my hands. It felt awesome! This went on for about 2½ months.

During this time, I shot a lot of 75s that should have been much lower. I was missing at least five or six putts that were three feet or less every time I played, including several three-putt greens on a regular basis. It was horrific! Had I been making these short putts like I should have been I would have shot 69s and 70s. Despite my putting woes, I played well enough to get my handicap back down to 4.

My putting was so bad I ended up getting the "yips." Basically, this is a nervous condition that golfers sometimes get when they are really having problems with their putter. Golf is a difficult game, and it can drive you crazy if you let it. Putting alone almost drove me nuts! I would get over a putt, and then I would think about it way too much and freeze. Get stuck. It was extremely hard to even get my putter in motion. My hands would shake, and I took way too long to hit my putts. I would be trying so hard you would think that each and every putt was for a million dollars. Putting became like an anxiety disorder. I was aware that it was taking me such a long time to hit my putts, so I would get worried about the other players in my group. I knew they would be thinking "C'mon, hit the fucking putt already!" This added to my stress.

MY TWO LOWEST ROUNDS: 68 & 69

I broke 70 for the first time in my life at Whispering Palms. Then I did it again soon after. The first time, I scored a 3 under par 68, and the second time was a 3 under par 69. It felt great to finally achieve this goal. I don't recall doing anything spectacular during those two rounds. As far as I can remember, I just played solid, steady golf. I hit most of the fairways and greens in regulation. It was during the time when I was hitting my irons so well. I think the main factor was that I wasn't missing a half dozen three-foot putts. By putting half decently, I brought my usual score of 75 down to a 68 and 69.

When I found out I had been accepted to become a student at the San Diego Golf Academy, I decided it was time to get my shit together and get serious with my life. The two-year party I had been on was over. I thought anyone who would be going to this prestigious golf school would be serious too. The legal drinking age in the United States is twenty-one whereas in Canada it is either eighteen or nineteen. I would be underage for the first five months I lived in California and wouldn't even be able to get into the bars there. I wasn't too concerned about this because I wasn't planning on drinking when I got there. I was going to go on the wagon and focus on my studies and my golf game.

I had good intentions, but they didn't last long. My first night there, I got drunk with my two new roommates, Lance and Rudy. The three of us drank a bunch of beer at the apartment we shared in Escondido. We were all excited to be there and looking forward to embarking on our new journey. I loved Rudy's Oklahoma accent. Several times in the first year, I called some of my friends back in Edmonton and put them on the phone with Rudy so they could hear him talk. In fact, I partied with guys from all over the place with all these different accents, so I put a number of them on the phone with my buddies back home. We all had a lot of fun doing this.

It didn't take long to find out that I didn't have to be an "angel" while I was a student there. I met a lot of guys who liked to party. There was drinking and toking on a regular basis. California had some really good weed! It turned out I didn't have to wait five months to turn twenty-one to get into the bars either. One of my classmates, Joe Novis from Georgia, did me a big favor. He had also lived in Florida and had driver's licenses from both states. Joe was kind enough to let me use his Florida license for ID, which enabled me to get into all the drinking establishments immediately. I used it until I turned twenty-one in June. Joe was a year or two older than me, and we looked like each other enough for me to use his ID. I never had any problems doing this — it worked great! I got asked for my ID a lot too. They are very strict with their drinking-age policies.

I lived with Lance and Rudy in Escondido for the first semester. It was twenty miles inland from the coast and got over 100°F during the summer. I didn't want to live there when it was so hot, and I wanted to live closer to the ocean (and beaches) where it was cooler. There were quite a few students living in Escondido because the apartment rental rates were cheaper than those closer to the ocean, and the SDGA referred us there.

My good buddy, Darrell McDonald, used to spend part of his winters playing golf down in Orlando, Florida. His parents, Bud and Mary, owned a condo there. In 1985, during my first semester at the SDGA, Darrell came to visit me in Escondido. He drove by himself all the way from Florida to Southern California. He had quite a suntan/sunburn on his face when he arrived, as he was driving his MG convertible sports car. I couldn't believe he drove three thousand miles to come see me. But he did! Incredible! Darrell wanted to take a different route home to Alberta because he was tired of driving the east coast, but the main reason was to visit me. I appreciated it immensely, and it's a good example of how close our friendship was.

The first night Darrell was in Escondido, we went out to the bar and got drunk. We had a great time! I've only seen Mac drink more than a couple of beers on a few occasions. The next day, we just hung around our apartment. It was hot, we were both hung over, and we didn't have air-conditioning. We suffered that day. We played golf at Whispering Palms as well. Mac continued his journey home five days later. It was so good to spend time with him.

I didn't want to stay in Escondido much longer. Rudy wasn't exactly the ideal roommate, and we didn't hang out with each other at all. Lance and I decided to make a change and move to Carlsbad with a new roommate. Rudy had no problem finding another place, and there were no hard feelings between any of us.

I liked living in Carlsbad a lot more than Escondido. We lived in a nice community, and it was a very short drive to the beach. Our complex was quite large with a swimming pool and three hot tubs. Lance arranged for one of our classmates, Gavin Hibbert from Delaware, to become our new roommate. He was only eighteen, one of the youngest people at the school. Lance liked Gavin and they got along quite well, but I didn't and having to live with him was brutal. I don't know how I got talked into this arrangement. Because our apartment had only two bedrooms, Gavin slept on his mattress in the living room. Lance and I may have charged him less money for his portion of the rent because of this.

My buddy Dave Lambert came to visit me when I lived in Carlsbad. I didn't have any wheels, so we rented a cheap car from one of those "rent a wreck" places. The car was indeed a bit of a wreck. The driver door didn't work, so the driver had to get in from the passenger side. It ran a little rough and was kind of shabby in general. We called it our "Mexican Unit."

One night, Dave and I had a double date with a couple of girls we met. We drove to Dave's date's home to pick them up. As we pulled up the driveway in our Mexican Unit, we saw that her home was more of a mansion. Our car was quite a contrast to this. The parents invited Dave and I in for a drink. No doubt they wanted to check us out for themselves before letting their daughter leave with these two complete strangers from Canada. We had one drink with them while we talked. I guess they thought we were pretty good guys, as they allowed their daughter and her friend to go out with us.

Dave's date was a good looking girl. She wore a beautiful dress and had these long, white gloves on, like she was a movie star or something. I think Dave was pleased with her. My date couldn't have been remarkable because I don't remember anything about her at all or what we did on our date either.

Dave and I played golf at Torrey Pines in La Jolla during his visit.

I didn't bring a car to California, a decision I immediately regretted because for the first semester and a half, I couldn't drive anywhere. For the most part, I rode with Lance in his car. I hated the loss of independence, so after four months of this, I'd had more than enough. I needed a car! My mom owned a 1976 Toyota Corolla she wasn't using, so I flew home, and we drove it down to San Diego. She stayed at my place in Carlsbad for a while and then flew back to Edmonton. It made a huge difference to have my own wheels!

Shortly before I moved to San Diego, I met Jackie, a girl I was smitten with, at Goose Looney's nightclub in Edmonton. She was about four years older than me and was working as a nanny. Jackie had done some modeling, so she was a pretty girl. It seemed like there were two sides to her. If she was drinking, she was kind of on the wild side. When sober, she was somewhat religious and a lot more reserved. I liked her much more when she was sober. She was smart, and we got along well. She was not easy, and I had to work hard to win her over. Just when things were starting to go really well between us, I had to leave. That wasn't easy either.

During my first few months in California, I wasn't having a lot of luck with the ladies. I hadn't developed any relationships, and I really missed Jackie. I talked her into coming to Carlsbad to see me and helped pay for her flight. It was so great to see her! She was there for about two weeks, but the time went by too quickly. I took her to the San Diego SeaWorld (which she loved), and we spent time at some of the local beaches. We also hung out at the pool at my apartment complex. Mainly, we just enjoyed being together again. It was tough when she had to leave.

I then moved into a two-level, three-bedroom apartment in Leucadia with Kyle Rogers and Norm Claffey, other SDGA students. They were both in their third semester. Kyle was from Ohio, and Norm (whom I met at a beach party for SDGA students) was from Edmonton. Living with Kyle and Norm was great — way better than my previous roommates. They were both easygoing, we all got along extremely well, and we had a lot of fun together. There was a swimming pool right outside our front door, but for some reason we hardly ever used it. We hung out in our apartment a lot.

Kyle wasn't a big drinker — he usually just had a beer or two — but he loved to smoke pot. A lot of it! Norm drank more than Kyle, and I drank more than Norm. Usually, we stuck to beer. Norm and I also smoked pot. Our bedrooms were upstairs, and it was quite common for me to come downstairs on a school morning at 7:00 a.m. to see Kyle sitting on the couch in the living room smoking pot from his water bong.

"Hey Donny, come over and have a hoot with me, man!" he would often say, but that was a little too early in the day for me, especially when classes started in an hour.

People like Kyle can get stoned and still function normally. Not me. Sometimes, the three of us would get high and get the munchies for ice cream.

We flipped coins to determine which one of us had to go and pick it up. I usually lost. Driving stoned for the short distance to go pick up the ice cream and come back to our apartment was quite challenging for me. Looking back, I never did like driving when I was stoned.

My luck with the ladies changed when I moved to Leucadia. One day, I went for a haircut. The girl who cut my hair, Donna, was a good-looking blonde girl. I asked her out and she accepted. We hit it off right away. She was twenty-three and owned the hair salon. Donna and I quickly developed a really good relationship. She was very smart, had a good sense of humor and was fun to be with. She fit right in with my friends and me. She was very generous as well. She would often bring groceries and beer over to our apartment. Kyle and Norm liked her too.

After classes, I would play golf and get home around 6:00 p.m. Often Donna would already be there with Kyle and Norm preparing dinner for us. She was a good cook too. We would have dinner, a couple beers and a few hoots. We spent most of our evenings doing this. It was very enjoyable and relaxing. When we had school the next morning, we usually went to bed early. Donna had to go to work in the morning as well. Usually, she would go home about 4:00 a.m. before going to work, so she wasn't getting much sleep. She did this on a regular basis and didn't seem to mind the inconvenience. She never complained. After she left, I would fall right back to sleep for a few more hours before I had to get up for school. I wasn't complaining either.

I met Donna's parents a couple of times, and we liked each other. I think they were quite wealthy because they had a beautiful home and some expensive "toys." We all went to the beach one day, and they had their motor home there. One time, Donna and her parents went to Lake Tahoe, Nevada, to go on a vacation with legendary country music artist Glen Campbell and his family. Donna gave me a picture I still have in my photo album of her relaxing on Glen's boat.

I had a student visa, which allowed me to live in the United States legally while attending SDGA. I was informed that several Canadian students in the past were able to live down there an additional six months by applying for a certain permit. The SDGA administration told me most Canadians had little trouble getting approved for this extension request. I loved living there and didn't want to go back to Canada after I graduated. I was thinking of trying to get a permanent green card or dual citizenship so I could live there forever if I wanted to.

I filled out all the forms with the Immigration Department in San Diego about six months before graduation so I would be approved for my six-month stay well before the end of my fourth semester. If I was approved, I needed some time to find a job (hopefully as an assistant golf professional) for those additional six months. During the "bonus" six months, I thought I could make all kinds of connections that could help me stay there on a permanent basis. I also thought that if things continued to go well between Donna and me, who knows? If I ended up marrying her, I could probably get a permanent green card. I really didn't give this option a lot of thought though. I was only twenty-one and not even close to considering such a huge commitment. Just being in a monogamous relationship was a big deal for me.

I went back to Edmonton for the Christmas holidays. Before I left, Donna asked me if I thought I would be seeing anyone there. Being my honest self, I told her that I might be spending some time with Jackie. Donna had been so good to me, and I felt I owed it to her to be straight up. I guess I wasn't able to fully commit myself to Donna at the time, either. Having said this, we were still planning to see each other when I got back. I spent some time with Jackie, partied with my friends for two weeks, and I didn't talk with Donna during that time.

A couple of days before I was scheduled to fly back to San Diego, I called Donna to see if she was going to pick me up at the airport. Not only was she not going to pick me up, she also informed me that she was seeing another guy. Our relationship was over, which I didn't see coming. I was shocked. She had just bought a new condo, and I didn't even get to see it. It sounded like her new boyfriend would be moving in with her. I guess I can't blame her for ending our relationship and moving on with her life. I told her about Jackie, and I didn't keep in touch with her while I was in Edmonton. I was looking forward to continuing where we had left off when I returned to San Diego, so I was really surprised at how fast she had moved on to this other guy. I was also heartbroken for a while afterward.

I went to a pub in La Costa by myself to drown my sorrows in margaritas. At first, I was in a sullen mood thinking about Donna but, after drinking for a couple of hours, my spirit began to rise. There was a table of four women who looked like they were having a lot of fun, so I went over and introduced myself. They asked me to join them. It turned out that it was a mother with her three daughters.

Over the next few hours, we drank a bunch more margaritas and the five of us danced like crazy. We were having a great time! The pub was about to close at 1:00 a.m. but we were having too much fun to stop partying right then, so the ladies invited me back to their place for a hot tub and some more drinks. I shouldn't have been driving, but I followed them to their condo in La Costa. The next thing I knew, I woke up on a lawn chair near the hot tub in the dark. I had obviously passed out. Maybe they had tried to wake me up and I was just totally passed out cold so they had to leave me? I will never know for sure. It was about 3:00 a.m., and I was extremely cold. It was January, and all I was wearing was shorts. The ladies must have let me use these to go in the hot tub because I was wearing jeans earlier. I don't remember being in the hot tub with them, but I must have been because the shorts were still wet. Whatever happened when we got back to their place is foggy to me. I really don't remember anything until waking up on that lawn chair.

Speaking of foggy, when I woke up it was so foggy out that I could barely see three feet in front of me. I didn't need this extra challenge, as I was in enough fog of my own. I started walking and, not being able to see where I was going, I soon ended up inside a tennis court. The fog was so thick, it took me a considerable amount of time just to find my way out of there. Now the real challenge was to begin. I had to find my way back to the ladies' condo and, basically, I had no clue where it was. My clothes, wallet and car keys were there.

As I began my search, the fog started to dissipate somewhat, so I could see a little better. But it was still very dark outside. I saw the condo complex, but I was faced with two problems. First, I didn't know their condo number. Second, it was a huge complex and the condos looked identical to me. How the hell was I supposed to find out which one was theirs? It was like the blind leading the blind. After walking around and checking countless condos for well over an hour, I finally found it. I looked in the window of this one condo and could see my clothes and shoes on the floor inside the front door. I couldn't see anyone in there and assumed they would all be fast asleep by now. I just wanted to get my belongings so I could go home and sleep. I didn't want to wake anyone up, so I didn't ring the doorbell or knock on the door. I tried the front door, which was locked. This made sense. I had just met them, they were going to bed, so why leave the door unlocked for a stranger? There was no other door I could try to get in. I had no other choice, so I rang the doorbell. No response. I kept ringing it. Nothing. I knocked on the door. No reply. I kept knocking louder and louder. Not a thing. I kept ringing that doorbell and knocking on that door for about fifteen minutes. No one came to the door. I thought that either they weren't there, or they were totally passed out drunk.

It was close to 4:30 a.m., I had wet shorts on, and I was freezing. I was extremely tired, miserable and still drunk. And I was desperate. Because of these things, I made a really bad decision, and I'm lucky it didn't cost my life.

THE POLICE HAD THEIR GUNS POINTED RIGHT AT ME

I broke the window with my right hand and crawled into the kitchen from there. I knew I had just done something really stupid. There was still no sign of anyone, and I still thought that either they weren't there or that they had passed out. I didn't check any bedrooms or other areas of the condo. I thought at least one of them would have heard the glass breaking if they were there.

I never went farther than the kitchen. There were pieces of broken glass all over the counter, in the kitchen sink and on the floor. I started to pick it all up and put it in the garbage under the sink. I was sitting on the kitchen floor picking up pieces of glass when two police officers rushed through the front door, guns drawn and pointed at me. I almost shit myself!

I did a lot of fast talking to explain the situation. One of them checked to see if anyone was there. The officer woke the mother and told her what I had done. Luckily, she vouched for me and didn't want to press charges. Thank God! I could have ended up in jail.

"You're lucky you're not lying in a pool of blood right now," said one of the officers. Apparently, homeowners (and tenants) in California can shoot someone to protect themselves and their property. I was extremely lucky that this didn't happen to me.

Looking back, I must have unlocked the front door as soon as I got into their condo because the police came in through the unlocked door. The cops told me to get into my car and leave. I asked them if I could just sleep on the couch for a couple of hours. The answer was a very firm "no." I told the cops that I would pay the lady for the window I broke. Then, I gathered my belongings and left. I couldn't believe they told me to drive because they knew I had been drinking excessively. I didn't trust them and thought they might be trying to set me up. I was extremely worried that if I started driving, they would charge me with Driving Under the Influence and I would end up in jail anyway. By this time, I was exhausted and wasn't thinking very clearly. I just wanted to get home and go to bed. I got into my car and drove home like the cops told me to do. Once again, I got lucky because they didn't follow me. No DUI. No jail. What a night.

After getting some much-needed sleep, I went back and paid the lady for the window I broke. She was very understanding. I have a little "souvenir" from that infamous occasion: a ¾-inch scar on my right wrist. I cut myself on the glass when I broke the window.

In my third semester, Kyle, Norm and I moved into a three-bedroom house in Encinitas, where I would live until graduation. They stayed there until they graduated, so in my fourth semester, I had to get two new roommates from SGDA. They were brutal. It was so much better living with Kyle and Norm. Kyle and I didn't keep in touch after he left, but Norm and I did. We became lifetime friends.

Several students caddied at Fairbanks Ranch Country Club on the weekends to make some money. This was an exclusive and ritzy private golf course located pretty close to the golf academy. Most of the members, like

Dean Spanos who owned the San Diego Chargers NFL team, were very wealthy. It was a course owned by Douglas Fairbanks and his family, who were in the Hollywood movie industry. In order to caddy, we had to be there by 6:00 a.m. Caddies were chosen randomly unless a member specifically asked for a caddy who had worked for him before. I didn't caddy often enough to develop this kind of rapport with anyone. I got paid $40-$50 on average for 18 holes. As a bonus, it was always cash and US dollars, which turned into my pub money for Saturday nights. As another bonus, Mondays were "caddy day" at Fairbanks Ranch, which meant SDGA students who caddied there could play for free.

One time, I caddied in a celebrity tournament at Fairbanks Ranch. There were people from the TV and movie industry, as well as many professional athletes there. There were several players from the San Diego Chargers and the MLB Padres. Some of my classmates and I talked briefly with famous game show host Alex Trebek as he warmed up on the driving range. It turned out to be the easiest caddying job I ever had. The golfers I was with used power carts, so I didn't have to carry anyone's clubs. I drove their carts quite a bit myself. I helped them find their balls, gave them the yardage to the green, advised them on club selection and read the greens for them. I raked the sand traps too. It was a very enjoyable day, and I got paid $100.

On another occasion, I caddied for one of the amateurs at the pro-am in the Money Tournament of Champions at the La Costa Golf Resort. This used to be the first tournament of the year on the PGA Tour. Back then, amateurs paid $2,000 to play 18 holes with a PGA Tour player in these pro-ams. I imagine it costs a lot more today. The pro in our group that day was Gay Brewer. I watched the tournament as well, following Jack Nicklaus for a while. I saw many other players such as Tom Watson, Tom Kite, Corey Pavin, Hal Sutton, Fuzzy Zoeller, Calvin Peete, Greg Norman and others.

Dick Rudolph was one of the instructors at the SDGA. He was the head superintendent at La Costa and instructed our Turf Grass Management course. Through Dick, our class was able to play golf there a couple of times. What a treat!

Jack Nicklaus is one of the greatest golfers in the history of the game. One of his records is for winning eighteen majors, the most of all time. Tiger Woods has won fifteen as of the writing of this book. In 1986, Jack won The Masters for the sixth time. He was forty-six years old, which makes him the oldest player to ever win a major. I watched him on TV in the final round on Sunday — it was absolutely incredible! It may be the most exciting round of golf I have ever seen, and I was thrilled when he won! He's a living legend.

When I was following Jack around at La Costa in 1985, he was having some problems off the tee. His drives were going in the rough and the trees.

With just a few holes remaining, he finally hit a good drive right down the middle of the fairway. The large gallery following him applauded. I was standing beside the tee box about twenty feet away from him. As soon as he hit his good drive, I said, "What causes that, hey Jack?" He looked right at me, smiled, then laughed. He said, "Yes, what causes that?" With that, he strolled down the fairway. I will never forget this brief encounter I had with The Golden Bear. The best part was that he totally understood my "golf savvy" and replied right back to me immediately. I was thinking, "Holy shit. I conversed with Jack Nicklaus! Wow!"

My friends and I went to a Beach Boys' concert at Jack Murphy Stadium in San Diego on each Mother's Day I lived there. There was a Padres' baseball game, followed by the Beach Boys' concert. It was about 85°F both times, and there were 60,000+ people there. Thousands of people "tailgated" in the parking lot prior to the event — barbecuing, drinking beer and throwing Frisbees — it was one huge party! I've never been a big baseball fan, but I have loved the Beach Boys since I was young. They put on an awesome show! I felt like I was in heaven on those two occasions.

THE DEL MAR CAFE

One of our favorite pubs was the Del Mar Cafe. It was close to the SDGA and to where a lot of students lived in the North County of San Diego. It often had good live music, and I liked the type of people who went there. It was quite common to have to stand in line to get in on Friday and Saturday nights. Even weeknights could be busy. Of course, my buddies and I were always scouting out the ladies and there were usually several there.

One night, it was totally packed about 10:00 p.m. when I noticed this group of people sitting at a table. One guy was wearing a shirt with a Canadian logo on it, and it was always interesting to run into a fellow Canadian, so I wanted to know what part of Canada they were from. I went straight over to this guy's table and told him that I saw the Canada logo on his shirt and that I was from Canada. I asked him if he was as well. He and the people he was with seemed very friendly and didn't seem to mind my intrusion. It turned out that he was from Montreal, Quebec, in eastern Canada. After talking for a few minutes, I learned his name was Joe Hesketh and he was a pitcher for the Montreal Expos (Major League Baseball). The Expos were there to play against the Padres. Joe was also a golfer, so I told him I was attending SDGA. I made a quick phone call to my friend and classmate, Robert Noel, who was working in the pro shop at the Rancho Bernardo Golf Resort early the next morning. I explained the situation and asked if he could get Joe and I out on the course. He said to come the next morning, and he would look after us. I informed Joe about this, and we agreed to play early in the morning at Rancho Bernardo.

Joe told me the name and location of his hotel and his room number. I was supposed to pick him up at 7:00 a.m., so I had to wake up around 6. As usual, I ended up drinking too much the previous night and only managed four hours of sleep. I absolutely didn't feel like getting out of bed and going golfing. If it was Wayne Gretzky, Mark Messier or Michael J. Fox, I would have honored my commitment and showed up no matter how rough I was feeling. But it was Joe Hesketh, a baseball player whom I had never heard of before. And I wasn't even a baseball fan! I decided to stay in bed and get some more sleep — I pulled a "no show." I felt really bad and have always hoped that maybe he had a late night too and decided not to get up early to play golf.

Another night at the Del Mar Cafe, I was standing by the bar. This guy walks by and accidently trips on my foot. He stumbles a bit, turns back towards me, and said, "Sorry man!"

"No problem," I said.

This guy beside me said, "Do you know who that was?"

"Nope," I said.

"That was Reggie Jackson!"

I didn't recognize him. Jackson was one of the best baseball players to ever play the game. Even I knew that. I thought it was kind of cool that we had this little exchange.

My buddy, Indiana Jack Geopfrich, and I were out at another favorite pub of ours called The Rusty Pelican, in La Jolla. It was Wednesday night, which was $1 Long Island Iced Tea night. Compared to Canada, buying alcohol in the United States is significantly cheaper. You can get drunk for a lot less money down there. La Jolla is one of the richest communities in the San Diego region as far as real estate is concerned. A lot of wealthy "cougars" — a lady in her thirties or older (I was only twenty-one then) — went to the Rusty Pelican. I was talking with a lady and told her I was from Canada. She asked me if I played hockey, and when I said "yes," she said she had just been talking to another guy from Canada who also played hockey. She pointed to a guy with dark hair, so I went over to say hi. I was thinking he might be playing in a men's commercial league — a "beer league" similar to the hockey that my friends and I played in Edmonton. I asked him who he played for.

"The Montreal Canadiens," he said.

I was extremely surprised. I said, "The Montreal Canadiens! Wow! I wasn't expecting that. I'm really sorry, but I don't recognize you. What's your name?"

He said, "Chris Chelios."

"Chris Chelios! No way! Oh my God. I'm sorry Chris, I should have recognized you. I'm a big Canadiens fan, and I know who you are."

CHRIS CHELIOS OF THE MONTREAL CANADIENS

Hockey is like a religion in Montreal. Montrealers take it very seriously and being a player on this team is like being a god. Montreal has won more Stanley Cups than any other team in the history of the NHL, so they are the most revered hockey franchise of all time. I watched the Canadiens play a lot, especially throughout the 1970s and 1980s. They had many all-star players such as Guy Lafleur, Steve Shutt, Jacques Lemaire and Larry Robinson. There were many others as well. Before my time, they had superstars such as Maurice Richard and Doug Harvey.

When I met Chris, he was only twenty-four years old. We hit it off immediately. Chris was staying at his parents' home in Rancho Bernardo. We talked about playing a game of golf together, so he wrote down his parents' phone number on a Rusty Pelican napkin for me. I kept it as a souvenir. Thirty-five years later, I still have it in one of my photo albums. A few nights later, Chris called me. He wanted to play golf, so we decided to play at Rancho Bernardo. I told him I would make the arrangements, find two other guys to complete our foursome and call him back.

I called Robert at Rancho Bernardo Golf Resort again right away. This time I told him I had met a famous NHL hockey player and that we wanted to play there. Robert pulled through again. He said he would look after the four of us. In "golf language," this meant he would "comp" us. It's always nice to have some pull, and he did this for my mates and me on a few occasions. I called Chris back and told him we had a tee time booked in a couple of days. We would tee it up around 12 p.m., so we agreed to meet at the golf course around 11:30 a.m.

Now I had to find a couple of guys to play with us. I knew I wouldn't have any trouble because a lot of guys at the academy would love to play with Chelios. I thought I could be quite picky with my selection. I really wanted to get a couple of guys who I thought Chris would like. We'd be on the course together for at least four hours and playing with Chris was a once in a lifetime opportunity, so I wanted to invite guys who would appreciate the significance of this occasion and who would be a lot of fun to play with. I decided to ask Dan Bosquet and Mark Hansen from the SDGA. They were one semester behind me. They were good old Canadian boys, both hockey fans from Vancouver. They were quite eager to play with Chris. We weren't best buddies, but I liked them and thought they would be a good fit for our group.

When we got to the course, Chris was on the practice green. It was a beautiful, sunny, hot day. I went into the pro shop to talk with Robert. True to his word, he "comped" all four of us for everything. It was a great start to the day.

Chris rode with me for the 18 holes. He had only been golfing for a few years at the time. I was more than happy to give him a few tips along the way. He was about a 20 handicap. I was a little nervous at first but after a few holes, I started to relax. The front 9 went great. We had a good group. We stopped at the snack shop on our way to the 10th tee. Chris said he wanted to buy some beer for us for the back 9 because he didn't have to pay for his golf or power cart rental. With a dozen cold beers on board, things were getting better and better. And even more relaxed. The back 9 went well also. It was a very fun and enjoyable game of golf for all of us. I didn't play my best, but I did OK — I broke 80, anyway. I'm not sure what Chris shot, but I think he did quite well. I hope I was able to help him with his swing and overall golf game.

After the game, we went to a local pub for happy hour and had beers and margaritas on the patio. Chris told some great stories about the adventures of being an NHL player, and more specifically of playing with the Montreal Canadiens. He was living a very exciting life. After a couple of hours and a lot of laughs and much fun, we left. Chris invited me to his parents' house in Rancho Bernardo for dinner. I was thrilled, and I happily accepted. Dan and Mark went on their way, and I went with Chris in his car.

Chris' parents had a really nice home and were very nice people. They're Greek and served us a delicious dinner and some wine. I really enjoyed spending some time with the Chelios family.

By this time, I had a lot to drink, mostly in the hot sun. Chris may have had a little glow going too, but we weren't done yet. We had just been getting primed up. After dinner, we decided to go to the Del Mar Cafe, a place he hadn't been to before. I visited with his parents while he had a shower and got ready. Chris drove us to my place in Encinitas so I could have a shower and change my clothes. I cracked him a cold beer to have while he waited for me. Shortly after, we carried on.

We arrived at the Del Mar Cafe around 9:30 p.m. It was packed, as usual. We were all set to have a fun night together. As soon as we got there, I went straight to the bar to order a couple of TKOs, a.k.a. Technical Knock Out, which are made with tequila, Kahlúa and ouzo. Well, that's what happened to me because I don't remember much of the rest of that night. After we had our TKO, a woman beside Chris started to flirt with him a bit. We weren't in "hockey territory," so I'm sure she had no clue who he was. Regardless, he wasn't interested. He just gave her the brush off. Mainly, he was enjoying the music, chatting with me and otherwise was just minding his own business.

While I was getting hammered, it seemed that Chris was staying quite sober. He was bigger than me and could probably handle his alcohol better. He was about 6' and approximately 190 pounds, all muscle. I was 5'11" and 175 pounds. Chris bought us a couple of beers, and that's the last thing I remember about that night. I don't have a clue what time we stayed until, and I don't remember how I got home. I thought I was doing pretty well, then the booze hit me all of a sudden. It had been a long day of drinking in the hot sun.

During our golf game, Chris told me that if I was ever in Montreal, I could stay at his place. I had no idea if I would ever be going there, but I really appreciated his kind offer.

I was really embarrassed the next day. I couldn't believe how drunk I got and how I had lost my memory. The fact that this happened the first time I was hanging out with Chris Chelios made it even worse. I should have called him and apologized, but I didn't. I was too embarrassed. I'm sure Chris has seen a lot of hockey players, including his teammates, get drunk. Anyway, I guess he wasn't too impressed with me because I never heard from him after that. I've never tried to contact him either. I wish this little story had a happier ending. But, in the end, it's another good example of how drinking too much had a negative consequence with me.

Chris went on to have a very lengthy and successful career. Renowned for his remarkable physical fitness, he ended up playing in the NHL for twenty-six years, tying a record with legend Gordie Howe. At forty-eight, Chris was the second oldest player of all time. Gordie Howe was the oldest at 52. He won three Stanley Cups. One with Montreal (1986) and two with the Detroit Red Wings (1999 and 2009). He officially retired on August 31, 2010. Chelios was inducted into the Hockey Hall of Fame on November 8, 2013.

Some friends and I went to Disneyland a couple of times, which was a cool experience and a lot of fun. One time, we stayed in a motel in Anaheim. About 3:00 a.m., there was an earthquake. It didn't do any serious damage, but it scared the shit out of us!

I experienced another earthquake while living in Encinitas. Once again, it happened during the middle of the night. I was sound asleep when all of a sudden, the ground started shaking. Then our house began to shake somewhat violently. I thought the ground was going to open right up and swallow us! The shaking only lasted for 45-60 seconds, but it seemed like an eternity. It really scared me!

On other occasions, I felt some minor tremors, which always made me feel quite uncomfortable.

My buddies and I went to LA to watch Wayne Gretzky and the Edmonton Oilers play the Los Angeles Kings at the Forum one year. This was another great experience. Hockey wasn't big in California until years later when Wayne was traded to LA from Edmonton. Because of Wayne Gretzky's influence, hockey became much more popular in LA and across the southern United States in general.

Just down the road from the Del Mar Cafe, was the Del Mar Racetrack, a place we loved to hang out at to watch and bet on horse racing. Stretch limos pulled up in front and big league people got out. They bet a lot of money on these races. There were all kinds of people there. Several thousands of them. It was an electric atmosphere that got my adrenaline going. Norm Claffey, my friend and roommate, spent more time at the racetrack than he did on the "golf track"! None of us were high rollers. I only spent about $20 when I went. I never won a lot of money, but it was great fun!

During my time down south, I went to Palm Springs a few times. It was only about a two-hour drive from San Diego, and it is a golfing mecca. They have all these beautiful, lush, green golf courses right in the middle of the desert. It's pretty cool. I loved playing the desert courses. One time, a few of us went there over Easter. We thought we would enjoy a quiet, relaxing weekend. The majority of the population and vast numbers of tourists that go there are seniors. When we got there, the whole city was going crazy! Turns out it was Spring Break, and thousands of college and university students from across the country descended upon Palm Springs to party — an annual event for them. Everyone was drinking and partying in the streets and all over the place. The bars were nuts. It was wild! Of course, my crew and I fit right in. Our "quiet weekend" turned into a three-day party.

Dave Strong, a guy I knew from Wetaskiwin, had moved to San Diego. He was about seven years older than me, so we weren't friends when I grew up there. He was my brother Jim's age. When I found out he was living in San Diego, I gave him a call, we hooked up, and a new friendship quickly developed between us. We were a couple of small town boys living it up in Southern California. Dave was a really good guy. He was smart and personable, had a good sense of humor, was good looking and took care of himself physically by biking and running. He liked to go out for a few beers, but I never saw him get carried away like I did. He was working as a chartered accountant in San Diego and lived in an apartment close to the beach.

He also lived close to my favorite nightclub in San Diego, fittingly called Diego's. The "scenery" was always very nice there. It was about a forty-minute drive from my place in Encinitas to Dave's apartment, which was not a drive I wanted to make after drinking. Dave was nice enough to let me crash at his place when we went there a few times. The next day, we would go to the beach for a while. It was awesome! A couple of times, Dave came to our place when my roommates and I were having a party.

One time, Dave and I drove to LA in his BMW. He went there to pick up his friend's Mercedes Benz, which was shipped from Hawaii. Dave drove the Benz back to San Diego, and I drove his Beamer. It was fun cruising down the I5, especially for a twenty-one-year-old kid from Wetaskiwin!

After my slow start with California girls, my luck changed for the remainder of the time I lived there. I dated Lisa for five months. She was twenty-four and didn't have the qualities Donna had, so I never considered her a serious girlfriend. It was more of a lustful romance. There were no broken hearts when we stopped seeing each other. I think I would have been more "successful" if I'd had more money. It seemed that many of the women there were attracted to guys who drove Porches and did cocaine. I did neither of these things. As it was, I still had several flings when I lived there. I was young and determined, so I put a lot of effort into these "relationships" back then.

CAR ACCIDENT

One time, I was still drunk from the night before and hadn't had much sleep, but at least I left my car at the Del Mar Cafe. Around noon, one of my classmates gave me a ride there to pick it up. I talked him into going in the pub for a beer with me. I ordered a pitcher of draft, he had one glass and left so I stayed there by myself. I was going to finish that pitcher. Before I got that far, the bar staff cut me off, which has only happened twice in my life (that I can remember). It must have been obvious that I was extremely inebriated. Then, I made a stupid decision to drive myself home. I hadn't had very much to drink on this second day, but I still had a lot of booze in my system from the previous night.

I drove through "The Ranch" (Rancho Santa Fe) on my way home to Encinitas. The roads were twisty and windy. Usually, I didn't drive very fast. Even if I had been drinking, I drove slowly and carefully. Not on this day. I must have been in a hurry to get home. I was driving way too fast, like a maniac. My tires were squealing as I tried to negotiate the curves in the road. I was out of control. By the grace of God, I made it home without causing an accident. Other drivers in my vicinity must have been shocked and appalled.

All I wanted to do was to go to bed, and I got within about two minutes from doing this. As soon as I got in the door, the phone rang. I was the only one there, so I answered it. It was some girl I had met a few days earlier at Diego's. Obviously, I had given her my phone number. She and her friend were there again, and she wanted me to join them for happy hour. If I had been using my head at all, I would have politely turned down her offer; I needed sleep. If she would have called five minutes later, I wouldn't have answered because I would have been in my bed sound asleep. Instead, I told her I would love to join them and would get there as soon as I could. It was about a forty-five-minute drive, so I took a cold beer from the fridge to drink along the way. I got back in my car and raced off down the road.

I was driving like a complete idiot. I was going way too fast and shouldn't have been driving at all in the condition I was in. I got about a mile down the road when I came to a major intersection with a stop sign in front of me. I didn't notice the stop sign until it was too late. I tried to stop for it at the last second, but I was going too fast. I hit my brakes and skidded into the intersection. In a split second, I got hit by a five-ton truck going about 40 miles/hour. The impact from the truck sent my car spiraling down the road. When my car stopped spinning and came to a stop, I quickly got out. I think I was in shock. I had just caused quite an accident. The beer I brought with me was in my car, still unopened. I just left it there. I didn't try to hide it or anything. I knew I had just pulled a major fuck-up. I decided to stay right there and face the consequences of my actions. My initial thought of fleeing the scene didn't seem like the right answer, and I couldn't have driven my car anyway because it was a write-off. The truck had hit me on the driver's side where the engine was and did a lot of damage. Both front tires went flat as well. What a wreck.

Within about two minutes, the police were there. Within five minutes, there were four police cars and a fire truck. Bystanders began to gather at the scene. I was on full display and felt like a total idiot. There was nowhere to hide.

The doors on the Corolla were quite thin. One of the cops told me that if I was hit there, I could have been killed. Most importantly, I didn't kill or injure anyone, including myself. I was extremely lucky because I plowed right into three lanes of busy traffic, traveling at least 40 miles/hour. It could have ended up a lot worse than it did. I think my angels helped me on this day. The police gave me some sobriety tests. One of the tests was to say the alphabet out loud, backwards, starting with "Z." I had some trouble doing this. Hell, I can't even do this when I'm dead sober! I'm not denying that I was impaired, but I think this is an unfair test. Anyway, I failed the tests and was charged with a DUI.

When the cop put the handcuffs on me, I gave him a bit of a struggle. I was kind of fighting it. It was just an impulse reaction. I think I was scared more than anything else. I was worried I might get sent back to Canada without being able to finish my schooling or that the SDGA faculty would hear about my incident and punish me. The next thing I knew I was in the cop car with my hands cuffed behind my back and my feet tied together with rope. It was pretty obvious that I was screwed.

As we drove away, I tried to reason with the cop. I told him that I was actually a pretty good guy and was a student at SDGA. I also told him my mom was going to kill me when she found out. Nothing I said resonated with him, and he drove me straight to the North County Jail. They took my blood alcohol level (which was .22) and put me in a cell with six other guys. They kept me in there until 6:00 a.m. the next morning, and I called one of my roommates to come pick me up. Being behind bars is a degrading and humiliating experience. And I deserved to be there. I had to pay the consequences for driving drunk and causing an accident. In the end, I got off really lucky. I plead guilty to my DUI and was fined $500. I had to do sixteen hours of "community service," and I didn't lose my driver's license. Back home in Alberta, I would have lost it for at least six months.

For my community service, I had to pick up garbage for sixteen hours with a group of ten other convicts. We had to wear orange vests and pick up all the garbage in this huge park. We rode in the back of a large "prisoner truck" to get to the park and back. To say I felt out of place with this crew is a major understatement. They looked at home in the back of that truck, as if this was nothing new or out of the ordinary for them. There were people of all races, and I kept to myself the whole time and didn't talk with any of them. I did this for two Saturdays in a row. It was a very long sixteen hours.

One of my main concerns was about rumors spreading regarding my accident. Most importantly, I didn't want any of my instructors to find out what happened. I also didn't want a bunch of gossip going around amongst the other students. I got lucky and remained unscathed in both regards. There were no repercussions — a huge relief!

During my scuffle with the police when they were arresting me, one of my dress shoes came off and was left behind at the scene, so I only had one shoe on when I went to jail. Two weeks later, I was going by the location of my accident and saw my lost shoe. Someone had put it on top of an electrical box on the corner of the road, so I got out of the car and picked it up. I couldn't believe it was still there!

My car was towed to a junk yard. A few weeks later, I had it towed to my place where it sat in the driveway for as long as I lived there. For a long time, I got a sick feeling in my stomach every time I looked at the damage from my drunk-driving accident. I realized that things could have ended up much worse; I could have killed someone or myself. I went on a major guilt trip because of all of this. I was ashamed and embarrassed, and I stopped drinking for a while. I bought an early 1970s Datsun 240Z for $400 to replace the Corolla. It was kind of a junk car, but it got me where I needed to go.

The very first week I was a student at the San Diego Golf Academy, one of our instructors told our class: "You guys may not realize it right now, but when you look back, these are going to be two of the best years of your life." He was right! My two years at the SDGA were simply incredible. Most importantly, I received a great education and graduated with a diploma in golf operations and management. Having this on my resume helped me get every job I applied for, with only one exception. The lifestyle I was able to lead while getting this education was amazing, especially because I was in my early twenties.

First of all, the weather was phenomenal. Based on temperature and amount of sunshine, San Diego is hard to beat. At one point when I was there, it didn't rain for months. It was beautiful every day, and I actually hoped it would rain for a change. For the first time in my life, I was able to play golf all year round. I absolutely loved this! The Alberta golf season is only six months long whereas the San Diego region is a golfing mecca. I played at a lot of beautiful courses down there.

The beach season lasted for several months as well. There were many white sandy beaches to choose from. My friends and I spent a lot of time relaxing, tanning, swimming in the ocean and boogie boarding at these beaches. I loved to run along the beach for a couple of miles also. Checking out all the California girls wasn't hard to take either. It was a paradise.

Sometimes we brought a golf club and a bunch of balls with us to tee-up on the beach and hit into the Pacific Ocean. We made a game of calling our shots: intentional hooks, slices, draws, fades, etc. The loser had to take a drink of beer. It was a fun game.

The pubs, bars and nightclubs were great. I was in my prime for this type of lifestyle, and there was an abundance of spots to choose from.

I graduated from the San Diego Golf Academy in August of 1986. My mom and brother, Doug, came all the way down from Edmonton for the ceremony.

DESERT HILLS GOLF CLUB

After I graduated, I had been back in Edmonton for a few weeks when I received a phone call from Dick Jones, the head pro at Desert Hills Golf Club in Green Valley, Arizona. He was looking for an assistant golf professional to work for him. He had contacted the San Diego Golf Academy, and they had referred him to me, which I really appreciated. I explained that I had applied for a six-month extension of stay with the US Immigration Department in San Diego several months earlier, but that I was still waiting to hear back from them. I told Dick that several Canadians who attended the SDGA before me had been approved for the same thing, and that I didn't think this would be a problem. I was quite confident I would be getting my own approval very soon. We took a chance on my pending situation, and he hired me over the phone.

Green Valley is a small town about twenty minutes south of Tucson, Arizona, and close to the US/Mexico border town of Nogales. My mom was a huge help for me once again. I left my Datsun 240Z in San Diego, as it was only worth a few hundred dollars. Because of this, and because the Corolla was a write-off, I didn't have a vehicle. Mom drove with me all the way from Edmonton to Green Valley in her 1983 Toyota Tercel. She stayed with me for about two weeks, helping me get set up in a one-bedroom apartment. Amazingly, she left the Tercel for me to drive. I couldn't have made this move without her help. She was incredibly good to me.

Desert Hills Golf Club is a private 18-hole course. The vast majority of the members were wealthy seniors. I started working in the pro shop as an assistant golf professional around the beginning of October 1986. I was excited to be there and looking forward to the next six months in the beautiful Arizona desert. I was under the impression that Dick was making pretty good money. He likely had a sizable salary and ownership of the merchandise in the pro shop, which would have increased his income substantially. Two of us assistant pros worked for him. The other guy's name was Allen Stewart. Allen had been working for Dick for some time before I arrived on the scene. I don't know how much Dick was paying Allen, but he was only paying me $1,200/month. It was my first experience of what I would consider being paid an unfair salary as an assistant golf pro, working for a head pro who could have — and should have — paid their assistants more money. After tax, I had to live on about $1,000/month. My apartment rent alone was $400/month, which left me with $600/month for food, gas, utilities and everything else. Thankfully, alcohol was really cheap down there. I could go to a bar and get drunk for $20. Looking back, I shouldn't have agreed to work for such a small amount of money. It wasn't a smart financial decision.

After working there for only about two weeks, I realized I had made a big mistake. I shouldn't have accepted the job, period. Both Dick and Allen were arrogant. I could easily sense this from their attitude and demeanor. There will be many accounts throughout my book that describe my hatred towards arrogance. It drives me crazy! On top of this, Allen had no personality whatsoever. Working with these two individuals in the small confines of a pro shop all day long, five days a week, was extremely difficult.

To make matters worse, Dick's wife, Gladys, also spent time in the pro shop. She didn't like me. I didn't do anything to cause her ill feelings towards me, but one time, she lost it on me. She got really pissed off and almost started yelling at me for no good reason. Being my boss' wife, I had to bite my tongue.

Because of the stress and unhappiness of my work environment, I always really looked forward to my days off. There wasn't much to do in Green Valley because most of the population were seniors. It was legal for them to drive their golf carts around town as long as they had license plates. There was only one decent bar there, which I only went to a couple of times. Rumors spread fast in a small town. I didn't want to get drunk at this place in case my boss heard about it or if a member at our course saw me there. I went to Tucson to have my fun.

I found out that a guy from Wetaskiwin named Jeff Williamson lived in Tucson and was attending the University of Arizona. We made contact, started hanging out and became pretty good friends. I also got to know a couple of Jeff's close buddies, who were also good guys. Jeff and his friends were good golfers, so we played together a few times, and I enjoyed playing with them. They were also fun to party with. They introduced me to a couple of great pubs where university students went. I stayed overnight at Jeff's apartment a couple of times because I didn't want to drive all the way back to Green Valley after drinking a bunch of beer.

One time, we went to a football game in Tucson between the hometown University of Arizona Wildcats and the Arizona State University Sun Devils from Phoenix. It was a nationally-televised playoff game, and there was a huge rivalry between the teams. There must have been 50,000 people, mostly university students, at the stadium. The place was going crazy — it was so much fun! It was my first and only time attending a football game at this level. I forget who won, but I clearly remember enjoying the occasion immensely.

Around the middle of December, I finally received a letter from the Immigration Department saying, to my surprise, that they refused my application. Not only that, I had to leave the country within thirty days. I only ended up working at Desert Hills for about ten weeks. I didn't even have time to become an "official" PGA Assistant Professional, as I hadn't got involved with their apprenticeship program, which included the PGA business schools and playing ability tests. When I received this letter, Dave Lambert happened to be in Green Valley visiting me. We discussed my situation and decided there wasn't much sense in staying there for another thirty days. Dave said he would drive back to Canada with me, and I took him up on his offer. There were a couple of members at the club who expressed an interest in "sponsoring" me so I could stay down there, but by this time I had already decided I was going back to Edmonton.

Dave and I packed as much as we could into my Tercel hatchback and hit the road. We went to Tucson on our first day of travel. On our second day, we went to Phoenix to meet up with his parents. We went to a bar that night and had a good time. We stayed at the same hotel where his parents were staying. The next day, we met them in Las Vegas. After a couple of days, they went back home to Calgary. Dave and I were having a blast, and we stayed in Vegas for four days. From there, we drove to Salt Lake City, Utah.

We spent a day skiing at Mount Alta, which was a pretty nice ski resort. After that, we drove straight back to Calgary. We may have stayed one more night somewhere along the way (Idaho or Montana), but mainly we just drove for that last leg of our journey. As always, Dave and I had a tremendous amount of fun traveling together. Dave stayed in Calgary, and I went back to my mom's house in Edmonton.

I was home for Christmas, which I should have been looking forward to, but I wasn't. In all honesty, I was dreading it. Christmas meant that my brothers would be there. As always, they would be drinking heavily. And, inevitably, this would lead to fighting between them. Sometimes fist fighting. I hated this more than anything else. The stress this caused me was very detrimental to my mental and emotional health. Being exposed to this type of behavior far too much in my life did a lot of damage to me. My friends and I drank a lot, too, but at least we had a good time. We didn't argue or fight with each other, or anyone else for that matter. Alcohol has done a lot of damage in my life. Some people just shouldn't drink at all, period.

DATING GREG NORMAN'S DENTAL HYGIENIST

One day, I was at West Edmonton Mall with my friends, Darrell and Mike. At one point, the three of us were watching these three really cute bear cubs in an enclosure. There was a good-looking blonde girl doing the same thing by herself. She was smoking hot and had a great suntan, which really stood out for someone in Edmonton at that time of year. I had her on my radar immediately. I led the charge, as my friends and I went over to talk with her. She was surprisingly friendly. I had tried this type of approach countless times and usually got shot down. But this girl was different, and I soon found out why. She was from Australia. Aussies are generally very friendly people. I loved her accent too.

I told her that Darrell and Mike were golf pros, and that I was in the process of becoming one myself. Upon hearing this, she asked us if we were familiar with Greg Norman. Of course we were. "The Shark" is a legend. He is from Australia, and during that era he was one of the best golfers in the world. He played on the PGA Tour for many years and was very successful. The girl said her name, which sounded like "Nerada." She went on to tell us that she was a dental hygienist, and that Greg Norman was one of her patients. He was very famous, and I thought this was pretty cool. I think they were both from Queensland.

Nerada was traveling by herself. After leaving Australia, she spent some time in Hawaii. From there, she flew to Edmonton. She was only going to be there for one night, then leave the next morning for Toronto. After that, she was going to do some traveling in the US before going back home. Darrell and Mike were my "wingers." They did a great job of promoting me and gaining Nerada's attention. I appreciated their support, and I think it helped me. Knowing she was by herself and that she was leaving the next day, I asked her if I could take her out that night. I was surprised and elated when she said "yes." She was staying at a hotel in Edmonton's west end. There was a nightclub called Denny Andrews close to her hotel, so we decided to go there.

I picked her up around 8:00 p.m. When she opened her hotel room door, she was a beautiful sight — dressed really nice, absolutely gorgeous. She gave me a souvenir koala bear from her homeland. It was really cute. I told Nerada I only had $50, and she told me not to worry. She said her grandma had recently died and had left her a bunch of money.

We had a great time at Denny Andrews, had several drinks and enjoyed each other's company. The night went by fast. At the end of the night, I escorted Nerada back to her hotel room. She invited me in, and I ended up staying there with her. Early the next morning, Nerada made a phone call to cancel her flight to Toronto that day. We were having such a good time that we wanted it to last longer. I spent the next few days with her and stayed with her at her hotel each night. It was a great experience. We kept busy doing things together and spent some time socializing with my friends. Nerada was very generous. She didn't mind paying for my expenses at all.

After four days together, she flew to Toronto. I hated to see her leave because I was really starting to like her a lot. Apparently, the feeling was mutual. Just a few days later, she called me from Toronto saying she wanted to come back to Edmonton and spend more time with me. I couldn't believe it!

When she returned, she stayed with my mom and me. We partied with my friends for a couple of nights and things were going well. On the third night, a few of my friends were over having some beers and wanted to go to Barry T's to party again. Nerada also wanted to go, but I was tired and didn't feel like going out. I told her to go have fun if she wanted to, but I was going to stay home and have an early night. She went, and I went to bed.

Nerada didn't get home until about 10:00 a.m. the next morning. When I asked her where she was, she said "I stayed with Ron [not his real name] at a hotel last night." She said this nonchalantly as if there was nothing wrong with it. It was a dagger in my heart. I trusted her to go to a nightclub with my friends to have fun and she ends up fucking one of them? Her actions didn't sit well with me. I put her suitcase by the front door and called a taxi to pick her up. I never saw or talked with her again after that.

I was pissed off at Ron, too, but I didn't hold a grudge against him for too long. I knew that guys were infamous for thinking with their dicks, especially when they've been drinking. I've done it myself.

THE CRAZY GOLF PRO

After having strong feelings for Nerada, her betrayal was what hurt me the most. I guess our relationship had to end one way or another. She was going back to Australia, and my future was in Canada. I can still say that I had quite a fling with The Shark's dental hygienist!

CHAPTER 7
1987
CPGA ASSISTANT GOLF PROFESSIONAL

It takes five years to complete the CPGA Assistant Pro apprenticeship program. The first year's status is "B5." Each year after that there's the "B4," "B3," "B2" and "B1." After this, an individual can try and get their Class "A" qualification and become an "Associate" or "Head Golf Professional." The CPGA gave me a one-year credit towards my apprenticeship program because I was a graduate of the San Diego Golf Academy. I've always thought this should be a two-year credit, as the SDGA was a two-year program, but at least it was cut down to four years.

The City of Edmonton Parks and Recreation Department ran adult "learn to golf" programs during the winter months, and the instructors were Alberta PGA golf professionals. Ken Ingoldsby from the Riverside Golf Club organized these lessons and was one of the instructors. I had known and liked Ken for a few years, and he was nice enough to allow me to become one of eight instructors. Some guys were head pros, and others were assistant pros from local golf courses. We taught indoor lessons, mostly in school gyms, all over Edmonton. We used plastic whiffle golf balls — the ones with holes in them. Our students hit the balls off hard rubber door mats, which were far from ideal. It would have been a lot better to hit off an AstroTurf mat. We used rubber tees as well. It wasn't the greatest setup, but it worked OK. Each group of students had one ninety-minute lesson a week for five weeks. Each class had two instructors for two groups of students, with about ten students per group. The instructors got paid $30 per hour, which was decent back then. I ended up doing this for three winter seasons.

At the first lesson, there were about twenty students for two instructors. I immediately noticed that one of the students was really good looking. She had long blonde hair, blue eyes and a great body. I wanted her in my class. I also noticed she was with another woman, so I would keep them together. Inconspicuously, I made sure I got the paperwork with all the students' names before the other instructor did. If I didn't do this, there was only a 50/50 chance the one I was eyeing-up would be in my class for the next five weeks. I wanted to be 100% sure. I learned their names and made sure I was the one who divided our two classes. My little scheme worked perfectly! I had Linda Koral and her friend, Pat, in my class.

The golf lessons were scheduled on weekday evenings and on the weekends. The lessons went well for me, and after our fifth and final lesson, we gave all our students the opportunity to rate our performance as instructors. Each student could be totally honest with their ratings of poor, fair, good, very good or excellent (and any comments they might have) because they didn't usually put their names on the forms. Approximately ninety percent of my ratings were "excellent," which made me feel really good.

I enjoyed having Linda and Pat in my class. They were a lot of fun, and we shared a lot of laughs. I had my eye on Linda. I didn't flirt with her a great deal during the lessons or make it obvious that I was interested. Then, I got a break. The class she was in wanted to take me for a beer after the final lesson. Eight of us, including the two girls, went to a nearby lounge. The majority stayed for one beer, but Linda, Pat and I stayed awhile longer and ended up having a few more beers. We were having a good time, and Linda invited us back to her place to continue the fun. I picked up a case of cold beer on my way there. Linda owned a home in Millwoods in southeast Edmonton. It was a three-level split that included a finished basement with a bar, which is where we ended up. Pat left around midnight, which left Linda and I alone. It was perfect. By then we'd consumed several beers and began kissing on the couch. Shortly after, she led me upstairs to her bedroom where we spent the night together. Linda had to work in north Edmonton at 8 a.m. the next morning, so we both got up at 6 after getting very little sleep. I don't know about her, but I was still half drunk when I left her house that morning. Linda gave me her phone number, but I didn't call her until about two weeks later.

In many ways, I'm an "old school" kind of guy. A little old fashioned you could say. To me, it's extremely important to have a lot of respect for a girlfriend or wife. It's also very important to completely trust them. To gain this respect and trust takes time. It doesn't develop in one night! Total honesty is also big on my list. Again, it takes time to get to know someone before you know for sure if they are truly an honest person or not. Guys are notorious for thinking with the wrong head. When I was younger, I thought about females and sex constantly, and I'm sure this applies to a lot of guys. If I was attracted to someone, my priority was to figure out a way to have sex with them. It was like a game, a challenge. When I "succeeded," the game was usually over, as I usually didn't continue the relationship after that. There was no time for respect, trust and honesty to develop.

As it was, Linda and I did get together again. We saw each other on a regular basis, and it turned into a steady relationship. She became my first serious girlfriend when I was only twenty-two and she was twenty-nine. We got along great in the beginning, had great conversations and discovered we were both Geminis. It was pretty cool that our birthdays were only one day apart. Besides being so attractive, Linda had several really good traits. She was extremely intelligent, hilarious and very personable. Over time, I learned she was an honest and trustworthy person. Domestically she was fantastic. Among other things, she was an excellent cook and kept a very clean house. Before long, I moved in with her.

Linda had a pretty good job as a bookkeeper with Canadian Concrete. She was very good at her job and had been working there for several years making pretty good money. Linda also cleaned the office building on the weekends, which paid her another $200/month. Her gas was paid for, and she even had an expense account that she used for things like taking clients out for lunch. She drove a blue Camaro Z28 Iroc with a T-roof and 5-speed manual.

In many ways, I had it made. Linda was the whole package.

CPGA PLAYING ABILITY TEST

At the same time, I was readying myself to become an official CPGA Assistant Golf Professional. The first thing I had to do was pass a 36-hole Playing Ability Test (PAT), which was scheduled twice a year in the spring and the fall. I couldn't get my pro card until I met this requirement, and I couldn't teach golf for money or play in professional tournaments for money until I attained the card. It's a crucial stage in becoming a golf professional in the first place. For most aspiring pros, trying to pass a PAT is a pressure-packed experience. People who play golf for a living are called "professional golfers." They play on tours to earn their income. Before an individual can do this, they have to obtain their pro card for that particular golf tour by playing in qualifying tournaments/events. The most difficult tour to attain a "tour card" for is the PGA Tour. Many golfers have to play several qualifying rounds in order to achieve this. The pressure is immense.

My first PAT for my CPGA card was held at the Sturgeon Valley Golf & Country Club in St. Albert, Alberta, in the spring of 1987. It was an 18-hole layout, and not a very difficult one at that. The par for the course was 36-36=72. I had to shoot a one-day 36-hole score of 162 or lower. I've always thought it should be lower than that because if you're going to be classified as a "golf professional" you should at least be able to shoot in the 70s. The number should be a 36-hole score of 158 or the equivalent of 79-79=158, or lower.

I was playing terrible golf prior to my PAT and had very little confidence in my game. As the day arrived, shooting a pair of 81s didn't exactly seem like an easy thing to do. I knew it would be a struggle. I played awful on the first 18. My drives, irons and putting were all brutal. I thought I had played as bad as I possibly could have and shot as high as I could have as well: an 83. I realized that all I had to do was shoot 4 shots lower (79) on the last 18 holes for a 162 and I pass my PAT. As bad as my first round went, I knew I still had a chance!

After a lunch break, I returned to the course with a new sense of hope. It was a sunny, warm, beautiful day for golf. There was very little wind, if any. The conditions were perfect. The first hole was an easy and relatively short par 5. It would be a good birdie opportunity for most players. There was "out of bounds" (OB) to the right of the fairway and was totally wide open with no trouble to the left. Because I had been hitting my driver so poorly, I decided to play it safe by hitting my 3 iron off the tee with the hopes of gaining more control and avoiding the OB. To play it even safer, I aimed for the far left side of the first fairway so that even if I hit my ball fifty yards to the left of that, I would be fine. Obviously, hitting the fairway would be even better.

I went through my normal pre-shot routine as I prepared to hit my tee shot. I took my swing and "blocked it" — my ball went way right and out of bounds. I was stunned. I had to tee-off again, but with the 2-stroke penalty I was taking my third shot. I took a deep breath and swung again. OB right again and another 2-shot penalty. I blocked yet another OB and was penalized 6 strokes in total for this debacle. My fourth tee shot was my seventh shot of a par 5 hole! I was not only shocked, but I was very embarrassed as well. The other players in my group had to wait for me and watch my catastrophe firsthand. Finally, on my fourth attempt I hit the fairway! From there, it took me 2 shots to get on the green and 2 putts to get my ball in the hole. I made an 11 on the first hole of my second round. Not exactly the start I was hoping for.

A lot of guys would have self-destructed after that. They would lose their temper and get totally pissed off. Some would quit right there and walk off the course, withdrawing (W/D) themselves. Fortunately, I kept my emotions in check. I wasn't happy with my performance thus far, but I didn't lose my mind. I collected myself and kept cool.

For the remaining 17 holes I couldn't shoot higher than 1 over par, a daunting task. I was under a tremendous amount of pressure, and I knew I had to bear down immediately. After my disastrous start, I rebounded by playing 14 consecutive holes at 3 under par. After this good run, I had a little breathing room with 3 holes left to play. All I had to do was play 16, 17 and 18 at 4 over par or better. Shouldn't be a problem.

Standing on the 16th tee box, I became very nervous. I knew I was in a great position to pass and thought that if I could just hold it together for a few more holes, I would accomplish this.

I bogeyed #16.

Then I double-bogeyed #17.

My nerves were getting the best of me, and now I had to make a bogey or better on the final hole. I was putting intense pressure on myself on the 18th tee box. It was a par 4 with a water hazard in front of the green. My tee shot was in the fairway. I was about 175 yards from the hole for my second shot, so I hit a 6 iron, catching it a little fat. I prayed it would make it over the water. If it didn't, I would receive a one-shot penalty and most likely make a double-bogey on the hole, eliminating my chance of getting my pro card. My heart was in my throat. Luckily, my ball cleared the water hazard by about ten feet and ended up on the grass between the water and the green. I pitched my ball to within about three feet of the hole. I missed my short par putt and tapped my ball in the hole for a bogey 5. I let out a huge sigh of relief. After shooting 83 on my first 18 holes, I shot 79 on my last 18 (40-39). I had passed! I had shot exactly 162. Because of the pressure this event puts on an individual, I think those who are trying to qualify will shoot an average of at least 6 shots higher than their average score would normally be for 36 holes. Playing the last 3 holes at 4 over par was only 1 shot away from being a complete meltdown for me. I was so happy that things turned out in my favor. I went into the clubhouse and joined some of the other guys to celebrate by having a couple of cold beers.

Gary Meyers was the head golf professional at the Belvedere Golf & Country Club in Sherwood Park, east of Edmonton. He was also on the board of directors for the Alberta Professional Golfers' Association (APGA). Gary was asking each individual who passed the PAT that day why they wanted to become a golf professional and other similar questions concerning our future in the golf industry. I knew that some of the other guys were a little nervous regarding this meeting. I wasn't. I had met Gary several times and had socialized with him on numerous occasions. I got along with him well and felt quite comfortable with him. When it was my turn to be interviewed, I went into the office and sat down across from him. The first thing he said to me was "Hi Rock. Get laid lately?" I just laughed. Then, looking at my score card, he said "Nice 11." Overall, it was an easy interview. I became a member of the CPGA and the APGA that day.

ASSISTANT GOLF PRO AT THE JASPER PARK LODGE GOLF CLUB

I then landed a job interview at the world famous Jasper Park Lodge Golf Club (JPL) in Jasper, Alberta. It's about four hours west of Edmonton in the heart of the beautiful and majestic Canadian Rocky Mountains. My interview was with Ron MacLeod, the head pro who was looking for an assistant. I had told some of my golf pro friends in Edmonton that I was thinking about applying for this job, and they advised against it saying I wouldn't be happy working for him. I thought he couldn't be that bad of a guy, so I went against my friends' advice and arranged to meet him.

The interview was at 1 p.m., and my mom came along for the beautiful drive. It is common to see wildlife there, including deer, elk and the odd bear. People from all over the world golf there. Ron called me a few days later to offer me the job for May 1, and I accepted. It was my first job as a CPGA assistant professional, and one of my top priorities was to build a good resume to help me land better jobs in the future, especially as a head golf professional. I thought that starting my apprenticeship as an assistant at Jasper Park would look excellent on my resume. I was excited! My professional status was official, and I was working at the Jasper Park Lodge Golf Club. It was a great start to my career.

After working there for a few weeks, I was becoming unhappy. My friends were right about Ron, my boss. He was arrogant. We didn't get along that well right from the start. Then things went from bad to worse. From my interview, I was under the impression that as his assistant pro, I would mainly be working in the pro shop. Instead, he had me cleaning clubs and power carts, working in the club storage area and picking up range balls by hand. This was not what I had in mind. Ron's wife, daughter and son (another assistant pro) worked in the pro shop, and I didn't like any of them. I didn't like the other guys I worked with either, they weren't my kind of guys. There were four of them, aged 19-25. At least one of them had never worked at a golf course before. Despite this, Ron didn't give me any seniority over this guy or over any of the others for that matter. Basically, I was just a back shop guy like the others. My experience and credentials didn't seem to mean anything to Ron, so I wondered why he had hired me.

The parking lot was a bit of a long walk from the pro shop. As back shop guys, we would clean the golfer's clubs when they finished playing and would often drive them to their vehicles in a power cart. I didn't mind being a part of this "valet" service because I met a lot of interesting people from all over the globe. Although I felt more like a bellhop than a golf pro, at least we usually received a small tip of $2-$5 for our service, which brought in an extra $300/month. I needed this little bonus because Ron was only paying me $1,200/month.

Ron was in his early 60s and had been the head pro there for about twenty-five years. Jasper Park Lodge was owned by Canadian Pacific Railway (CPR). In 1987, it was still quite common for CPGA head pros to own the power carts and the pro shop merchandise. Having this arrangement with the golf course owner meant that the pro would receive the revenues generated from these concessions. Ron owned both of these. It was like he had a license to print money. Someone told me that Ron became a millionaire while he was there. I have never heard of this happening with any other club pro, but I believe it could be a fact, nonetheless. He mainly made his fortune off the power carts. When I was there, he had eighty-two of them, and during peak season all eighty-two would be rented out. Often, many of them would get rented twice in one day. Ron was charging $22.50 per cart if they paid cash and $24.00 if they paid by Visa for 18 holes. This was a discrepancy I had never seen before or since. In all the years I worked at golf courses, our customers paid the same price regardless of whether they were paying with cash or a credit card.

Ron also made a lot of money by selling his pro shop merchandise. Most of the items, including clothing, hats and souvenirs, had the JPL crest and the famous "Jasper the Bear" logo on them. These things sold like crazy. Some of the best customers were Asians (mostly Chinese and Japanese) who came there in busloads. I don't know how much revenue this generated for Ron, but I'm certain it was a significant amount.

Years later, golf course owners started realizing how much money these guys were making from these concessions and began keeping them for themselves. It's much more common now for the pros to be salaried employees of the golf course. This arrangement makes more sense and is how I would operate if I owned a golf course. Especially with the power carts.

At JPL, my guess is that Ron also received a "retainer fee" or was paid a monthly or annual salary for his services as the head professional. If so, I would imagine that this would also be a significant amount of money. He must have signed quite a contract with JPL and/or CPR. It certainly appeared that he was getting the maximum benefit out of his position.

I didn't like Ron because of his personality and attitude. As I mentioned earlier, he was arrogant, which drove me crazy. He wasn't personable or very friendly with the golfers or other customers. I couldn't believe he'd had this job for twenty-five years! I worked six days per week, a minimum of fifty hours and received $1,200/month (about $5.50/hour, which was the minimum wage back then). Employers like Ron paid their employees a monthly salary, so they didn't have to pay overtime wages. I don't think this is fair to the employees, but I have worked for a couple of head pros who operated this way. I believe that the more money a business and an employer makes, the more money their employees should make. Ron obviously didn't share this philosophy. My friends and I used to refer to these type of people as "one dog, one bone!"

I don't know how much Ron was paying the other back shop guys, but our work schedules and job descriptions were basically the same, so I would think it was the same as me. My experience, diploma and professional status didn't seem to resonate with Ron when it was time for our pay checks.

Jasper Park Lodge was a pretty big place that employed about 650 people, a lot of whom were from eastern Canada. Most of them lived in wood cabins at the lodge that were designated specifically for employees. Most of these cabins weren't very big, and they were mostly shared accommodations. There was usually between two and four people per cabin/room. The majority of the staff were 18-21 years old, which was probably a lot of fun. I think most staff rooms were $300-$400/month, paid for among its occupants.

I was lucky in this regard. Being a golf pro there, I had my own room and didn't have to pay rent. This was the best benefit of working there. If I was working somewhere else and had to rent an apartment, it would have cost me about $500-$600/month. Free accommodation was the deciding factor when I agreed to work there for such a low salary.

My small cabin/room was one of many located inside the longest wood cabin in the world. The worst part was that I had to share a common bathroom and shower with my neighbor. My room was rustic — not fancy by any means. The walls and ceiling were constructed mainly with old logs and wood. The room itself was only about 400 square feet. The only furniture in there when I moved in were two old single beds. I put them together to create a makeshift double bed. It wasn't the greatest, but it worked. With proper sheets, comforter and pillows, it did the trick! I added a table and a couple of chairs, then I purchased a small fridge and a microwave oven. Of course, I had to have my tunes to listen to, so I had my ghetto blaster as well. I didn't have much time to watch TV, so I didn't have one. That's all I needed. Just the basics. I didn't spend a lot of time in my room anyway. Mostly just to sleep. I have always been pretty adaptable to my environment no matter where I'm living.

There was a pub/dance hall for the JPL employees situated beside the cabin I lived in. It was a busy place, and I heard loud music coming from there every night. It didn't really bother me much because I was always so tired when I went to bed that I would just fall fast asleep. I only went there a couple of times myself. Even though I had just turned twenty-three, most of the others seemed really young to me.

There was a staff cafeteria called The Beanery. The food wasn't very good, but it was only $2/meal, so I ate there often.

The best part of my time in Jasper was that Linda came to see me almost every weekend. As I said earlier, I wasn't happy with my job and didn't like the people I was working for and with, so I always looked forward to Linda's arrival. It was more than a breath of fresh air. It was more like a huge relief. Linda was amazing. She worked until 4 p.m. in her west Edmonton office, then made the four-hour drive to Jasper to be with me. She arrived Friday nights around 8, and to get the most out of our time together, usually didn't leave until 4 a.m. on Monday mornings. She drove straight to work for an 8 a.m. start. I had it so good with Linda in many ways. She cooked healthy food for me and brought it when she came. She also did my laundry.

I had to work on the weekends (usually the open shift, which was 5:30 a.m. to 2 p.m.). Linda and I spent the remainder of the afternoon and evenings together. It was still early in our relationship, and we just loved being together as much as we could.

At one point, the old tractor used to pull the range picker broke down, and Ron was too cheap to pay to get it fixed. So, for a while we had to pick up the driving range balls by hand with a shag bag. Finally, the golf course mechanic fixed it and all it cost Ron was a case of beer.

After about ten weeks, I couldn't take it anymore. Working for Ron made me miserable. I hated it. I felt that my job description wasn't conducive to my apprenticeship as a CPGA Assistant Golf Professional. I wanted to quit, but I was extremely worried about any repercussions regarding my professional status and reputation. This wasn't how I wanted to start my career!

One morning I called Bill McDougall, my old boss from the Wetaskiwin Golf Club. At the time, Bill was the head pro at the Elk Island Golf Course in the Elk Island National Park, located northeast of Edmonton. I had stayed in touch with him over the years and knew him quite well. We always had a good relationship, so he answered my call right away. I was so upset, I started to cry over the phone (it takes a lot to make me cry). It was hard for me to even try to speak with him. Choking on my words, I did my best to explain my situation. Bill was great. Not only was he understanding, he also told me that I could work for him at Elk Island starting as soon as I wanted to. And I would be working in the pro shop! I took him up on his offer with much appreciation. I think Bill may have already had an idea what Ron was like. He knew I was a pretty good guy and a good employee.

I wanted to make this transition properly. I spent three days working on a professional letter of resignation for Ron. I was also giving him two weeks of notice. Besides Bill and Linda, I only told Brady, a guy I worked with, that I was going to quit. I asked him to keep this information confidential. When I went into the pro shop to give Ron my letter of resignation and my notice, he already had my pink slip and my last check ready for me. Brady went behind my back and informed Ron about my plans. Ron was swaggering as if he had fired me.

Around the middle of July 1987, I went to work for Bill at the Elk Island Golf Course, which I enjoyed. He was a good employer and was like a friend as well. He was a pretty easygoing guy, which suited my personality well. My job there was pretty mundane. Mostly I collected green fees and sold pro shop merchandise. At least I was a CPGA Assistant Professional and working the full season, so I received credit for my apprenticeship program. It was also important that I got along well with the other staff members. The course was 9 holes, and I only played it a couple of times. I would say it was a decent course, but not spectacular. I lived with Linda at her house in Millwoods, about a forty-five-minute drive to work.

Elk Island is a national park, and there are numerous huge buffalo there! When I drove into the park, they would often come very close to my car. Their heads alone were massive. It was pretty cool to see these enormous creatures up so close. Sometimes I got a little worried, but I never saw them get aggressive and was never in any real danger.

One Friday afternoon around 3 p.m. when I normally would have been working in the pro shop, I was out cutting fairways for some reason. I hadn't done this since I was thirteen years old at the Wetaskiwin Golf Club. I guess it was like riding a bike because I still knew how to do it. I was cutting the 18th fairway when I noticed how ominous the sky was. The clouds were almost pitch black. At first, I thought there was going to be a major thunderstorm. It was getting incredibly windy. I kept watching the sky and began to get an eerie feeling. I started to sense that something catastrophic was going to happen. I went straight to the maintenance shed and parked the tractor and fairway mowers. It started raining heavily, so I ran to the clubhouse as fast as I could.

The TV was tuned to a local station in the clubhouse. It turns out a tornado had just touched down on the southern outskirts of Edmonton! This was very unusual as Alberta is not "tornado country." Several of us kept looking out the clubhouse windows, keeping an eye on the weather. At the same time, we were all glued to the TV. The report was that the tornado was moving fast and traveling to the north — towards us! The park wardens wouldn't let anyone leave the park until a few hours after everything had calmed down. In the meantime, most people went into the basement cellar of the clubhouse. Knowing the tornado was coming our direction, another staff member and I poured ourselves a couple of rum and Cokes. We kept a close watch on the weather and kept watching the TV. We got lucky, and the tornado didn't reach us. After a few hours, we were allowed to leave.

I took the Sherwood Park Freeway going home. The traffic was backed up for a couple of miles and was just barely crawling along. Then I saw the devastation caused by the tornado. It was unbelievable! I hadn't seen this when I was watching TV at the clubhouse. I didn't realize the severity of the tornado until I got to this point. There were cars, trucks and RVs scattered all over the place. Many of them were upside down or laying on their sides. They were on the highway and in the ditches. Many vehicles were in a field 50-60 yards and farther from the highway. The power and force generated by this tornado was incredible. There were people everywhere. It was total chaos. Emergency personnel had more than their hands full — I had never seen anything like it. It was a somber experience, and an example of how powerful Mother Nature can be.

The place that was hit the hardest by the tornado was the Evergreen Mobile Home Park located in north Edmonton. I drove through there a few weeks after it happened. The entire park was annihilated! It was totally demolished. All of the mobile homes were gone. Only the cement foundations remained of this large mobile home park. I would guess there were over one hundred units in there. Seeing the destruction this tornado caused firsthand was a shocking and sad experience. The tornado killed several people, and the day went on to be called "Black Friday."

I had an interesting job working for a company called "Dial-A-Bottle" in Edmonton during the winter of 1987/88. I delivered alcohol all over the city. It was a totally legitimate business. We charged our customers the same price as the liquor stores, and then charged them a delivery service fee that averaged around $5-$6 per delivery. There were several drivers, and we used our own vehicles. The drivers were paid approximately sixty percent of each delivery cost plus tips, which averaged about $2/delivery. I ended up making about $5/delivery for 20-30 deliveries/day, which was $100-$150/day. We worked liquor store hours. I needed this money to get me through the winter months.

One of the best things about this job was that I was basically my own boss. I never had to deal with the owners at all. Our office was on the south side of Edmonton, and a dispatcher worked there taking orders and then relaying them to the drivers. At first, we used pagers, which was a pain in the ass. The dispatcher would page us, and we would have to find a pay phone in the freezing cold and call them back for the order. Using outdoor pay phones wasn't fun. It was hard to write down an order without the pen freezing up, so I used indoor pay phones when I could. Sometimes I would get a little lonely from driving by myself for eight-hour shifts, so once in a while Linda would come to keep me company.

Most of our customers were "regulars," and there were a lot of serious alcoholics amongst our clients. Most of them ordered from us every day — many of them twice! The liquor store opened at 10:00 a.m., and our dispatcher's phone would be ringing off the wall right on ten bells! It was amazing how many people started drinking first thing in the morning. I guess they were trying to avoid a hangover or withdrawal symptoms. I've seen people shaking really bad, especially in the morning. Then they would start drinking again. I saw a lot of people in rough shape from years of heavy drinking. It was sad. I know that I drank too much, but these were hard-core drinkers. Compared to them, I was an angel. Sometimes I felt guilty about contributing to their addiction, but I knew if I didn't deliver the alcohol, somebody else would. The good thing was that these people weren't drinking and driving. Dial-A-Bottle offered a great service. A $5 delivery fee would ensure that someone wouldn't get an impaired driving charge and/or into a car accident. Most of our customers lived in apartment buildings. Many of them didn't own a vehicle and didn't drive at all. Thank God for that!

The busiest time was near the end of every month when the welfare checks came out. As soon as our customers had some money, they spent it on booze.

This job made me think about my own drinking habits. I certainly didn't want to end up like so many of my customers.

During this same winter, I taught indoor golf lessons again for the City of Edmonton Parks and Recreation Program. I enjoyed doing this much more than delivering alcohol out in the cold weather and driving around on the city streets with bad winter conditions. Teaching gave me more experience and confidence. The money I received from doing this was also a big help.

I think Linda was truly in love with me and ready for a serious, long-term relationship. She was thirty, and I was only twenty-three. She was my first serious girlfriend and the first one I had ever lived with. (To this day, I've only lived with two women.) Linda was a great person, and she was extremely good to me. I cared deeply for her, but I wasn't in love with her. I also wasn't ready to commit to a monogamous relationship. Looking back, I realize I wasn't mature enough to make this kind of commitment. I still had many seeds to sow!

In some ways, I was quite mature for my age. I had grown up playing golf with adults and spent a lot of time with older people in general. Most of my friends were older than I was. At the age of thirty-six, I finally realized that settling down with someone monogamously requires a different kind of maturity. Now in 2020, my wife and I have been together for over twenty years. We have a remarkable relationship. In large part, our success comes from my maturity.

Back in 1987, I wasn't ready. I was a bit wild. I felt kind of chained down, and I wasn't happy, so I decided to move on with my life.

I ran into Norm Jackson, an associate professional at the Edmonton Country Club, at David's one evening. He told me there was an assistant pro job opening on Vancouver Island at Glen Meadows Golf & Country Club, which was located in Sidney, a small town north of Victoria. I played there once when I was about ten years old. Norm knew Doug Mahovlic, the head pro at Glen Meadows and would provide a reference if I wanted. I sent Doug my resume along with several references, including one from Norm. Shortly after, Doug and I spoke over the phone. He had two assistant pros at the time and offered me the job to become his third. I accepted to start on March 1, 1988.

The most difficult part of this transition was having to inform Linda that our relationship was over and that I was moving to Vancouver Island. I knew it was going to be hard for her, and it was. I felt really bad about that. It was hard for me, too, but I had made up my mind. I was looking forward to a fresh new start, both professionally and personally. I was moving to "Beautiful British Columbia"!

CHAPTER 8
1988
GLEN MEADOWS GOLF & COUNTRY CLUB

The first thing I had to do was find a place to live. I thought I would just rent a one-bedroom apartment in Sidney. After a thorough look, there was nothing available in the region, so I ended up renting a motel room very close to the famous Butchart Gardens for the first month I was there while I continued to look around.

After that first month, I was able to get on a waiting list in an apartment complex, and I kept a close eye on the vacancy rates for Sidney and the surrounding area. Basically, it was around 0-1%. It was extremely difficult to find rental accommodations. Then, I had an idea. Why not buy a place and rent out a couple of rooms? I found a half duplex for sale in Sidney that was very close to the Victoria International Airport and only a five-minute drive to Glen Meadows. It had three bedrooms upstairs and two bathrooms. There was a small yard and a carport. It came with a fridge and stove, and washer and dryer for $73,000. I calculated all of the costs and convinced my mom it would be a smart decision to buy this place. The apartment rent was at least $500/month. I qualified for a BC First Homeowner's Grant, which required a down payment of approximately $3,650 (5% of $73,000). Even though my mom loaned me the money, I still had to do a lot of talking at the TD Bank in Sidney to convince them to approve this sale in my name, but I was bound and determined to get this deal done. It felt great when all the paperwork was done and I was officially a homeowner.

I put an ad in the local paper for "rooms to rent," and within a week, I was getting calls. My mortgage payments were $650/month, so I charged $325 per room. With my roommates paying my mortgage, all I had to pay for was the utilities. Having roommates again wasn't exactly ideal, and I would have preferred to live by myself. However, just a couple of years earlier, I had lived with roommates when I was at the SDGA and having good "roomies" can be enjoyable. Perhaps more so when you're young. I was only twenty-four. The bottom line was that I couldn't afford to live by myself because Doug was only paying me $1,400/month. Even my own apartment would have been difficult for me to afford. I needed these two roommates to help pay my mortgage.

At least I had some control over who lived with me. I received several calls from people who were interested, and I got lucky. The first two guys I interviewed, I liked. Their names were Al and Cameron (Cam). We agreed they would rent from me on a month-to-month basis, and they moved in immediately. Al and I were about the same age, and Cam was just a couple of years younger, so the three of us got along well. They turned out to be pretty good roommates. I never had any problems with either one of them, and there was always $650 cash sitting on my kitchen table on the first of every month. Every time this happened, my mortgage was paid for another month. I loved this part of the deal. Al and Cam must have thought I was a pretty good roommate also because I didn't spend much time there. Basically, I just slept and showered there. The rest of my time, I was working, playing golf or at a pub or nightclub.

The two assistant pros working for Doug when I arrived were Dave Cormier and Scott Dickson. Glen Meadows was an 18-hole, semi-private course with a driving range. Most of the golfers there were members. There was a large dining room in the clubhouse for special occasions, such as weddings. Every Friday night, Head Chef Anthony prepared excellent dinners for the members. A curling rink with several sheets of ice was attached to the clubhouse, which was busy during the winter months. The golf course was open all year round. In the winter months during periods of heavy rain or occasional snowfall, the course would have to be closed for a few days. Because the golf course was a lot quieter during the winter, I was employed from March 1 to November 30.

During my first week of work, Doug and I were in the pro shop, and I asked him if he would like a coffee. He said "yes." I went upstairs to the restaurant and got two coffees in Styrofoam cups. When I handed his coffee to him, he got really pissed off at me, and said "Don't ever bring me a coffee in a Styrofoam cup again!" I couldn't believe it. I thought, "What did I get myself into?" This was my first taste of Doug's personality, and things got worse from there.

I mention several times throughout my book how much I hate arrogance. It just rubs me the wrong way, and I can usually detect it quickly. I don't have much tolerance for it. I always hoped Doug would be in a good mood when I went to work because it was so much better. When he was in a bad mood it was brutal — like walking on eggshells.

Because of our differences, we butted heads on occasion. We had a bit of a tumultuous relationship. For the most part, I kept this turmoil inside of me, so it would fester and build up inside like a volcano. I felt like erupting and unleashing a verbal onslaught towards Doug countless times, but I always refrained because I knew I would get fired if I did. I could feel how stressful this was, but I didn't realize how detrimental to my health it was.

Dave Cormier's nickname was "Pooch," and he had been working for Doug for a number of years. He was an easygoing guy, and we usually got along. I went to his house for a couple of parties, but aside from that, we didn't socialize outside of work.

After the first few months, Scott Dickson and I began to have a good working relationship. The more he got to know me the better things got between us. Eventually, we had a blast working together. Scott and I became good friends outside of work as well. We were both young and single, and we liked to go out for a few beers together. We went to some of the best nightclubs in Victoria and always had a lot of fun. He was full of personality and had a great sense of humor. Scott was one of the best pros on the island and did well in some of the tournaments against other CPGA pros.

Mike Wallace and I got along really well. He mainly worked in the back shop cleaning clubs and looking after club storage. I would guess he was in his early 40s and was a bit of a hippie. He was easygoing and funny, so we hit it off immediately. Mike and I went to the lounge at the Sidney Hotel many times after work for a few beers, and I always enjoyed his company. His son, Brian, was a good guy too. He was about twenty and was a very good golfer. I think he was a scratch handicap.

There were some good players at Glen Meadows. Ed Beauchmin and Don Gowan may have been the two best amateurs on Vancouver Island. Ed worked on the grounds crew. He was a quiet and humble guy. I liked him. His brother, Bob, was the commissioner of the Canadian Golf Tour during that era. Don was an accountant and a member of Glen Meadows. Ed and Don battled each other for the title at most tournaments. Both were scratch players or close to it.

After I had been there for a couple of months, I really started missing Linda. I hadn't met anyone new to be interested in and was feeling kind of lonely. I was thinking about how good it was with her and hoped she didn't have a new boyfriend yet. I called her and, luckily, she wasn't with anyone new. We both still had very strong feelings for each other, so she flew out to see me. We ended up having a long-distance relationship over the next several months. Linda flew from Edmonton to Victoria on a pretty regular basis during this time. I really appreciated her faithfulness and commitment towards me, and I was always excited to see her. We cherished our time together.

Linda was a pretty heavy smoker. There were countless times that I gave her a hard time about it. I didn't smoke, and I wanted her to quit. She had emphysema from smoking, and I was concerned about her health. Plus, it just really annoyed me. I don't really know why. I grew up in a smoking environment and knew a lot of people who smoked, which didn't bother me at all. I was brutal with Linda in this regard. It was like I was possessed or something. Looking back, I'm kind of perplexed as to why I acted this way towards her. I knew Linda smoked when we first got together, and I should have just accepted this fact. At the very least, I shouldn't have been so controlling and persistent with this issue. Linda tried to quit, but as long as I knew her, she just wasn't able to. Two years later, I started smoking myself! I went on to love it and was a smoker for the next twenty-five years! Linda would flip if she knew this. In hindsight, I'm much more understanding towards Linda's smoking habits, or anyone else's for that matter. Sorry Linda! Having said this, I quit smoking in 2015 at age fifty. I'm glad I did.

Unfortunately, things with Linda didn't work out in the end. Our long-distance relationship was too hard to maintain, and I guess it just wasn't meant to be. Around the time Linda and I split up, my friend Angela Babb was living in Vancouver. I worked with her at the Windermere Golf & Country Club in Edmonton in 1983 and 1984, and we had stayed in touch after that. After Linda was out of the picture, Angela and I started seeing each other on a pretty regular basis. Quite often, she took the ferry to the island and stayed at my place for a few days. On a couple of occasions, I went to Vancouver and stayed with her at her apartment for a couple of days. During this time, our friendship escalated somewhat. We became intimate but didn't get overly serious. Things were pretty casual between us. Still, our relationship was monogamous. Above all, we were good friends.

The owner of Glen Meadows was Percy Criddle. His sons, Larry and Greg, worked on the golf course, and his daughter worked in the office. I liked the Criddle family. They were all good people, and they were always good to me while I was employed there. The brothers liked to have a couple of beers in the clubhouse after a hard day's work, and they were hockey fans. They were down-to-earth people.

One morning when I arrived at work, Doug said, "You're playing golf today." He explained that there was a pro/ladies' tournament that day at the Victoria Golf Club in Oak Bay. Jim Rutledge was supposed to play in it, but he was a late cancellation for some reason. Doug told me that I would be taking Jim's place. I became nervous immediately. Jim Rutledge was from Victoria and one of the best Canadian golfers in history, among the ranks of Dave Barr, Jim Nelford and Dan Halldorson. He played on the PGA Tour for several years. My first thought was, "The ladies whose group Jim was supposed to be in are going to be very disappointed when they find out the pro in their group is me. Don who?" To make matters worse, my golf game was terrible at the time. I had very little confidence in it, if any, which wasn't good for the nerves factor.

My hands trembled as I hit my tee shot on the first hole, and it took a few holes before my anxiety started to settle down. Despite Jim Rutledge's absence, we ended up having a very enjoyable day on the golf course. It was sunny and warm, with very little wind. A perfect day for golf. I was hoping to break 80 that day and missed by only one shot, shooting exactly 80. This obviously wasn't a very good score, but under the circumstances I wasn't too upset.

The Victoria Golf Club is a private and exclusive facility with a number of very wealthy members. I was lucky enough to play there a few times. It is one of my favorite golf courses because it is right beside the Pacific Ocean. Some holes are right along the ocean, and several holes have an ocean view. The scenery is breathtaking. I enjoyed playing there so much, I wouldn't get upset if I didn't play well.

After the golf tournament with the ladies, we went into the clubhouse for the prize presentations and dinner. All things considered it was a good day.

I worked at Glen Meadows until about the end of November. Doug laid me off for a few months, and we agreed I would return to work on March 1, 1989. At the time, I was happy he wanted me to work for him again the following season. Looking back, returning to work for Doug may not have been the best decision. I had just gone through nine months of stress, and now I was signing up for more. I didn't realize how this stress was affecting my health.

CHAPTER 9
1989
CANADIAN TOUR QUALIFYING SCHOOL

I spent the winter of 1988/89 in Edmonton, where I partied with my friends. I also taught golf for the city again. As usual, this was mainly done at school gymnasiums all over Edmonton. I enjoyed teaching golf, and it was nice to get paid to do this. It supplemented the meagre unemployment insurance benefits I was receiving during the three months I was laid off from Glen Meadows. My time off from work went very quickly. Before I knew it, I was back at my home in Sidney and had started my second season.

For the most part, my employment as an assistant golf professional was pretty standard. It was my job to help run golf operations, and I enjoyed it. I still found it difficult working for Doug, and our differences created a tremendous amount of stress for me.

The Canadian Tour Qualifying School was held at Glen Meadows that year. Guys from all over the world came to our course to try and obtain their Canadian Tour pro card. The successful qualifiers earned the right to play in Canadian Tour events across Canada. The Canadian Tour is considered a stepping-stone for professional golfers who want to play on the PGA Tour. Doug told our pro shop staff that, "These guys aren't anyone special, so don't treat them like they're special." It was quite condescending. My attitude towards our guests was much different than my boss. Having this special event at our golf course was kind of exciting. It was cool to meet a lot of these guys. Many of them showed up early so they could play practice rounds and get familiar with the golf course before their qualifying rounds began. This was serious business for these guys. Their future of playing golf for a living was on the line.

STEVE "TEX" PARKER

One of these early arrivals was Steve Parker from Houston, Texas. He was playing practice rounds and using our driving range to prepare for the big event. I first met him when he came into the pro shop, and we hit it off immediately. Because of his obvious "Texas drawl," I nicknamed him "Tex" right away. A friendship developed quickly between the two of us.

Tex had driven all the way from Houston and was staying at a nearby motel. I knew this would be quite expensive, so I invited him to stay at my place. Not having to pay for accommodation and being able to eat meals at my place would obviously help him financially. He happily accepted my offer and stayed with me for about a week. Luckily, my roommates were OK with this arrangement. We all got along well, and Tex and I especially bonded. We had a lot of laughs and good times when we were together. We also played golf together on one occasion at Glen Meadows. I was quite impressed with his game. Tex was a true professional, and I really enjoyed playing with him. Tex successfully qualified for his Canadian Tour pro card and competed in Canadian Tour events across Canada for two years (1989 and 1990). After this, he lived full time in Houston and resumed his career as a PGA golf professional.

We have now been friends for thirty years. I went down to Houston in '93, '95 and '96 to visit my brother, Jim, who lives there, and I socialized and played golf with Tex as well. On one occasion when I was with him, I was starting to go manic. I had been diagnosed by that time and Tex knew, but he never held it against me. He was always very good to me no matter what. I've always appreciated that about him. There have been several people in my life over the years who I thought were my friends, but when I really needed them to be there for me, especially because of things related to my mental illness, they made the decision to avoid contact with me altogether. If I was a drunken idiot, like I was on countless occasions, my "friends" always used to just accept me the way I was and vice versa. But, if I was "mentally ill," that was a whole different story. Most of my "friends" were nowhere to be found! The world needs more people like Steve Parker. People who are more accepting and less judgmental.

JACK NICKLAUS JR.

Jack Nicklaus Jr. was one of the guys who was trying to qualify to play on the Canadian Tour. I have a good picture of him and I together. Being the son of perhaps the greatest golfer in the history of the game, Jack Jr. attracted a lot of attention from the locals. Of all the players, he had the largest gallery following him. I didn't get a chance to watch him play, as I was usually working. I felt kind of bad for Jack Jr. He must have been under a tremendous amount of pressure. How do you follow in the footsteps of your father when his name is Jack Nicklaus? In the end, he qualified and earned his right to play on the Canadian Tour.

After the ceremony for the successful qualifiers, I organized a small celebration for them at Merlin's, a really good nightclub in Victoria. I arrived there first and explained to the doorman that there were going to be several pro golfers joining me, and I gave him some cash incentive to make sure he wouldn't make any of these guys wait in a lineup. Shortly after, about a dozen guys showed up. Merlin's was packed like usual, and my little bribe worked perfectly. They were all extremely happy and ready to party! The next thing I knew, I was sitting at a table with a few of them, one of whom was Jack Nicklaus Jr. I couldn't believe it! I wish I could say I had a great conversation with Jack Jr. or that we really hit it off and had a lot of fun partying together that night, but that didn't happen. From my perspective, he seemed like kind of a quiet guy and was somewhat guarded. Having said that, I think he was still having a good time and enjoyed being there with the rest of us. Regardless, I gave him his space. I didn't even really try to talk with him. I just didn't want to bother him. A few of us let loose a bit — dancing and partying and really having a great time together. It was a fun night.

Three years earlier, in 1986, Jack Jr. caddied for his dad at Augusta when Nicklaus became the oldest player to ever win The Masters at age forty-six. In 2017, Nicklaus was reported to be worth $280 million.

CHAPTER 10
SUMMER 1989-WINTER 1990
UPS AND DOWNS

Having the Canadian Tour Qualifying School at Glen Meadows was a special time for me. I really enjoyed hanging out with some of the guys. Tex, Jack Nicklaus Jr. and the rest of the guys who had just received their tour cards went to the Uplands Golf Club in Victoria where they played in the Victoria Open. It was the first event of the year on the Canadian Tour schedule and the beginning of an exciting journey for these professional golfers.

When I met a lot of these guys, they would have known me as a pretty normal guy. I was twenty-four years old and in my third year working as a CPGA assistant pro. They were better golfers than me, but we had a lot in common. Their future looked bright, and so did mine. I had no signs or symptoms of mental illness at this time. A week or less later, all of this changed literally overnight. I suddenly had to experience the symptoms and consequences of manic depression, also known as bipolar disorder.

Becoming mentally ill changed everything very abruptly. After the episode I described in Chapter 1, my family and I decided I would go back to Alberta with them. This meant that I would be living with my mom again, in her house in Edmonton. I really had no choice in the matter. I love my mom very much, and we got along extremely well. I was very lucky to be able to live with her.

MEETING MARK MESSIER

In October, I went to the two-day APGA seminar at West Edmonton Mall. After the seminar, we played a hockey game at the mall. The golf pros from southern Alberta played against the golf pros from northern Alberta. I played on the northern Alberta team, and we had some good players, including a few former NHLers. None of them were "big name" players, but they were still a nice asset to have on our team. My good friend Darrell was on our team and often played on my line. We recruited my buddy Dave to play defense for us. Most of us were quite competitive, and both teams wanted to win for the bragging rights. It was fairly good hockey, and we had a lot of fun. I don't remember who actually won the game.

After the game, Dave and I went to Club Malibu for a few beers. It was a weeknight, and it was quiet. Around midnight, Wayne Gretzky, Mark Messier and some of the other Edmonton Oilers players showed up. By this time, Wayne was playing for the Los Angeles Kings. He was traded from Edmonton to LA on August 9, 1988. It looked like Wayne had already had a couple of beers. He seemed to be in a great mood and looked like he was really having a lot of fun with his ex-teammates. I found out later that Wayne had just broken Gordie Howe's record for scoring the most points in the history of the NHL. It was October 15, 1989, and Wayne's new record was 1851 points. No wonder he was having such a good time.

"This one's on me, boys!" said Messier as he and ten Oilers sat at the bar.

If there were any girls there that Dave and I might have been eyeing up, we could now forget about that. With the Oilers there, we didn't stand a chance!

I asked our waitress to serve Mark a shot of ouzo, hoping he would like it. I watched as she gave it to him at his seat up at the bar. The waitress pointed towards me, indicating to Mark that I was the one who sent it to him. He looked over at me, and our eyes met. I raised my beer in a "cheers" motion to him. A few minutes later, Mark came over to our table and sat down with Dave and me. He brought three shot glasses of ouzo with him. Apparently, I had made the right call. Mark visited with Dave and I for about 15-20 minutes. It was one of the greatest honors and thrills of my life. I was already a big Messier fan before this, but even more so afterward. I was really impressed with his actions that night. The fact that he took the time to come and join Dave and I like he did really means a lot to me. Myself, and many others, consider Wayne Gretzky to be the best hockey player ever. In a recent interview on TV, Wayne said that Messier was the best hockey player he had ever played with. That's quite a statement. I'm not impressed with superstardom alone. But, if a superstar can remain humble and possesses other important qualities and traits, there is a much better chance I will be impressed by him. From what I know about Mark Messier, he falls into that category.

Anyway, back at Club Malibu on Gretzky's record-breaking night, I thought I might get to meet Gretzky. I could have asked Mark if he would introduce Dave and I to Wayne. Or, because Wayne was in such a good mood, I may have been able to approach him and introduce myself. Regardless, I decided not to push my luck. I didn't want to infringe upon him, and I respected the fact that he was there to celebrate with his friends.

Later on, someone said there was going to be a hot tub party at Kevin Lowe's house in Riverbend. (Kevin was also a former teammate and one of Wayne's best friends. After he retired as a player, Kevin became the head coach and then president and general manager of the Oilers.) I was well oiled and thinking that maybe Dave and I might get invited to Kevin's place to party with the Oilers. Maybe I would still get to meet Wayne! I was hoping someone would give us Kevin's address.

I saw Messier leave Club Malibu and thought the best chance to be invited to the party would be through him, so I followed him out. By the time I got outside, Mark was already in his black Porsche, which was parked right out front. I went to the driver's side window. It was a little frosty from the cold. I saw a female in the passenger seat and knocked on the window to talk with Mark. He completely ignored me and sped off. He obviously had other priorities. Regardless, I understood. Besides our visit a little earlier that evening, I was just a stranger to him. We never went to the party, but we had a good time that night anyway.

Point of Interest: Earlier that evening, LA had a game against the Oilers. The Kings won the game 5-4 in overtime. Wayne had two goals and an assist, including scoring the OT winner. His goal in the third period tied the game and set a new record for NHL all-time career points with 1851, breaking Gordie Howe's record of 1850 points. Fittingly, the game was in Edmonton. After this, Gretzky played ten more years in the NHL. He retired with an incredible 2857 points, making him the all-time leader. Wayne won four Stanley Cups when he played for the Oilers. Messier is second on the list for most total points in history with 1887. He won six Stanley Cups (five with Edmonton and one with the New York Rangers). Gordie Howe is in third place, close behind Mark. He won four Stanley cups with the Detroit Red Wings.

DEPRESSION

In November 1989, I went into my first major depressed episode. This lasted for four months. I had been depressed before, but that was what I would call "normal" depression. Life is full of ups and downs, and I think we all get them. There are many reasons why someone may become depressed. Losing a loved one might be the number one reason. I'd had a few people die that were close to me, and I'd had my heart broken a couple of times when relationships with girlfriends didn't work out. When I experienced these losses, I became depressed. I think it is totally natural to do so. A normal period of time for someone to be depressed could range anywhere from a few days to a few months. If someone is really depressed for longer than three months, they might have to seek treatment.

Bipolar disorder is a chemical imbalance in the brain. Both the mania and the depression occur when there is an imbalance. A lot of people need to be educated about this illness. One time when I was severely depressed, my brother Jim got really pissed off and told me to "snap out of it!" This was a very ignorant thing for him to say because I'd had my illness for several years. He had seen me go through lengthy periods of depression a few times. He should have known by then that depression was a major component of my illness, and that I couldn't just "snap out of it." I sure wish it was that easy!

When I am feeling well, I am naturally an upbeat, positive and optimistic person. In general, I have a pretty good attitude. People need to understand that when someone has manic depression and becomes very depressed, it's very likely that this symptom is being caused from a chemical imbalance, as in my case. It's most important for the family and those closest to the individual to realize this possibility. Psychological issues may also contribute toward the depression. A health professional may recommend the assistance of a psychiatrist or psychologist. Often, the combination of having "talk therapy" and taking antidepressant medication(s) can help an individual.

During my first episode, I didn't know about any of these things until I experienced them. My family had no knowledge either. It was like the blind leading the blind. I wasn't seeing a psychiatrist or taking any psychiatric medication(s). I don't remember exactly, but I think the psychiatrist who was treating me at the Eric Martin Pavilion in Victoria either wanted to see me again after I had been released from the hospital or he gave me a referral to see another psychiatrist. The referral would have been to see someone in either Victoria, Sidney or Edmonton. I didn't follow up on this recommendation. I'm not even sure I finished taking the psych meds I was prescribed when I left the hospital in Victoria.

No psychiatrist, no psychiatric medications. Not exactly the best way for me to be treating a very serious brain disorder. But, then again, what did I know? I was only twenty-five years old and still wanted to drink and party. I was only three years into what I thought was going to be a very long and successful career. My family didn't know any better either. We all learned together as things happened and time passed by. We ended up learning the hard way.

After my episode in Victoria, I was incredibly embarrassed. Rumors and gossip can get around the golf industry quickly. I was relieved to leave Sidney and Vancouver Island as soon as possible. We had about 650 members at Glen Meadows, and I knew many of them would have heard rumors about me — and that was bad enough — but my #1 concern was about the CPGA and the pros. The pros I was working with knew parts of the story — that I ended up as a patient in the local psych ward.

There are a lot of golf courses in the Victoria region and many more all over Vancouver Island. Most golf courses in Canada employ CPGA professionals to run their golf operations. After working in a specific region for a while, you quickly get to know the other pros in the area. I was only at Glen Meadows for about sixteen months, but I had met several pros from different courses. News of this magnitude would spread like wildfire. They would probably be saying something like, "One of the assistant pros at Glen Meadows went crazy and ended up in the psych ward!" The facts can get twisted around pretty easily when rumors are going around. Some of the things people would have been saying about me may have been true and accurate, while other things may have been completely false.

One of my main concerns was that the British Columbia Professional Golfers' Association (BCPGA) head office and/or the national head office would become aware of my situation. Some of the pros I knew in the Victoria region served on committees for the BCPGA and CPGA. I worried about what they would do if they heard what happened. What would the repercussions be? Would I be shunned from the CPGA? Would I lose my pro card? Would this be the end of my career? At the very least, I thought this would be detrimental to my reputation. I talked with one friend, a CPGA pro in Edmonton, shortly after I arrived back there, and he told me that there were already rumors regarding my manic behavior in Victoria. Apparently, that kind of news travels fast! Thankfully, no one from either the CPGA or the BCPGA tried to contact me, which was a huge relief. It looked like my status would remain intact.

I ended up just lying around my mom's house all winter. I was too depressed to do much of anything else and definitely not up to working. I became isolated and seldom went out anywhere. My social life, usually very active, became non-existent. This type of behavior was totally out of character for me. On top of all that, I was so embarrassed about what happened in Victoria that I didn't want to talk with anyone or see anyone anyway.

The only good thing that happened was that my half duplex in Sidney took about two months to sell, and I even made a profit. After the realtor's fees were paid and everything was settled, I ended up with about $16,000. Obviously, this didn't make me rich, but I was more than happy with this outcome. As pleased as I was, it didn't do anything to improve my mood disorder. I was still very depressed. Over the next several years as I learned more about the depressive side of this illness, I learned that having a lot of money doesn't mean anything if the individual is suffering from a chemically-imbalanced depression. Money simply cannot fix this problem.

As soon as I received the money, I repaid my mom for the down payment. I had also racked up about $2,500 in unpaid bills and other debts during my manic episode on Vancouver Island. Mom paid off these debts for me, too, so I reimbursed her for this money as well. It felt great to square up with her. After I paid her back, I still had $10,000 in my bank account.

Some of the depression I was experiencing could have been classified as "normal." I did have some psychological issues to deal with because I lost my job and was basically forced to sell my home and move back in with my mom. Dealing with the ramifications of my mental illness was depressing in itself. I later learned that the manic depression mood disorder usually cycles from extreme highs to extreme lows when an individual is chemically imbalanced. That is exactly what I experienced during my first episode. I went from this incredible euphoric manic high to this dreadful depression. It only took about a month to go from one extreme to another. I found out then, and many times after, that when I was feeling really depressed, each day seemed like a year. That 1989/90 winter seemed like forever to me.

CHAPTER 11
1990
FROM HEAVEN TO HELL

Around the beginning of March 1990, I started feeling much better. After being so down and out for the previous four months, this was much more than just a welcome relief. It was exhilarating! There was a major improvement in my mood, and I had a lot more confidence.

The first thing I wanted to do was to go back to work. I found out they were looking for an assistant pro at the Vernon Golf & Country Club. Vernon is in the beautiful Okanagan Valley in the heart of BC. I wanted to get out of Edmonton and move to an area where no one would have heard about my incident in Victoria. I really wanted to move back to BC and thought the Okanagan would be ideal. Ross Bogg, the head pro, would be doing the hiring, and he was originally from Edmonton. Some of my very closest friends who were CPGA pros in Edmonton knew Ross. When I told them I was thinking of applying for the job, they strongly advised against it because they didn't like Ross. These were the same friends who advised me not to go work for Ron MacLeod at the Jasper Park Lodge Golf Club. I guess I was young and somewhat naïve back in those days, and I thought, "Oh, he can't be that bad. I can get along with almost anybody!" As you know, I quit working for Ron after about two brutal months, and I should have listened to them. Apparently, I didn't learn my lesson, and I decided to ignore their advice again.

The instructors at the SDGA advised us to always have a contract for our golf professional jobs. I knew this was very good advice, but I still worked without a contract for my jobs from 1987-1989. I have always been a "look in my eyes and shake my hand" kind of guy when it came to making a deal with someone. I guess I thought this was good enough. I wanted to feel more secure and protected, so I wrote my own contract. There wasn't a lawyer or notary involved, so I didn't know if it would even be considered any kind of legal document. Mainly, it just made me feel better to have something in writing about the terms and conditions of my next job.

I called Ross and told him I was interested in applying for the position. He wanted to interview me, so my mom and I made the ten-hour drive from Edmonton to Vernon. My mom and I were very close, and she was a great companion. Mom was just a great lady, period. She had a great sense of humor and had many positive qualities. Sadly, she passed away on January 3, 2009. I miss her immensely. I love her so much!

It was a long way to drive for a job interview, but I felt pretty confident that I had a good chance at getting it. Just having some confidence again was a great feeling. During the whole time I was depressed, I had absolutely no confidence. Just the fact that Ross wanted to interview me was good news at the time. Apparently, he hadn't heard about my infamous manic episode in Victoria the previous summer, which was a huge relief. I had my interview, then mom and I went back to Edmonton.

About one week later, Ross called and offered me the job. I accepted. This meant another move for me. To Vernon this time!

Before I officially started work, I made a copy of the contract I had written up. Both Ross and I signed the original document and the copy. I kept the original in my briefcase, and Ross had his copy. He agreed to the conditions and knew my main concerns related to my job description and work schedule. When I was hired as an assistant pro at Jasper Park, I was under the impression I would be working mainly in the pro shop. We know how that turned out. I also didn't like working six days a week and 48-60 hours. When I was hired, I was not informed I would be working so much. I wanted to make sure that something like this didn't happen again, so it was great to agree to terms with Ross from the start.

Money isn't just a major issue for golf pros but for contracts in general. This wasn't true in my case because I wasn't too worried about the money. At this early stage of my career, my focus was on building a really good resume and working towards completing my CPGA five-year Apprentice Training Program. I thought I would start making some decent money after I had worked for a few more years. In the meantime, if I was getting paid enough to cover my basic living expenses, I thought I would be OK. A lot of people think golf pros make a lot of money, but this is often far from true. My salary at JPL is proof. Even though it was 1987, $1200/month was still way too low for that time. It turns out there were some big differences between how much CPGA pros were being paid — both head pros and assistant pros. The majority of CPGA golf pros are not as well off financially as many people think they are.

THE VERNON GOLF & COUNTRY CLUB

I started my new job as the assistant pro at the Vernon Golf & Country Club in mid-March 1990. This is an 18-hole, semi-private facility with mostly members. I was the only assistant pro at the time, and Ross Bogg had been the head professional for several years. Almost immediately, Ross confessed that he'd had some problems with his assistant pros in the past, and several of his assistants quit over the previous couple of years. Someone later told me that as many as six had quit working for Ross during the previous two to three years. Many of them ended up working at another local golf course called the Spallumcheen Golf & Country Club. I thought, "Oh no, this isn't good at all! I could easily become another one!" Ross tried to reassure me by saying he was to blame for some of this, and that he was going to make an effort to become a better person and a better employer. It was still a major "red flag" for me. Maybe I should have taken my friends' advice back in Edmonton and not even applied for this job in the first place? Had I made another big mistake by working for someone even though I was advised against it? Time would tell.

I wasn't the only new employee at the club that year. They also hired a new general manager named Ralph Williams. Ralph was the former GM at the MacDonald Island Recreational Facility and the Miskanaw Golf & Country Club in Fort McMurray, Alberta. Ralph was now the new "head honcho" and was also my boss' boss. Ralph and I got along well right from the start. He was only about five years older than me, and he was just a nice guy in general.

Besides starting my new job, my number one priority was to find a place to live. My original plans were to rent an apartment. I stayed at a hotel for the first four or five days while I checked out the vacancy situation. I quickly found out there was next to nothing available that I was interested in. I think the vacancy rate may have been only 1-2% at the time. Somehow, Ralph heard I was having some trouble finding a place to live and told me I could live with him if I wanted to. We had known each other for less than one week when he made this offer. He said that if I did move in, it would be temporary — maybe three or four months. He was renting a townhouse in Vernon and was living by himself because his wife and kids were still in Fort McMurray. They would be moving to Vernon in July, so I had to be out by then. Ralph's townhouse was two levels. His bedroom was upstairs, and he only had his bed. I would have to sleep on the couch down on the main level, but my rent would only be $200/month. I couldn't afford to stay at the hotel much longer, so Ralph's offer looked like a lucky break. It was very easy to move in with him because I didn't have any furniture or a lot of personal possessions to worry about. I didn't mind sleeping on the couch, and the very low rent really helped me on the financial side.

One day, Ralph and I both had a day off, so we decided to go skiing at the Silver Star Mountain Ski Resort near Vernon. Silver Star is a world-class ski resort about a forty-five-minute drive from downtown Vernon. We hit the slopes on a beautiful warm and sunny day. There was a ton of snow, and the skiing was awesome! We had a great day together! That is one of the many benefits of the Okanagan Valley. During the springtime, you can go golfing and skiing on the same day.

Within about an hour's drive southeast of Vernon is the Big White Mountain Ski Resort, another world-class hill. The Okanagan Valley has an abundance of golf courses, many of which are of championship caliber. You can play 9 or 18 holes in the morning, then go skiing for a few hours in the afternoon, or vice versa. It's the best of both worlds!

Back at the pro shop, Ross and I were getting things ready for the golf season. The new inventory he had ordered was coming in, so we were busy going through all the merchandise and stocking the shelves. We also got the power carts and pull carts organized. The course had just opened for the season, so we were starting to book tee times as well. Basically, just doing the mundane tasks of a golf pro.

The first few days of working for Ross went OK, and I was cautiously optimistic. At the same time, I reminded myself that several of Ross' assistant pros had quit the previous couple of years, and they must have had good reasons. In the beginning though, it seemed as if Ross was making an effort to get along with me. Not knowing him well at the time, I wasn't too sure if his "niceness" was genuine or if he was just trying to make a good impression on me.

While I was getting to know Ross, I was also getting to know many of the members of the club. Conversing and socializing with the members and golfers in general was always one of my favorite aspects of working as a pro. There was almost always contact with someone and many opportunities to develop interpersonal relationships. As always, I made friends quickly and easily.

One of my favorite members was Herb Wilms. He was also a member of the board of directors for the club and a really good guy. He invited Ralph and me over to his place on a few occasions to have a hot tub. Herb and his wife lived in a really nice home overlooking beautiful Kalamalka Lake. Herb, Ralph and I got along well, and I really enjoyed relaxing in the hot tub and "shooting the shit" with the boys.

Kari Wilms first caught my eye when she walked into the pro shop one day. She was twenty-one and quite attractive, tall with a nice figure. She had beautiful, long, thick brown hair. We played golf together once and skied at Silver Star. We had a lot of fun together. She was intelligent, personable and had a good sense of humor. Kari was a former member of the BC Junior Girls' Curling Team and was a lifeguard at the local swimming pool, so she was quite athletic. As we got to know each other better, we started dating. Kari was special.

Ross knew that I was living with Ralph and that I was becoming quite friendly with Herb Wilms and other prominent members. Ross became insecure and perhaps felt threatened by the relationship Ralph and I had, and his behavior and attitude towards me became increasingly negative. This escalated rapidly over a short period of time. Despite this, I made sure I was doing a good job. If things went from bad to worse, I wanted to protect myself. I wanted to make sure he had no valid reason to fire me.

When I found out I was hired for this job, I decided to "jump on the wagon" and stop drinking. Having a tendency to drink too much, I just thought it would be in my best interest not to consume any alcohol at all. I had been on the wagon several times in my life prior to this, but always fell off. The longest period of time I had been on the wagon was about three months. I wanted to go on longer this time. I didn't smoke cigarettes then, but I did like to smoke some of the "wacky tobacky." I always found that a little pot or hash didn't hurt me too much. Actually, it didn't hurt me at all. I can't say the same thing about alcohol. When I got stoned, I became very relaxed and sometimes got the munchies. When my friends and I got stoned, we would just laugh and have a good time. I have never seen a fight or any serious problems arise because someone had been smoking pot or hash.

My decision to go on the wagon was a smart one. However, I was not prepared to become an "angel." Hence, I brought a really nice chunk of black hash with me to Vernon. Smoking some hash was my reprieve from all the stress I was experiencing in the pro shop with Ross. I didn't let anyone know that I smoked dope — this was my little secret. After work or on a day off, I would really enjoy smoking a joint by myself and spending time relaxing. Sometimes I would drive down to Kelowna while listening to great music and enjoying the beautiful scenery. I only had enough hash to last me for the first month. I didn't smoke it every day, and I never toked during my work hours.

Even though my living arrangement with Ralph was going well, I still wanted my own place. I had no success finding an apartment to rent, so I checked the housing market. I wanted to do the same thing as I did with my place in Sidney. Obviously, the house price and mortgage payments would have to be feasible. I quickly found an ideal two-level home that was considerably larger than my half duplex. It was 15-20 years old but was in pretty good condition. Most importantly, the main level was a suite of its own. It had a kitchen, laundry, appliances, bedrooms, etc. My plan was to rent this suite for $500/month. My mortgage payments were approximately $900/month, so I could live upstairs by myself and only have to pay $400/month towards the mortgage.

The upstairs was pretty nice. There were two bedrooms, a fireplace and a huge deck that wrapped around three sides of the house. I would have a lot of room for myself. The asking price was $120,000, and it was a perfect time to buy. Several years later, house prices in the Okanagan Valley skyrocketed. In 2019, the average house price in Kelowna was $780,000, and the average price in Vernon was $515,000. I could have made a very nice profit on this deal. Even at that time I was very confident that house prices in Vernon would continue to escalate. I just knew it would be a smart move and a very good investment. In addition, there was next to nothing available to rent in the area, so I thought I would have no problem finding someone to rent the suite. This whole thing really enticed me. I wanted to buy this house!

My mind was made up, and I was extremely determined to own this house. If you really want to achieve something or accomplish a goal, having the three "Ds" will really help you in becoming successful. To make owning this house a reality, I had all three "Ds" working for me. First, I had an intense desire. I also had the necessary determination. Finally, I had the dedication to persevere towards my goal until it was accomplished. Eventually, I was approved for the mortgage, and I was a very happy camper!

I put an ad in the local paper to rent the main level suite and had success almost immediately. I took possession right away and made arrangements for some tenants to move in within the first two weeks. I was really looking forward to moving into my new home, and my financial plan would work as I had envisioned it.

Immediately after I finalized my house deal, I leased a new 1990 Nissan Pulsar NX. It was a white two-door, T-top convertible sports car with dual exhaust and a 5-speed manual. It went like a bat out of hell. Very fun to drive. However, leasing this car was a stupid idea because I couldn't afford it, and I didn't even need it. I owned a reliable '85 Honda Accord that was totally paid for. I ended up trading it in on this deal, which I regretted later. At first, the car dealership wasn't going to approve my lease agreement because my financial status didn't meet their criteria. They had correctly calculated that after I paid my mortgage, I wouldn't have enough left for the $300/month car payments. I was very determined to get this car, and in those days if I wanted something badly enough, I would usually find a way to get it. I could be very persuasive and convincing when I needed to be. The only way I got approved for this lease was because the salesman was a member at our golf course. After getting to know each other, we started to become friends. I think he kind of put his neck on the line for me. He may have bent the rules a bit and done some "creative financing" on my behalf. The bottom line is that I was approved when I really should have been denied.

Working full-time in the pro shop, getting my house situation settled and dealing with the car dealership took up most of my time, so I wasn't playing much golf. Despite this, I entered a CPGA Assistant Pros tournament at

Spallumcheen. It was a one-day 18-hole event. I did OK considering my lack of practice and play up to that point — I shot a 75. I didn't make any money.

In the pro shop, things between Ross and I were going from bad to worse. There was tension in the air, and it was very uncomfortable and stressful. It was very clear that he did not like me and wanted to get rid of me. His behavior became strange, so I was suspicious. We kept working together, but he was quiet and evasive with me. At times, it seemed like he was sneaking around and acting secretly. I didn't trust him. I noticed he was coming and going from the pro shop a lot more than usual. I wasn't sure why, but then something came to me. Has Ross been going to see a lawyer to get advice on how he could legally terminate me as his employee? Is my contract valid as a legal document? Even though this was a stressful situation, I was able to remain pretty calm throughout. Ross, not so much. He had become very high-strung. He was fidgety and tense. He would have these outbursts. During one of his outbursts, he accused me of wanting to take his job.

I had only been working there for a couple of months, but because we worked together in the small confines of the pro shop for 40-50 hours a week, we got to know each other quickly. It didn't take long to figure out why several of his assistant pros quit. If I had been aware of this or listened to my friends I probably wouldn't have applied for the job. As far as wanting to take his job, I think he was becoming paranoid. Perhaps his ego had been threatened. He was acting somewhat childish. As he was in his mid-forties, Ross should have been more mature than I was. If anything, my attitude and behavior was more mature than his. And it's just a fact that I wasn't even in a position to be hired as a head professional because most head professionals are a Class "A." An assistant pro who is a Class "B" must work for a Class "A" head pro in order to get credit for their apprenticeship. The CPGA Assistant Pro/Apprenticeship program is five years. Ross was a Class "A," and I was a Class "B." It would be two more years before I would get my Class "A" status. In a rare situation, a Class "B" apprentice might be hired as a head golf professional, but this was not my intention at the Vernon Golf & Country Club. In addition, Ross had held his position for several years before I arrived on the scene, so it wasn't feasible for me to take over his job when I had only been working there for a couple of months.

The next thing I knew, Ross wanted me to resign. He came right up to me in the pro shop and told me this. I told him that hell would freeze over before I would do this. I have had a lot of jobs in my life, the vast majority at golf courses. I had quit a few times, but I had never been fired. Being asked to resign was a first. I thought it was strange that he wanted me to resign. Why didn't he just fire me? Then I quickly realized that this might have something to do with my contract. Maybe he couldn't just fire me.

I made sure I never gave Ross any legitimate reason to terminate my employment based on job performance. I always arrived a bit early to start my shifts and always worked a little longer after my shifts had expired. There was no problem with my job description and work duties. I was more than qualified, and I was doing a good job. Despite the conflict between Ross and me, I managed to keep my composure and my professionalism toward the members and guests when I was working in the pro shop. Overall, I was doing what I was hired to do, and I was doing it well.

I wasn't about to give into Ross' wishes and simply resign and just walk away. Besides, I had just purchased a new home and leased a new car. I really needed this job! And I was planning on living in Vernon for a long time. I thought I had better read over the contract I kept in my briefcase at all times right away. I always took my briefcase to work and left it unlocked in Ross' office in the pro shop. It didn't occur to me that I needed to keep it locked. I didn't keep anything valuable in there (besides my contract), and I assumed that Ross's office would be a safe place for it.

I went into Ross's office when he wasn't around and opened my briefcase to get my contract. I took a thorough look, but it wasn't there! I could hardly believe it! My mind raced. I was bewildered. I knew for a fact that I didn't take it out. I can only assume that Ross must have. Who else would have? And why? I didn't approach Ross to discuss this matter, nor make an accusation. I had no proof that he did this. Ross had been acting desperate, and desperate people do desperate things! I wished I had made another copy of my contract and kept it in a safer place. With my only copy gone, I was pretty much screwed. I could hardly believe this was happening to me.

I began to think I might have to get a lawyer, and I started to prepare for a lawsuit against Ross. My main objective was to not give him any legitimate reason to terminate my employment. I decided to keep a "working diary" with detailed records from that point on. Every evening after work, I wrote down everything I did at work that day and exactly what time I arrived and left. This whole thing was very stressful for me, and I was literally losing sleep over it. Often, I would wake up on Ralph's couch in the middle of the night and start writing things down about Ross and work in general. I recorded my daily work activities for approximately three weeks. I had accumulated about thirty pages of notes and intended to show them to a lawyer if things went that far.

The situation between Ross and I had gotten crazy, but it would become even crazier. Ralph knew what had been happening right from the beginning, and he got involved. I liked and trusted Ralph. I had confided in him and felt like he was the perfect person to talk with regarding my growing concerns with my employment situation. One day, Ross said he wanted to have a meeting with me at a specific time in two days. This sounded serious. I discussed my situation and expressed my concerns to Ralph when I got home. I already knew Ross wanted to get rid of me, but I wasn't willing to just quit and walk away. I felt I was doing a good job and that Ross didn't have any reason to terminate me. If he did, he would have tried to fire me already. I thought my contract would have protected me to some degree, but then it went missing from my unlocked briefcase. Ross must have stolen it, but I couldn't prove that.

I don't remember if it was Ralph's idea or mine, but one of us thought I should secretly tape record the meeting between Ross and me. This was totally confidential between Ralph and I. It would be a risky thing to do, and the idea of it made me nervous. However, I simply didn't trust Ross, and I thought this would be a crucial meeting. After the meeting, Ralph could listen to the tape, and if things went far enough, I could present the tape to a lawyer as evidence of my case.

The morning of my meeting with Ross, Ralph helped rig me up with a simple recording device. We used a small cassette recorder and put in a new cassette. Ralph taped the cassette recorder to the left side of my waist under my golf shirt, and I put on a golf sweater to further conceal this device. We were sure Ross wouldn't notice. All I had to do was to press the "play/record" buttons right before I went into Ross' office. It was a 120-minute tape, and I thought our meeting would be no longer than thirty minutes. I felt like I was an FBI or CIA agent doing an undercover sting operation!

I walked into the pro shop and, after making sure no one was watching me, pressed the "play/record" button on the cassette recorder and went straight to Ross' office. He was already there, and I was right on time for our meeting. My recording device was secure and well concealed under my golf shirt and sweater, but I was tense. I had never attempted anything like this before! Under the circumstances, I was relatively calm at the beginning of our meeting. Ross was a different story. He was completely stressed out and appeared to be a bundle of nerves. His eyes looked crazy! While he was kind of "losing it," I just stayed calm. To be honest, I don't remember what was said between us, but Ross badly wanted me gone. Since I wouldn't quit and I wasn't willing to resign, what would happen? There was the issue of my "missing contract," and Ross didn't have a legitimate reason to terminate my employment anyway. We seemed to be at a stalemate.

About ten minutes into our meeting, there was a loud "beep" noise made by my cassette! It scared the shit out of me! Ross instantly and shockingly said, "What's that?" I must have put the tape into the machine incorrectly, and after only ten minutes of recording, the tape came to the end. I jumped up and ran out of Ross' office, down the hallway and into the washroom. I tore the tape off that was securing the cassette recorder to my waist as fast as possible and threw the machine into the garbage. I was in and out of the washroom in only a few seconds. I thought that Ross would be following close behind me, and I wanted to get rid of the evidence. I don't think I had ever moved so fast before! It was a tall garbage can with a lid on it. I was desperately hoping that he wouldn't go into the washroom and not to have the inclination to look into that garbage can.

The next thing I knew I was sitting in the general manager's office. Ralph, Ross and I had a meeting to discuss the whole situation between Ross and I. As usual in a case like this, "politics" were involved. I had some positives going for me. I thought my biggest plus may have been the fact that I was living with Ralph and had a good relationship with him. I kept Ralph informed right from the beginning regarding the "pro shop politics." As I mentioned before, I was getting along very well with the members. I was becoming friends with some of the prominent ones, some of whom were also on the board of directors. What was not in my favor was the fact that I had only been working there for about two months.

I wondered how Ross was able to maintain his position for several years when it appeared that the members disliked him so much. Perhaps he had a lengthy contract. Maybe the terms and conditions of his contract would have made it too difficult for him to be fired. I don't know what his situation was, but I do know that Ross' father-in-law was a senior member on the board of directors at the golf club, and I'm sure he would have used all his clout to support his son-in-law.

During our meeting in Ralph's office, it was obvious that Ralph was quite uncomfortable with this situation. It was a difficult position for him to be in. Having only been the general manager for a couple of months, he had more than enough to deal with already. He didn't need to add the conflict between Ross and me to his list. I felt bad for him. I don't remember exactly what was said, but the bottom line was that Ross wanted me gone, and it was looking like he was going to get his way. I didn't want to force Ralph to make the decision, so I decided to make it a little easier for him by resigning. My tenure at the Vernon Golf & Country Club was over after only about two months.

I saw a lawyer the next day because I thought I might be legally entitled to receive some compensation for wrongful dismissal. I brought my working diary of detailed notes. It took a lot of time and effort to make them, and I thought they would help prove I was doing my job well. The lawyer didn't even look at my notes, he just gave me some advice. Basically, he said, "Don, you are still quite young and you have a long career ahead of you with the CPGA. I think it would be best for you to accept your fate and move on." He wasn't interested in taking on my case.

Vernon is a small town. I wondered if this lawyer knew Ross and if they had a good relationship. Maybe that was the real reason why he didn't want to get involved? Maybe it would have helped if I still had a copy of my contract? Perhaps he was truly giving me good advice. I will never know the answers to these questions. Regardless, I accepted his decision and somewhat reluctantly walked away from the whole thing.

I left my tenants in my house, but they were only paying half of my mortgage. In hindsight, I probably should have rented out the upstairs as well before I left Vernon, but I didn't. With very little money and no job, I decided to go back to Edmonton right away and decide what to do with my Vernon house from there. My dream of working and living in the beautiful Okanagan Valley was very short lived. I not only lost my job and was in a predicament with my house, I also had monthly lease payments for my new sports car. I had to get another job as soon as possible, and I was concerned this might not be an easy task. It was May, and most golf courses would have their professional staff in place already. Finding new employment as an assistant professional at this time of the season could prove to be very difficult.

Besides my financial woes, there was a personal issue to deal with. I had to leave Kari behind. I had been in a long-distance relationship before, which I found very difficult, and I didn't want to go through that again. The fact that Kari and I had only been dating for a very short time helped make this transition easier for me, but it still made me quite sad. In retrospect, I think that if Kari and I had met in later years, and if the circumstances were different, we may have had a very successful and long-lasting relationship. Kari stands out in my mind as one of the best girls I have ever dated, and I would have been very fortunate to have her as a girlfriend. I'm also quite sure that she would have gone on to become an excellent wife and a great mother if her life path ended up going down those roads. No matter what, I hope everything turned out well for her. She was a very special person.

Before I left Vernon, I went to the Spallumcheen Golf & Country Club where several of Ross' former assistant professionals ended up working. I introduced myself to the head pro and gave him a brief explanation of how things didn't work out between Ross and I. He seemed to be empathetic towards me and my predicament but not surprised. I don't know if he was one of Ross' former assistants, but I am quite sure some of his staff were. I told him I was looking for a job, but he informed me he already had his assistant professionals in place. With no luck there, I was forced to go back to Alberta.

My move back to Edmonton was very simple. Basically, I just had my clothes, golf clubs and some personal items to take with me. I would stay at my mom's house. As disappointed as I was that things didn't work out for me in Vernon, I was bound and determined to carry on and move forward. I had to.

I was back in Edmonton for about a week when I got a job at the Miskanaw Golf & Country Club in Fort McMurray, about 275 miles north of Edmonton. Unbelievable! Of all the golf courses in Alberta, I end up working at the same one that Ralph Williams was the general manager at before he took over as GM in Vernon. It was the last place I would have expected to find employment.

My old buddy Darrell McDonald was the head golf pro at the Millwoods Golf Course in Edmonton (as of 2020, he is the executive director at Millwoods). One day, Darrell let me teach a group lesson with two of his assistant pros at the driving range. After the lesson, I went into the pro shop to talk with him. He knew I was looking for employment, and I wished I could have worked for him, but he already had his staff in place. It just so happened that Darrell had Mark Shushack, the head pro at Miskanaw, visiting him that day. I knew Mark's name, but we had never met. Darrell introduced us and informed Mark I was looking for work. Lucky for me, Mark was looking for an assistant pro. Darrell put in a good word for me, and Mark agreed to an interview. He was flying back to Fort McMurray the next day and wanted to meet me at the airport before his flight. The interview went well, and Mark hired me on the spot. I didn't worry about a contract this time. I thought that if Mark was a friend of Darrell's he must be a pretty good guy. Plus, I was just happy to get a job for the rest of the season so I would get credit for my apprenticeship for that year. That was the most important issue. During the process of getting hired by Mark, I was very relieved that there was no discussion of my mental illness.

I would have rather lived and worked in the Edmonton region, but to my knowledge all the head pros in the area had already hired their assistants for the season. Golf courses in northern Alberta usually open around the end of April, but because Fort McMurray is so far north of Edmonton, theirs open around the middle of May. This is approximately when I started working at Miskanaw.

Mark had terminal brain cancer. I was told he'd had several operations and had already lived longer than expected. I had a lot of compassion for him and knew that he might not have much more time to live. When I first met him, I noticed two things right away. One was that he had some obvious scars on his head, which would have been from his operations. The second thing was that he appeared to be quite medicated; he seemed somewhat sedated. He may have been on pain killers and/or some medication that would help alleviate his symptoms. Despite this, I thought he was quite lucid. He was still thinking clearly and knew what was going on. I found it easy to understand him. This is the way it was during the time I worked for Mark.

TERRI COMRIE

About two weeks before I started my new job in Fort McMurray, I met a girl named Terri Comrie at Fast Eddie's nightclub. She was twenty-three, had blonde hair (my favorite), blue eyes and an excellent figure. I gave her a solid "9" on the 1-10 scale. She was absolutely gorgeous! This was my number one "criteria" for a girlfriend back in those days. One of my best friends, Johnny Morris, was a captain of the Edmonton Fire Department at the time. The fire department was holding a charity golf tournament at the Millwoods Golf Course, and he was one of the main organizers. He asked me and some of our buddies to find some girls to help out by doing some various tasks for the tournament. Terri was sitting with some of her girlfriends when I first noticed her. After watching her for a brief period, I made the bold decision to go over and introduce myself. Doing this took some courage because I was still on the wagon — completely sober. Usually, I would have needed to consume several beers or cocktails before I would get up the nerve to do this, but the golf tournament gave me a good excuse to approach her.

Things went well during that first meeting. After talking with her for a while, I gave her my phone number and told her she could give me a call if she was interested in helping out at the tournament. I didn't ask for her phone number or put any pressure on her at all. I just left it at that. Much to my surprise, she called me the very next day. Terri said she would like to come to the golf tournament. I was thrilled! Again, I didn't want to put any pressure on her, so I suggested we meet at the golf course. When I saw Terri a couple of days later at the course, it was a great feeling to have this beautiful woman there to meet me. The tournament was mainly a fun event — a "Texas Scramble" format, a team event. There was a full field of approximately 144 golfers who played 18 holes. Many of the golfers, volunteers and organizers dressed up in costumes. Johnny Morris dressed up as Dame Edna. It was hilarious! I was way too shy to dress up, and Terri didn't wear a costume either.

I didn't take Terri to the volunteers' committee because I wasn't sure what mundane task they would have her doing. I thought she might enjoy just coming along with our group. When I suggested this, she seemed happy with the arrangement. I was more than happy. Over the 18 holes, we would have at least five hours to get to know each other a little better. My plan was working perfectly so far! I knew this wasn't going to be one of Terri's most thrilling days, but I hoped she would enjoy herself. She didn't play golf, and I don't think she had any interest in the game either. Having her spend several hours on the golf course with our group would be a challenge as far as trying to make sure she was entertained and ensuring she didn't get bored.

I was hitting the ball pretty well that day, which was a relief, as I was hoping to play well in Terri's presence. Being a team event, we didn't keep track of our individual scores. Our team didn't win any prizes, but we still had a fun day together. Terri seemed pretty content. She walked along with our group and rode in the power cart at times. It wasn't a serious tournament for me, so I was able to chat with her quite a bit during the round.

After our game, there was a dinner and prize presentation ceremony for all the golfers in a banquet room. It felt really good to have Terri sitting right beside me. We were really starting to connect, and I thought there were "good vibes" between us. Terri probably enjoyed this part of the tournament better, as now it was more like a big party and the atmosphere was more relaxed. I have partied several times with many of the members of the Edmonton Fire Department, and I always had a great time with them!

At a later date, Terri told me that she was really nervous the day of the golf tournament. I'm not sure why, and I didn't ask her. Maybe it was because she was out of her element. She was a non-golfer surrounded by all these golfers. She also went there by herself without knowing anyone except me. She would have known I was a golf pro, so I don't know if this contributed towards her nervousness or not. While Terri may have been out of her element, I was in mine. I felt comfortable on the golf course and had played in Texas Scrambles several times. They were usually a lot of fun and I also knew some of the people there. It was easy for me to socialize with them, as well as with the other golfers. The only thing out of my element that day was the fact that I had a beautiful young lady come around the golf course with me and watch me play.

At the end of the day, everything went quite well. Terri and I both wanted to see each other again soon, so we agreed to meet at Fast Eddie's a couple of nights later. When we met again, a couple of Terri's girlfriends were with her. I brought my buddy Dave with me. I wanted Dave to meet Terri and see how good looking she was. Terri didn't disappoint. She looked awesome! Near closing time, Terri and I didn't want to leave each other just yet, so we decided to go somewhere for a coffee. Her friends and Dave went their own ways.

We went to a local hotel that had an all-hours coffee shop and stayed there from about 3 a.m. to 5 a.m. The time seemed to go very fast when we were together. We talked and got to know each other better. The feelings between us seemed to be getting more and more intense. There were moments when we didn't talk. We would just look into each other's eyes. At times, we would both have tears in our eyes. There were some extremely powerful emotions being stirred up between us, and I couldn't believe it was happening. I had never experienced anything like it before. Was I falling in love with Terri already? Was she falling in love with me? This was only the third time we had hung out. I believed in love at first sight and wondered whether this was what I was experiencing with Terri.

GRANDMA CLARK

I told Terri how special my love for my grandma was. I really wanted them to meet each other, so I made a spontaneous decision to drive to Wetaskiwin to visit her. Terri was game to do this and she had me drive her home first so she could change into a pair of jeans. We arrived in Wetaskiwin around 6 a.m. My grandma wouldn't be up for another hour, so I took Terri to the Wetaskiwin Golf Club for a coffee. It gave me a special feeling to bring her to the place where I grew up playing golf as a young boy.

It was after 7 a.m. when we got to my grandma's house, and she was already up. Besides being a little surprised to see us, especially that early, Grandma was her usual self. She was extremely warm and friendly and invited us into her home wholeheartedly. She was a very loving and caring person and had a great sense of humor. She was also very wise. Grandma Clark was eighty-seven years old and was doing very well for her age. She passed away at the age of ninety-two. I miss her dearly.

I don't remember for sure, but I think Grandma made breakfast for Terri and me that morning. This is something she would have naturally done because she always did this every morning when I had spent the previous night at her place. She would always cut up an orange for me, have porridge and make really good bacon and eggs. It was always delicious!

Grandma took a couple of Polaroid pictures of Terri and I. On the back of one of them, she wrote "Maybe?" I suppose she was being optimistic and referring to the possibility of Terri and I having a long and successful relationship. Was my grandma thinking about marriage? I don't know, but I wasn't. We had just met! I had only been in one serious relationship prior to this. Just calling someone my "girlfriend" was a big deal. I was definitely smitten by Terri, but I was just living and enjoying the moment. I wasn't making any big plans for the future. We had a very nice visit with my grandma for a couple of hours, then drove back to Edmonton. Terri and I were finally getting tired. Our new excitement for each other and our adrenaline must have contributed towards keeping us up all night, so we both went home to get some much needed sleep.

We had the commonality of recently moving back home and living with our parents temporarily until we figured out what our next move was. Terri's parents' house was also on the south side of Edmonton, about a ten-minute drive from my mom's house, which made it convenient for us to spend time together.

It didn't take long for me to realize that Terri had some brains to go with her beauty. She was managing a Kelsey's restaurant in Toronto prior to moving back to Edmonton. I thought that was a pretty good credential for someone who was only twenty-three years old. It wasn't just because of her work experience that I thought she had some smarts. I could tell she was intelligent from our conversations and our time together.

I think she moved back to Alberta when a relationship she was in with a guy in Toronto ended. When we met, neither one of us was looking for a relationship.

The fact that Terri was living with her parents and I was living with my mom didn't exactly create the ideal situation for us. We didn't have a place where we could be alone together and have some privacy. I hated that! It was very frustrating for me because I was used to having my own place. Even when I had roommates, I felt like I had quite a bit of independence when I was dating someone. Living with my mom was a whole different story. I loved her very much and had a good relationship with her, but on the rare occasion I would meet someone that I liked enough to bring home, it never seemed to go very well. I'm not sure why, but for some reason my mom wasn't very nice to them. This made things difficult for me, and Terri was no exception. Mom didn't treat her well either. She didn't like Terri.

The several times I went to Terri's home, it was a different story. Her mom and dad liked me and treated me well. Mrs. Comrie (Lois) was always very warm and friendly with me. Mr. Comrie (Don) was more serious and gave me the impression he was a man who you don't want to get pissed off at you. Having said that, he was always good to me and fair with me. Sometimes the four of us would watch TV or a movie together. In a general sense, I just felt comfortable with them and in their home.

Terri and her family are related to Bill Comrie, who is the founder and former owner of The Brick Warehouse. Don is Bill's cousin. The Brick is a large chain of furniture warehouse stores which also sells household appliances, TVs, etc. I thought it was kind of cool that my new girlfriend was a "Comrie" because of the connection with Bill Comrie and The Brick Warehouse.

Going to Fort McMurray and leaving Terri in Edmonton meant another long-distance relationship. I didn't want so much distance separating us, but I really had no other choice. The good news was that it would only be temporary because I was planning on working there until the end of the golf season then going back to Edmonton. It was only five months, and we'd decide what to do after that. Since she wasn't working at the time, she would be able to come up there once in a while to spend time with me, and there was a chance I might be able to make a couple of trips to Edmonton. We would work it out. I only had about two weeks to spend with Terri before I started my new job, and the time went very quickly. While I was falling madly in love, I was also in the process of making a huge mistake that almost cost me my life.

MISKANAW GOLF & COUNTRY CLUB

My move to Fort McMurray was very easy. As with all of my moves, I didn't have much stuff to bring with me. It was even more convenient that I already had a place to live as soon as I arrived. My new boss, Mark, knew someone whom I could move in with immediately, which was a huge help. His name was Mark Stiles and he was the sports director at one of the local radio stations. Lucky for me, he and his roommate had a spare bedroom in their house that I could occupy. My monthly rent was very reasonable, and the three of us guys got along well.

Miskanaw was a busy 18-hole public course with a driving range. It was a good course, but not a great one. Usually, two of the main duties for an assistant golf professional working in the pro shop at a public golf course are to schedule tee times and collect green fees. I didn't have to do these things there because they had a different setup. There was an area near the front of the pro shop where golfers booked their tee times and paid their green fees, and a couple of ladies managed these duties. My job was to help manage the pro shop, power carts and driving range as well as teach lessons. Another assistant pro named Craig Morton had been working for Mark for several years. I didn't get to know him well, as we never socialized together or became friends. He wasn't my kind of guy.

Mark played on the Canadian Golf Tour in the 1970s. After getting cancer and being unable to compete anymore, he organized a Canadian Golf Tour event to be played at Miskanaw called The Rotary Classic Golf Classic. I had mixed feelings about the event. I was really looking forward to it because some of the players would be the same pros who qualified for the Canadian Tour at Glen Meadows. Many of these pros also played in the Victoria Open at Uplands as well. I was sure I would see some familiar faces, and perhaps some of the guys I had gotten to know would be there. On the other hand, I was worried about whether the guys would recognize me and label me as "The Crazy Golf Pro" who lost his mind. Would Kelley Murray be there?

A few weeks before the tournament started, I was working in the pro shop when a local newspaper reporter came in and asked if he could take my picture. I was under the impression that he just wanted to do a brief article with a small picture of me in the local paper — just an update from the media to announce the hiring of the new assistant golf professional at the local golf course. This had happened before, and it wasn't a big deal; I didn't think too much about it at the time. The reporter wanted to take my picture on a green, posing as if I was reading a putt. We went to the nearest green, and he took the picture. Within a week or so, the 1990 Rotary Classic Golf Classic magazine came out, and my picture was on the front cover. It was a pretty big picture. This was a special edition of this magazine designed for this Canadian Tour golf tournament. There may have been several thousand of this particular magazine printed. I couldn't believe they did this! I was kind of shocked.

The day before the tournament started, there was an 18-hole pro-am event. This is a team event that combines professionals with their amateur partners, and I played to represent our professional staff. There was a member of the Canadian Tour on our team named Phillip Hatchett, who was from Kentucky, USA. There were also a couple of members from Miskanaw who were the amateurs. I was a little nervous because I was playing with a Canadian Tour player. Considering this, I did OK, shooting a 3 over par 75. I didn't make any "pro money," but Phillip did. I don't know how much he won, but he probably received a decent check. He might have even been the "low pro" for the event. Phillip shot a 7 under par 65. He smoked me by ten shots! He played a superb round of golf and really demonstrated why he was a Tour pro. It was a pleasure for me to watch him play such a fine round of golf. Phillip's 65 was the lowest score for 18 holes by anyone I have ever played golf with. You need to be able to "go low" like this if you want to make your living by playing tournament golf.

After the pro-am, one of our amateur partners thanked me for the game. He said it was one of the most enjoyable games of golf he had ever played. He was talking as if I had a lot to do with this, which made me feel really good! I don't remember who won the tournament, but it was kind of cool that these professional golfers from all over the world were coming all the way up north to Fort McMurray, Alberta. And for the second year in a row, they were coming to a golf course that I was working at.

Fort McMurray is famous for its massive, multibillion-dollar oil and gas production. Several thousands of people are employed there by huge oil companies such as Syncrude and Suncor, and the city has been booming for a long time because of this. As a golf destination? Not so much. I don't know exactly how Miskanaw became the host for a Canadian Tour event. Mark may have known Bob Beauchmin, the commissioner of the Canadian Tour at the time. Being the head honcho, Bob would have had a lot of input towards deciding where Tour events would be held. Having connections can be very helpful in many ways.

At one point during the Rotary Classic, Terri and I were having a coffee in the lounge of the clubhouse. Canadian Tour player Guy Boros sat down by himself at a table beside us to enjoy a cold beer after his round. I asked him if he would like to join us at our table, and he accepted. Guy seemed to be a nice person. We talked for about a half an hour, then I had to go back to work. His father, Julius Boros, was a well-known golfer who played on the PGA Tour back in the 1960s and 1970s. Guy ended up following in his dad's footsteps, as he also became a PGA Tour player.

I didn't see Kelly Murray there or experience any repercussions regarding my manic episode the year before in Victoria. What a relief! The Canadian Tour came and went. This time I didn't end up in the psych ward.

One day, I was working in the pro shop and this smoking hot woman came in and asked for a golf lesson. I told her I could give her one in thirty minutes when my shift was over, and she said she wouldn't mind waiting. We met at the driving range in mid-afternoon on a beautiful, warm and sunny day. She was dressed for the warm weather, wearing a summer top and short shorts. I have taught golf lessons to a lot of very good-looking women in my life, but she ranked in the top five. She had blonde hair, a very pretty face and the body of a Playboy bunny. I was in heaven! Her name was Eva, and she was from Switzerland.

What I remember the most about this lesson was when I had Eva do some stretching exercises. She was a beginner, but proper stretching before hitting balls is extremely important for all levels of golfers because it can help prevent injuries such as strained or pulled muscles, and it increases flexibility, which is very important for the golf swing. Any decent instructor would agree with this. I taught all of my students how to stretch properly. I felt somewhat guilty for getting her to do some of the stretches. I shouldn't have, as I didn't do anything wrong. In retrospect, I did everything right. It was the same routine I had all my students of all ages do. Eva was very voluptuous and had large breasts, and some of the stretches accentuated this fact. The driving range was busy that day, and I wondered if others were watching us. I guess I was somewhat self-conscious. Regardless, the lesson went well.

Dan Hodgson

Eva's boyfriend came into the pro shop to pay for her lesson, and I talked with him for a while. We hit it off right away. His name was Dan Hodgson, and he was a professional hockey player drafted by the Toronto Maple Leafs in 1983. After playing for Toronto for a short period of time, he played for the Vancouver Canucks. He continued to play professional hockey, but this time it was in Europe. When Dan and I met, he was playing for a Swiss team. He had come back to his hometown of Fort McMurray for the summer and brought his Swiss girlfriend with him. Dan and I became friends very quickly. With my roommate, Mark Stiles, being the sports director at the radio station, and my new friend, Dan, being a professional hockey player, I guess I was kind of hanging out with a couple of local "celebrities."

One night after we had known each other for a week or two, Dan was over at the house that I was staying at for a little get together with the boys. My two roommates, Dan, and myself were hanging out downstairs, and they were having a couple of beers. Dan was aware I was on the wagon, and he was determined to change that by getting me to drink beer too. He was very persistent. Relentless, actually. He wasn't going to take "no" for an answer. He kept trying to convince me to start drinking again. It was a classic example of peer pressure. Mark and my other roommate didn't say anything, and they weren't trying to get me to drink. I held my ground and stayed as strong as I could for as long as I could. I really didn't want to give in to Dan's wishes. I had been completely sober — not even a drop of alcohol — for about four months. I didn't have a goal set as far as how long I wanted to stay on the wagon — I was just taking it one day at a time — but my intention was to keep this streak alive. I really was enjoying being a non-drinker, and I wanted it to stay that way.

After rejecting Dan for a couple of hours, I finally gave in. I shouldn't have, but I did. A "victory" for him was like a "defeat" for me. I am totally against peer pressure, and I didn't like the tactics Dan used on me. At the same time, I don't blame him for this outcome. The final result of this situation was due to my own weakness. I'm the one who eventually said, "OK, I'll have a beer." As always, one beer led to another and another and another, etc., which is why I went on the wagon in the first place. Once I started drinking, I couldn't stop! I think Dan and I may have ended up going to one of the local bars that night and getting drunk. We had a lot of fun together and got along well. Like any friend of mine, he had a good sense of humor. He was intelligent and witty. We partied and played some golf together.

During that summer, I registered to play in an assistant golf professional tournament at the Stony Plain Golf & Country Club, which is just west of Edmonton. Dan wanted to caddy for me, and I was more than happy to accept his proposal. It turned out to be a very enjoyable and fun day with Dan "on the bag." I don't remember what I shot — I might not have even broke 80 — but I know I didn't play very well. In spite of this, I'm glad Dan was with me. The other three pros in our group were dead serious for the entire 18 holes. They hardly talked and didn't have many laughs, if any. They weren't very enjoyable to play with. Having this kind of demeanor didn't seem to help them much, as none of them had a great game either. I was serious too. I was very competitive, and I wanted to play my best, especially in a tournament. I wasn't out there to socialize or to joke around. I always tried my best on every shot. Having said this, it's still important to remain relaxed and calm. Golf is a game that requires an individual to control their nerves and temperament, especially in a pressure situation like a tournament. Obviously, I wish I had played better that day, especially after Dan took the time and effort to caddy for me. Even though I didn't have a great score, we still had a good time. Dan had a good attitude and was fun to be with. We had a lot of laughs together. He was a good caddy too.

On another occasion, Dan and Eva joined Terri and I for the long drive from Fort McMurray to Edmonton. It was a fun trip, and we enjoyed listening to a lot of great music along the way. About an hour north of Edmonton, I got pulled over by the RCMP for speeding. The speed limit was 100km/hr (60 miles/hr) and I was going 150km/hr (90 miles/hr). Normally, I don't speed. I am a very careful and safe driver who stays very close to the speed limit. I have only had three speeding tickets in my life. When I got that Nissan Pulsar NX in Vernon, I was pulled over twice for speeding within the first three months of having it. It just went so fast and was so fun to drive! With some luck, Dan and I were able to talk the RCMP officer out of giving me a ticket. I don't know how much the ticket would have cost, but it wouldn't have been cheap. The whole scene turned out to be pretty comical as Dan and I "worked our magic." Having two hot babes in the back seat may have helped us too. Maybe even more than our sweet talking did!

We went to the West Edmonton Mall, one of the largest shopping malls in the world. I only touched on it before, but it is so big, it's unbelievable! It's an amazing place to see and spend time at. You could easily spend an entire day there and still not see the whole thing. There is a countless array of stores, restaurants, attractions and features — overall, there's a lot to see and do. It's a great place to take your family. If you have children, they will love it! There is a good amusement park that even has a roller coaster. It also has a large indoor water park with a wave pool and several very cool water slides. As I mentioned before, there is also an official size NHL skating rink in the mall. The Edmonton Oilers used to practice there on occasion, and the public could watch them. The Alberta PGA used this ice surface a few times as well. As I mentioned, we held our annual seminar in one of the conference rooms at the Mall and then had a hockey game between the pros.

Shortly after we arrived at the mall, we came across this same ice surface. As soon as I saw it, I wanted to go skating. More specifically, I wanted to impress Dan with my skating ability. I guess I probably wanted to impress Terri as well. I hadn't skated for a couple of years, so I knew I would be more than a little rusty. Also, not having my own skates with me meant that I had to rent some crappy ones. Because of these facts, I knew I wouldn't be able to skate my best, but I would try anyway. Dan didn't skate. He just wanted to watch. I only skated for about fifteen minutes. I tried to wind it up a bit and show my "audience" some of my speed, but I couldn't go as fast as I wanted to because there were too many people skating. Someone would always get in my way! Plus, being rusty and using those crappy rental skates didn't help my cause. Doing this was still kind of exhilarating for me. Dan was probably more amused than impressed at my antics.

The great thing about West Ed is that all the amenities, from the amusement park to the ice rink and everything in between, are indoors and open all year round. After spending the day at the mall, we decided to stay at The Fantasyland Hotel, right at the mall! There were four theme rooms: Roman, Greek, Polynesian and another I don't remember the name of. Each couple rented a room with a jacuzzi and stayed there the one night. It was a fun and enjoyable experience.

Terri and I were making our long-distance relationship work. Over the course of the summer, I made a few trips to Edmonton, and I was always extremely excited to see her! It seemed we were madly in love. I had never felt this way about any of my previous girlfriends. Usually, I would only date someone for a very short time because I just hadn't found anyone who I wanted to get serious with. I thought Terri was different. I thought she was "the one" I was looking for. I thought she had the characteristics and qualities I wanted my partner to have. In my younger years I believed in love at first sight. As I have gotten older (and hopefully wiser), I have changed my opinion on this matter. I no longer believe in this theory. At this point, Terri and I had only been together for a couple of months. Was it "true love" already, or not?

On a couple of my return trips from Edmonton, Terri drove back to Fort McMurray with me. The long drive seemed to go by a lot quicker with her by my side. It was great to have her at Fort Mac with me. We didn't do anything special there. We just enjoyed spending as much quality time together as we could. If I had to work when she was there, I would let her use my car. We would drive to the golf course together and drop me off, then she would go back to my place. She always managed to keep busy doing something while I was at work. I usually worked the "close shift" at Miskanaw, which was from 3-11 p.m. Golfers could play until that late at night during the summer months because we were so far north that it stayed light until then. Sometimes Terri would come to the pro shop about half an hour before the end of my shift to visit with me, but it didn't interfere with my job at all. The pro shop was always very quiet that late at night. Most of the time, she would just come and pick me up around 11 p.m. We usually went straight home after that.

I had worked the close shift at other golf courses in Edmonton and Sidney. It was a great "party shift" and suited my lifestyle perfectly during those times. After work, some of us would go to a bar or nightclub to drink and party until 2 a.m., sometimes later, before going home to bed. Sometimes

I would get sidetracked and end up at a different destination. After a night of partying, I could sleep until noon the next day if I wanted to. I would still get at least eight hours of sleep and be in pretty good shape to start my close shift again the next day.

My close shift at Miskanaw wasn't a "party shift." Even when I fell off the wagon and started drinking again, I took it easy. I can remember getting really drunk once when I was out at a local bar with Dan. Terri wasn't there on this occasion — I never drank to excess in her presence. Because of this, the fact that I was drinking again wasn't an issue with her. Terri liked to have a few drinks herself. This wasn't an issue with me either, as I had never seen her become overly intoxicated.

One time, Terri flew from Edmonton to Fort McMurray, and I picked her up at the airport. I watched her walk off the plane. She looked stunningly beautiful. She was dressed really nice and was just simply gorgeous. It made me feel so good that she was my girlfriend! Having a girlfriend or wife who is extremely attractive can bolster a guy's ego. It can be a great feeling when "your woman" is a knockout.

I have made several remarks referring to Terri's good looks because it was extremely important to me at the time. I was only twenty-six years old. My viewpoint is much different now, and I don't think physical attraction and good looks should be the number one priority anymore. There are many other qualities and characteristics that are much more important.

Local Radio Station Interview

One night, a few of us were having some beers at our place. As part of his job as sports director, Mark hosted a sports talk radio program. Sometimes he did live interviews with sports figures either over the phone or in studio at the radio station. Mark told me he was supposed to interview the head coach of the Saskatchewan Roughriders of the Canadian Football League over the phone the next morning, but the coach cancelled last minute. He asked me if I would come to the radio station in the morning and be his guest on his talk show. He said Doc Knickerson, a former trainer for the Montreal Canadiens, would be co-hosting the program with him, and that the two of them would give me a live interview in their studio. I had never done this type of thing before. Discussing this with Mark made me feel quite nervous, but I was also very excited. After some more talking and another beer or two, I said OK. I wasn't drunk, but I did have enough "liquid courage" to make this bold decision.

The next morning, I arrived at the radio station around 9 a.m. Within a few minutes I was in the studio with Mark and Doc and had some headphones on. I was extremely nervous. This was really happening to me, and I was way out of my comfort zone. We would be going live on the air right away. The interview lasted for about twenty minutes, and Mark and Doc did a good job. They asked me some questions about my history and what it was like working as a CPGA pro. I described some of the education and training that was necessary to become certified. I talked a little bit about how I had some "extra education and training" by being a graduate of SDGA, and that I had a diploma in Golf Operations and Management from there.

During the interview, I said "It is an honor for me to be working for Mark Shushack" at the Miskanaw Golf & Country Club. This turned out to be a premature statement I would kind of regret saying later. Words are very important to me, and I try to choose them very carefully. Whether I am talking or writing, I try to "say what I mean" and "mean what I say." In retrospect, I wish I hadn't used the word "honor" when discussing working for Mark. I had only been there for about a month, and I didn't know him well at all. All I knew about him was that he used to play on the Canadian Tour, that he had terminal cancer, and that he was my boss. We hadn't had any kind of lengthy conversation that would have enabled us to get to know each other better, and I just didn't know much about him in general. I need to know an individual a lot better on a personal level and a lot more about that person before I can justify saying that I "honor" someone in one way or another. Saying, "It is an honor for me to be working for Mark Shushack" was more of an emotional statement at the time based on the compassion I had for Mark because of his terminal cancer.

Immediately after my interview, Mark Stiles called legendary hockey analyst Howie Meeker at his home in Parksville, BC, to interview him. It was pretty cool that my interview was followed by Howie Meeker! The listeners were probably thinking "Don who?" At that time, most of them (especially the hockey fans of that era) would have been familiar with Howie for sure.

Terri recorded my interview, and when I listened to it later, I was a little surprised. It sounded better than I thought it would. My nervousness wasn't as apparent as I expected it might be, and I thought I did a pretty good job especially since it was my first time. I let my mom and a few close friends listen to the recorded interview. It was just kind of fun to listen to. Unfortunately, I lost the tape shortly afterward. It was a bummer. I should have made a copy. I wish I still had it. It wasn't a major production or anything, but it was still special to me. The tape would have been a nice souvenir from "back in the day" when I was working and living life as a golf professional.

I played in the CPGA "Pro/Junior" tournament held at the Innisfail Golf & Country Club in southcentral Alberta that summer of 1990. It's not a very big town, but the course is pretty good. I have played there a few times. There are a lot of trees, which I like on a golf course, and it has a fairly difficult layout. It's a good test of golf. This format was for a CPGA pro to take a junior golfer (under the age of 18) as a partner. The pros usually bring one of the junior members from the golf course they are currently working at. I brought one of the junior members, Trevor Goplin, from Miskanaw to be my partner. Trevor was about sixteen and was a very good player — a handicap of 5. Trevor was a good looking guy, very intelligent and had a lot of talent. He also had a good sense of humor.

Unfortunately, neither one of us played very well. At least we had a good excuse. It was windy, raining and quite cool. The already challenging golf course was playing even more difficult because of this. The vast majority of the scores would have been higher than normal on a day like this compared to playing when the weather is nice. As far as our "good excuse" for not playing well, everyone in the golf tournament had to play in the same weather conditions. It was still a fun trip. Years later, I read in a golf magazine that Trevor had become a CPGA pro as well.

In 1991, a group of eight of us (mostly from Calgary) went to Innisfail to play the same course. One of the guys who played in my group was Mike Mohler, a hockey player for the Quebec Nordiques (no longer an NHL team). Mike's brother, Randy, was also an NHL player. They were from Red Deer, located in central Alberta. Thankfully, the weather conditions were a lot better on this day. It was warm and sunny with little wind, if any. My game was also a lot better this time around. I forget what I shot exactly, but I think it was in the mid 70s. What I remember most clearly about that day was smoking the ball with my driver! I hit several drives that were close to three hundred yards and was keeping the ball on the fairway for the most part. It was just one of those days when I felt confident and was comfortable over the ball. I could have easily shaved a few strokes off my score had my iron play and short game been a little better. Just like the old golf saying says, "Drive for show and putt for dough." Summing it up, it was just another fun day on the golf course, especially with Mike Mohler in my group! Mike and I really clicked. I'm pretty sure he even gave me his phone number so we could possibly connect in the future for another game of golf. Unfortunately, because of my life circumstances I never did call Mike or talk with him again.

I really enjoyed playing in those golf tournaments that summer of 1990 even though I didn't play very well. I always got really excited to be competing in those events.

My trips to Edmonton were all good ones. I always liked to visit my mom and to see some of my friends. Without a doubt, my number one priority during that time was Terri. I didn't mind the five-hour drive knowing I would get to see her when I arrived. After being apart for a few weeks, we both were extremely excited to see each other!

On my last trip, Terri was with me when I drove from Edmonton back to Fort McMurray to get back to work. As I mentioned earlier, I was mainly working the "close shift" at Miskanaw, so my shift started at 3 p.m. On my first day back at work, I arrived at the pro shop at 2:45 p.m. — fifteen minutes early to start my shift. Mark was in the pro shop when I got there and immediately said to me, "You're late!" I could tell by his voice and demeanor that he was pissed off at me. I was kind of shocked. I was early, not late! I always used to carry my day timer/journal with me in my front left pocket. I had my work schedule written down in there along with my lesson times with my students, as well as any important appointments and meetings. I took it out of my pocket right away because I wanted to double-check it to see if I had made a mistake. I hadn't. It said "3 to close" for that day, which was my normal shift anyway. I tried to show this to Mark, but he wouldn't even look. Our pro shop staff had our work schedule written down on a calendar in the back area of the pro shop. I went to look at it to confirm the time of my shift, but it wasn't there. Someone had taken it down from where it was pinned against the wall. I told Mark that I wanted to look at the calendar, but he denied my request. I thought "What the FUCK is going on here?"

Mark told me to come with him to the general manager's office. I hadn't met her before, and I didn't even know what her name was. This situation had become very serious, very quickly. I knew there must be some other reason why Mark brought me to her office other than my supposed lateness. In fact, no one said anything about being late. Instead, Mark accused me of giving free power carts to people. I readily admitted that I had indeed done so but only on a couple of occasions. Without hesitation, Mark fired me. He refused to let me explain myself and wouldn't listen to my side of the story. The GM just sat there and listened. She didn't say much of anything. I think she was there mainly to be a witness to the execution. It was a very short meeting. I couldn't believe this was happening to me. It happened so fast and totally out of the blue. I was shocked. I felt helpless. I went back to my place and told Terri what had happened. Then I went and laid in bed with her by my side. Losing another job was catastrophic for me. I was devastated and became extremely depressed.

I think Mark was unfair with me because what I did happens at golf courses on a pretty regular basis. It is simply a fact that golf pros will not charge someone for the use of a power cart once in a while. I have seen this done countless times at golf courses in Canada and the United States. The most ironic thing about me getting fired was that Darrell, my old buddy who referred me to Mark (and Mark's friend), gave more free power carts to golfers than any other pro I have ever seen. When I worked with Darrell at Windermere in 1983 and 1984, he gave out several free power carts. Most of the time he would do this with some of his friends who were members of the golf course. Despite it being a relatively common occurrence, I have never heard of any other pro getting fired because they didn't charge for the use of a power cart on a couple of occasions — not if they are otherwise doing a good job and are a good employee.

I don't know for sure, but I think Mark may have owned the power carts when he was the pro at Miskanaw. He struck me as the kind of guy who would demand to own the power carts as part of his contract, and he seemed to take the cart issue very personally. He fired me because of this! It was kind of like he thought I was stealing from him. I am a very honest person. I have several references from CPGA pros I have worked for and with and character references from golf pros and other people who have known me for a very long time. Every single one attests to my honesty and integrity.

Generally, there were only a couple of situations where I comped a power cart. The most common was when they had spent a lot of money in the pro shop. If someone purchased a set of golf clubs for $1,000, I might throw in the use of a power cart for 9-18 holes at no extra charge. Or if a member of the golf club routinely supported the pro shop and spent a considerable amount of money there, I might do the same thing for them on occasion. Usually, the merchandise in golf course pro shops is owned by either the golf course owner or the head golf professional. It is part of an assistant pro's job to sell this merchandise, and I never received any commission. I think Mark also owned the pro shop merchandise at Miskanaw. Any pro shop sales I made would have made him a profit.

It only cost a few dollars to operate a power cart for a round of golf. This applies to both gas and electric carts. I had learned from other CPGA pros I had worked for and with, before working for Mark, that it was a good thing to reward golfers for their patronage on appropriate occasions. Giving them the use of a free power cart for a round of golf is a great way to do this. Especially when the owner(s) of the power carts only have to pay $5.00 or less for this good deed.

Other situations whereby pros may not charge for the use of a power cart is when someone who is close to them is involved. This could be a number of different people, including family members and friends. I have seen this done countless times at many golf courses, and I have done this myself. Also, sometimes golf pros don't charge other golf pros for the use of their power carts. I think the course owners have clamped down on this practice over time, but I imagine this still happens quite frequently.

Any avid golfer who has played this game for many years and who has spent a lot of time at golf courses and in pro shops has likely witnessed some of these accounts and has maybe even been a recipient of a free power cart themselves on one or more occasions. I don't remember the exact circumstances of my power cart ordeal with Mark, but I admitted I had not charged for the use of a power cart on a couple of occasions. Apparently, when these transactions occurred there was another Miskanaw staff member present who reported the situation to Mark. Someone who knew they were being dishonest would have been a lot more discreet than I was. I had nothing to hide because I didn't think I was doing anything wrong. I wouldn't have jeopardized my job for something like this if I knew what Mark's reaction would be.

I have always been pretty intuitive and sensitive. I can pick up on the "vibes" very quickly, and I really thought things were going well at Miskanaw. Did Mark just get really pissed off and fire me because of the power cart issue? Or was there more to it? I wonder if some of the media exposure I was getting rubbed Mark and Craig the wrong way. If Mark did have other reasons for firing me, I am unaware of them. Anyway, it's why I regret my comments about him on the radio; I lost respect for him after this ordeal.

I didn't see this coming — I was totally blindsided. My short tenure at Miskanaw was over. It was time to move on once again. Before I left Fort McMurray, I asked Mark if he would sign my professional papers so I would get credit for my apprenticeship for the year, and I'm thankful he did because I deserved to get credit for the 1990 season. Obviously, neither job worked out in my favor, but it wasn't from a lack of effort on my part. I was employed for approximately six months, which met the criteria for getting credit for an apprenticeship year. (This length of time is based on the fact that the majority of golf courses in Canada are only open for approximately six months each year.) It was good of Mark to sign my papers. He did the right thing, and it meant a lot to me. Because of this kind and fair gesture, I never held a grudge against him for firing me. Getting credit for the year was a big relief and one bright spot from an otherwise disastrous golf season.

I was sad to hear that Mark finally succumbed to cancer a few years later.

I ended up back in Edmonton around the end of August. Once again, I stayed at my mom's house. For the next month, Terri was fantastic. She tried to encourage and inspire me. She often told me she was my "number one fan." She wanted me to get another job and continue with my life. Under normal circumstances, I would agree that this would be the logical decision for me. However, things were far from normal for me. Terri was a lot more positive than I was. As it was close to the end of the golf season, I knew I wouldn't be employed until the next spring. Not at a golf course at least. I thought about finding another job in the meantime, but I had no idea what I could do. I was so depressed that working wasn't a realistic option. Losing both jobs left me with zero confidence. I was worried that my reputation would be severely tarnished. My future as a pro was in limbo.

As bad as things were, it would get worse. A lot worse. I became worried, then obsessed, that I was going to lose Terri. It was all I could think about. My mind was totally consumed, and I felt like I had the weight of the world on my shoulders. In this depressed state, I became very quiet and didn't talk much. I wasn't acting like the confident, fun-loving guy Terri had known for the previous four months. My mind was not functioning properly. Despite this, my feelings for her didn't diminish, and I still treated her well. Unfortunately, I can't say the same thing about her.

After being loving and supportive for that first month back in Edmonton, Terri suddenly became cold hearted. During my second month of depression (October), it became more and more obvious that she was losing patience with me. Her attitude and demeanor had changed drastically, and she was pissed off because I wasn't seeking employment or attempting to get my life back on track. This situation escalated to the point where I felt that she despised me — an awful feeling. I understood Terri's reasoning, but that didn't make things any easier. I felt helpless and knew she would end our relationship soon. To have the love of my life treat me like this was the ultimate betrayal. By the end of October, Terri ended our relationship and told me she "had to move on." Not surprising. She stuck with me for about two months when I was having a really tough time, but after that, she wanted nothing to do with me. She wanted me out of her life forever.

A part of most marital vows is: "Will you take this man/woman for better and for worse?" Sometimes people forget the "for worse" parts of the marriage and, as far as I am concerned, this applies to all serious relationships. It's easy to stay in a relationship when all is well — steady work, robust financial situations and countless other important elements of a relationship — but life is full of ups and downs. Most of us are going to experience hardships along the way. During these rough times, it's nice to have some support. If you have a partner who is a good person and treats you well but is suffering from a lengthy bout of clinical depression or another hardship, I hope you won't end your relationship after dealing with the "for worse" for only two short months, as Terri did with me.

It has often been said that there is a fine line between love and hate. I used to believe this until I learned what "true love" really is. At the time, it seemed like Terri went from loving me to hating me, but I have a much different viewpoint now. When I look back (with that 20/20 vision) at our relationship and think about the reasons why I felt so strongly for Terri, I realize how and why it became a disillusion for me. I wasn't totally delusional, but apparently, I was destined to learn an important life lesson in this regard. I have been writing about Terri's good looks and the chemistry we had together — there is no doubt that we had extremely strong feelings for each other. I mistook this "chemistry" and these feelings for "love." Terri told me many times (and wrote in some letters to me) that she loved me too. I was sure that she did. There were several qualities I was looking for in a serious relationship, but my number one requirement was that my girlfriend was gorgeous. I had to have a very strong physical attraction to her. After that, I was looking for elements such as intellect, trust, honesty, loyalty, respect, compassion, patience, generosity, consideration, kindness and humor.

Physical attraction is often immediate, and I think way too many people get this confused with "love at first sight." I think this is more like "lust at first sight." Terri was hot, and we had a very strong physical attraction. It takes time to get to know someone well. Time is the teller. Terri and I only knew each other for about six months — the length of our relationship. The first four months were like heaven, the last two were like hell.

Despite being a relatively short relationship, it has had a profound influence on my life. It ended up being the hardest, but most valuable lesson I have ever learned. True love doesn't just come and go that quickly. Love takes time to build in the first place. It needs to grow, develop, be nourished and sustain itself. To really love someone is to love them for who they are. Hate is the opposite of love. I don't think there is a "fine line" that separates the two.

Guys are notoriously famous for thinking with the wrong head, which can be very powerful. A classic case of this was when US President Bill Clinton was found guilty of getting a blow job from Monica Lewinsky. "Sorry Bill, but you are a perfect example!" Maybe the main reason why I had such strong feelings for Terri was based on the same concept and I just didn't realize it at the time. Maybe I was thinking with the wrong head?

Our relationship probably looked promising to Terri in the beginning because I had a bright future with a house in Vernon and a solid job. I wasn't making a lot of money, but I was earning a decent wage. I was very entrepreneurial and had big ideas of making lots of money. Looking back, I think I may have been somewhat hypomanic during those first four months with Terri. I was full of confidence and had a lot of energy. I was exuberant and fun to be with.

I didn't tell Terri I was diagnosed with manic depression the year before. I think I was in denial about it and decided not to inform her. I think the psychological depression I was in became worse because my chemical-imbalance depression got added to the mix. Hence, my depression was a double whammy. Not knowing I had manic depression, Terri may have thought that she just made a big mistake by getting involved with me in the first place. She may have thought that I turned out to be a loser and that my lack of responsibility and motivation was just simply a part of my attitude and character. I can see that, but it's not true. I was under the control of "the wicked monster" — depression. A sad statistic regarding this depression is that approximately fifty percent of those with bipolar disorder attempt suicide at least once, and fifteen percent are successful.

I had a lot of rough times over the years, but 1990 was probably the worst year of all for me.

In the end, I can just say that it didn't work out between us, and that it wasn't meant to be. When she broke up with me, it felt like my heart was ripped into a million pieces. It fucked up my head really bad too. I was devastated. When she was giving me this bad news, depressed as I was, in a very cold and callous manner she said, "What are you going to do, kill yourself?" I hadn't thought about committing suicide over Terri before that, but I started to.

CAME CLOSE TO SUICIDE

About three weeks later, I decided to kill myself with the .22 caliber rifle in my mom's garage. The rifle was pretty shabby, and the wood handle was broken; I didn't know if it even worked anymore, but I intended to find out.

On a beautiful, sunny day around noon, I walked to the Heritage Shopping Mall and bought a box of .22 caliber bullets at the sporting goods store. Ironically, as I walked out of the mall with the bullets I intended to kill myself with, I saw my ex-girlfriend, her mom and her grandmother walking into the mall. They didn't see me. I knew my mom and Doug would be out shopping for a couple of hours that afternoon, so I would have a perfect window of opportunity when no one would be home. I would go into the basement and shoot myself in the head while they were out.

I walked back home, made sure no one was there, then got the rifle from the garage and took it down to the basement. I put a bullet into the chamber, laid down on the floor on my back and put the rifle by my side. All I could think of was Terri and how I didn't want to go on living without her. I was in so much pain. My heart was crushed, and my mind was severely depressed.

I lost track of time, but I think I laid there for at least two hours. I came extremely close to putting the rifle against my head and pulling the trigger. All of a sudden, I heard someone come into the house upstairs. This startled me, and I began to panic. I sure didn't want anyone to know what I was up to. I took a quick look around and spotted an empty golf bag standing upright on the floor beside me and quickly hid the rifle inside it. As I placed the rifle into the golf bag, the trigger caught on something and the gun went off! The blast was unbelievably loud. It scared the shit out of me! The bullet missed my head by a fraction of an inch. I came that close to what may have been called "an accidental suicide." Wouldn't that have been something? If it hadn't killed me, I'm sure I would have been critically injured and/or severely disfigured. I feel incredibly lucky that the bullet missed me. It's a miracle that I even survived this incident, let alone came out of it totally uninjured.

Gary had come into the house. After the bullet so narrowly missed my head and face, it went through the furnace duct in the basement ceiling, through the basement ceiling, through the flooring upstairs, and finally ended up lodged in the wall on the main level of the house. The bullet just missed hitting Gary as he came through the front door. I found out later that since he didn't know what I was doing, he thought I was shooting at him! I heard the front door slam, and I frantically ran upstairs. My mind raced, my heart pounded. I saw Gary running across our street. I ran after him and shouted, "Gary, stop! I didn't mean it! It was an accident! The gun went off accidentally." But he continued to run east on 23rd Avenue with me trying to catch up and repeating that it was an accident. Along with all the frantic emotions, I also felt embarrassed that Gary had "caught me in the act." When I finally caught up with him, I told him how the gun went off accidentally. I don't think he believed me at first. He was freaked out but settled down and we walked home together.

I couldn't come up with a good excuse for taking the rifle from the garage to the basement. Because of my extreme depression, I think my mom and brothers knew what my intentions had been, but we never discussed it openly. Most people don't feel comfortable discussing the topic of suicide with a loved one who may be suicidal. This is understandable, but also unfortunate. Talking about suicide with someone could help save their lives.

Gary threw the rifle away after that.

CHAPTER 12
1991
GETTING TO KNOW "MANIA"

<u>SILVER SPRINGS GOLF & COUNTRY CLUB</u>

After barely surviving 1990, my situation became a lot more positive in the early spring of 1991. The depression I was in seemed to eradicate itself almost overnight. This massive and swift shift confirmed that the severe depression I had experienced for the previous six months was indeed a combination of psychological factors and a chemical imbalance in my brain. The imbalance was probably triggered by the overload of stress I was experiencing. Coming out of my depression the way I did must have been an incredible realignment of my brain chemistry.

It wasn't a sudden change in my attitude that improved my mood, it was a sudden change in my mood that improved my attitude. Manic depression is a mood disorder. People with this illness experience major highs and lows when their brain chemistry is out of balance. These mood states usually cycle. I would always go manic first, followed by the depression. Normally, one would experience a period of wellness between these opposite mood states when they are balanced. Obviously, the longer a person can stay balanced, the better it is for them.

Having a mood disorder doesn't mean an individual is a "moody person." When I was manic, I would have the symptoms of mania. When I was depressed, I would suffer from the symptoms of depression. However, when I am balanced and stable, I am just my normal self. I am a very easygoing and even-tempered person, and I get along with most people just fine. My friends are similar. It's those "moody" people (without a mental illness!) who I don't like to be around.

I started to get my ambition back, and I immediately returned to work. I was hired as an assistant professional at the Silver Springs Golf & Country Club, a private 18-hole golf course with a driving range in Calgary, Alberta, at the beginning of March 1991. I was so happy I got hired, especially after my disastrous 1990 season. It felt great to be employed again.

My new boss was Darren Young, who had been an assistant pro at Silver Springs for several years. He was then promoted to the position of head golf professional when his boss, the previous head pro, retired at the end of the 1990 season. I initially thought Darren was a pretty smart and decent guy. The other assistant pro working for Darren was named Terry Carter. Of all the names out there, his name had to be the same as my ex-girlfriend's. I couldn't believe it! Luckily for me, I was in a good enough state of mind that this didn't become an issue. I liked Terry and we got along well. We went out for beers on a few occasions. The three of us were around the same age and seemed to work well together in the pro shop.

Around the middle of May, Silver Springs hosted an APGA assistant pros tournament, an 18-hole event. I was one of the participants, but home course advantage was not a factor for me, as I was new and hadn't played the course many times. It was pouring rain that day. They had us wait around the clubhouse for over an hour to see if it would let up, but it didn't. They decided we should play, so I put my rain gear on and prepared to battle the elements. My caddy's name was Ron Shymka, a member at Silver Springs. He was a big guy who used to play football for the Calgary Stampeders of the CFL. I tried to deter him from caddying because of the weather, but he insisted that he still wanted to. So, away we went into the rain.

Ron kept the grips of my clubs as dry as possible and was overall a good caddy. However, everything just got so wet, it was like fighting a losing battle. Eventually, I was just trying to keep my clubs from flying out of my hands as I hit each shot. It was brutal. The officials should have postponed the tournament and re-scheduled it for a later date. Because of the difficult conditions, many of the pros, including myself, didn't even break 80.

A couple of weeks after the tournament, I was in a convenience store located close to the golf course. There was a really good-looking woman in there at the same time. We seemed to catch each other's eyes, and we exchanged "hellos." I guess I was back to my flirtatious state, and she was extremely friendly with me. We talked briefly and seemed to hit it off. Her name was Debbie, and she was a realtor. I guessed that she was around my age. I told her I was working at Silver Springs as an assistant pro and suggested she come over there some day to say hi. A few days later, and much to my surprise, Debbie came to the course to see me. We had a short visit and exchanged phone numbers. Soon after, we started dating.

I was living with Darcy, whom I met through a friend, at his place in northeast Calgary at this time. He was a good guy and made a good roommate. Having said this, I didn't spend a lot of time there — mainly just to sleep and shower. I was working, playing a bit of golf and going to bars a lot in the evenings. Before long, I was spending some nights over at Debbie's place. I enjoyed being with her because she was very intelligent and a fun person to be around. Everything was going quite well for me, and I was pretty happy.

Just when I thought things were going my way, I was in for another big surprise. After working for Darren for only about 2½ months, he called me into his office for a meeting. He said there were some complaints regarding some ladies' group lessons I was teaching, and he fired me! I said he had to give me proof of these allegations — I wanted names, dates and times. I asked him to be specific and said he couldn't fire me without giving me more details. He offered me no further explanation. He didn't say anything with regard to my teaching method or technique. Basically, he disregarded everything I said because his mind was made up. Despite not producing any evidence, he fired me. I was shocked! Several hundreds of my previous students thought I was a very good instructor. This incident happened out of the blue. I thought "What the hell is going on here?"

My question was soon answered. What was "going on" was that I had started to go manic after only a couple of months of working for Darren. I didn't know I was having a manic episode at the time. I was completely unaware that anyone had complained about my teaching, and I have no idea of what the complaints were — there could have been many reasons. I guess I was just not communicating properly with the ladies I was teaching. I was probably very incoherent to them. They might have thought I was on drugs.

I have never held a grudge against Darren for firing me. He must have been in a difficult position because I hadn't told him about my manic depression diagnosis two years earlier. He must have thought, "What the hell is going on here?" Maybe he thought I was on drugs? It was Darren's first year as head pro at Silver Springs, and it was very unfortunate that he had to deal with this crisis. Sorry Darren!

Immediately after Darren fired me, I left the course. The first person I saw in the parking lot was Paul Baxter, a former NHL defenseman with the Calgary Flames. I don't know if he was a member at Silver Springs or if he was just there playing golf, but we didn't know each other. About twenty yards away from Paul, and in my bewildered state, I looked at him and said, "I just got fired!" Paul just looked back at me with a surprised look on his face. He didn't say anything. I kept walking, got in my car and drove away.

During my short tenure at Silver Springs, I became friends with Wayne Hall, the head pro at the Stettler Golf & Country Club in southern Alberta. I don't remember where or how we met — maybe at one of our golf tournaments or seminars — but we got along very well and had a lot of fun together. After I was fired, there ended up being a bit of a party at Debbie's place that night and Wayne was there. He stayed overnight and slept on the couch. The next morning, I thought Wayne and I should go and have a "Swedish massage" because of my Swedish ancestry. I had never had one before, but I managed to talk Wayne into coming with me. We each had a massage, but it wasn't a "Swedish" one. When I was getting my massage, I was having major back spasms. The pain was excruciating! I asked my massage therapist how bad she thought my back was by giving me a number on the 1-10 scale, 10 being the worst. She said, "a 9." No wonder it hurt so much!

After our massage, I thought we should go and bet on the ponies. So, off we went to Stampede Park to watch the horse races. I knew next to nothing about horses. I think Wayne had much more knowledge than I did, but we were there just to have some fun. We studied our programs, and he placed his bets. As I was looking at my program, I had a kind of premonition. There were ten horses running in the next race. One of the horses' names had "Captain" in it. As soon as I saw that I just knew he was going to win this race — it was a sign of a sure bet! All of this was based on the fact that my dad was a pilot — a captain! Unfortunately, he died in 1983 at the young age of 51. I was thinking about him at the races and thought I was getting a message from above. I put $300 on the "Captain" to win! This horse wasn't one of the favorites to win, so the odds were 10-1. If the Captain won the race, I'd win about $3,000. If he finished second or worse, I wouldn't win anything.

I had been to the horse races many times before this, mostly at the Del Mar Race Track when I was a student at SDGA. I would usually bet on the favorites, which pay out the least. Sometimes I would bet on a "longshot" just for the fun of it because it could turn a nice profit. I never bet a lot of money on the horses — usually $20-$30 for the day. I would be happy if I broke even. I was never lucky enough to win a lot of money. When I told Wayne about my $300 bet, he was kind of shocked and said, "Are you crazy Walin?!" He didn't know that I had been diagnosed with manic depression and that I was in the early stages of a manic episode. Neither did I. Going on spending sprees are a classic symptom of mania.

So, did I make a foolish bet? Yes! It was ridiculous! Stupid! I was far from rich. I only had about $500 to my name at the time (at least I didn't bet all $500!). I wish I could say I got lucky and won, but I didn't. The "Captain" finished seventh out of ten horses. It was like throwing $300 out the window. So much for a sign from above. The mania was running the show now!

GRANT FUHR

A couple of days later, I played in an assistant pros tournament at The Links at Spruce Grove Golf Course just west of Edmonton. It was one of our regular 18-hole events. I don't remember much about my round of golf that day, but I shouldn't have played. Playing relaxed is vital in golf. This was hard for me to achieve in my manic state. I wasn't "full blown" manic yet, but I'm sure I must have been acting peculiar enough for the other guys in my group to think something was wrong with me. Plus, I was having very painful back spasms. I couldn't relax mentally or physically.

For some of our tournaments, we would leave a couple of "media" spots open for sports writers from the local newspapers. Sometimes, other "special" people were allowed to play with us, and on this day, Grant Fuhr was playing. Fuhr was a famous goaltender with the Edmonton Oilers who won five Stanley Cups and was a six-time all-star. I had never met Grant before, but I had seen him being interviewed on TV many times. He always seemed to be a very confident guy with an easygoing and almost carefree demeanor. I never saw him get upset or angry. The hockey broadcasters were always talking about his easygoing attitude. These kinds of character traits could really benefit his golf game as well. Grant was known to be a bit of a golf nut. He absolutely loved the game. I even heard that he wanted to become a professional golfer on the Canadian Tour after his hockey career was over. I don't know how successful he was, but when he played in our events back in the day, he had a long way to go with his golf game. Grant played in 2-3 of our tournaments that I'm aware of and scored in the mid 80s — not even close to qualifying as a CPGA Club Professional, let alone for a Tour pro.

After all the other pros had left, I was still there drinking beer by myself and eating sugar. SUGAR! Some of the other pros were getting together at Denny Andrews, a nightclub, and I planned to meet them there. Not having had much sleep over the past week, I was starting to feel tired. I wanted to go to Denny Andrew's and party all night, so I thought I needed some energy. I noticed a bowl full of sugar packs on my table that were obviously intended for coffee or tea. At the moment, sugar meant "energy" to me. So, while drinking a few beers I ate about six packs of sugar. Whether it helped my goal or not is debatable. At least they didn't make me sick.

I went to Denny Andrews and met some of the guys. I saw Grant Fuhr with two girls at a table. Without any hesitation, I walked up to him and introduced myself. I think he and the two girls were drinking Dom Pérignon, which is very expensive. Grant and I had a brief conversation, which resulted in a bet. He said he had a tee time at 8 a.m. the next morning at the Edmonton Country Club, and we agreed to play an 18-hole medal play match for $400. It was to be even-up, which meant neither one of us would get any strokes, as if our handicaps were the same. This was not a big money bet for Grant, but it was for me. I don't think I even had that much money, but it wasn't a concern because I was sure I would win! All of this was based on my manic state. After I made the bet with Grant, I partied the night away and didn't get much sleep again.

I arrived at the course on time the next morning and went straight into the pro shop. I talked with Doug Hicks, one of the assistant pros and a former player with the Oilers. I didn't know him personally. I told him I was there to play with Grant Fuhr, and I wanted to confirm Grant's 8 a.m. tee time. Doug told me Grant didn't have a tee time booked. I was a little perplexed. Then I thought maybe the tee time was booked under a different name because I didn't know who else was supposed to be playing in Grant's group that morning. I told Doug I would go upstairs and wait in the clubhouse for a while to see if Grant showed up.

He didn't. Maybe he could tell I was acting a little strange and fabricated the story about the tee time to blow me off. All I know is that I showed up like I said I would. Even if I was acting somewhat strange, he shouldn't have made the bet if he had no intention of being there himself. Maybe he was just fucking with me, which isn't cool. Maybe this was my karma getting back at me for blowing off that round of golf with Joe Hesketh in southern California five years earlier. Doesn't matter because it's probably a good thing for me that we didn't play. I've played golf a few times when I was manic, and it was a disaster every time! Being out of control mentally on the golf course equates to a golf game that is out of control. If my health was good, I would have had an excellent chance of defeating Grant, but when I'm manic it is best to stay off the golf course altogether, let alone bet money. My back was killing me too. At 7 a.m., I was already drinking straight Southern Comfort and taking anti-inflammatory medication (Flexeril) for the pain. Looking back, I don't think I could have played for this reason alone.

The Edmonton Country Club is one of Edmonton's elite "private" golf courses. Many of the city's wealthiest people, including some of the Oilers, are members there. It's an "uppity" golf club. When I was sitting in the clubhouse waiting to see if Grant would arrive, I started to get major back spasms. The pain was wicked, and they tended to coincide with my manic episodes. When this would happen, I would usually lie flat on my back and flop around like a fish out of water as I was jolted with countless spasms. This usually happened around people I knew and they understood what was happening, but it was a different story at the Edmonton Country Club.

I knew I had to lie down and let the spasms do their thing, so I decided to do it outside on the deck. I thought there would be more room and fewer people out there. It was a quick decision, and I wasn't thinking clearly. It was a beautiful morning and there were more people out on the deck having coffee and breakfast than I thought there would be. I tried to go to an area where I would be inconspicuous, but at the same time, I was in my own little world, and I wasn't overly concerned if anyone saw me. I laid down on the deck on my back and the spasms caused my body to go into convulsions. It probably looked serious — perhaps like I was having a heart attack or an epileptic seizure. My physical symptoms were bad enough, but I was also very mentally ill. I must have scared the people who witnessed this scene.

After my "performance," I went back into the clubhouse, sat down and put my head on the table with my eyes closed. I felt a hand on my shoulder and heard a voice say, "Donny, are you OK?" I opened my eyes. The voice belonged to Bill Penny, the head pro at the club. Bill and I had met several times — he was a pretty decent guy. Obviously, Bill had been informed about my situation and came to check on me. He was genuinely concerned and had empathy for me. Shortly after, my mom and Doug came to take me home. I never did see Grant Fuhr.

A few months after this episode, I wrote an extremely difficult letter to Bill. I was incredibly embarrassed, and I apologized. I also explained my manic depression diagnosis and that my behavior was the result of me being on a manic high at the time. I was hoping I would get a reply — either a quick phone call or short note saying something like "Don't worry about it, Donny. No problem, buddy! I hope you're feeling better. I wish you all the best for the future." This would have meant a lot to me, but I didn't get a reply. I was very disappointed with him.

Grey Nuns Hospital in Edmonton

After my ordeal at the Edmonton Country Club, my crisis escalated. A couple of days later, I was aimlessly roaming the streets of south Edmonton in the early hours of the morning. I hadn't slept at all the night before. I felt like a lost soul. After walking around for a few hours, I ended up close to a firefighter friend's house and decided to stop in. It was only about 6 a.m., but in my state of mind, I wasn't too concerned about waking Tim ("Doc") up. Not only did I wake up Tim, but also his buddy, Johnny Mowatt, who was sleeping on the couch. I knew Johnny as well. He was also a firefighter. They must have been wondering why the hell I was there so early! I was really fucked up. I was delusional and in a state of psychosis. I thought there was some kind of "life force" or energy (almost alien-like) being transferred back and forth between Doc and Johnny. It was very strange to say the least. This might seem spooky to some people, but it didn't scare me. If anything, I was fascinated.

The next thing I knew, Rick and Gary arrived with one of their friends. Doc had called them to come pick me up. Not knowing my illness, Doc and Johnny must have thought that I had completely lost my mind. I went with my brothers. Shortly after, we walked into a hospital. I didn't know what was going on at first, so I just went along with them. Suddenly, I was in a room by myself with a stretcher, and it didn't take long for me to figure out that this stretcher was for me. I didn't like this idea, and I got pissed off. The door to this room was open, and suddenly there were security guards, hospital staff (possibly including a psychiatrist and a psych nurse), my brothers and their friend at the door. My anger escalated quickly, and I went ballistic! I unleashed a torrent of foul language and threatened to take them all on. No one — not even the security guards — stepped into the room. I picked up the stretcher like it was a feather and threw it at them. Then Gary blindsided me with a hard punch to the jaw when I was looking the other way. Not a very brotherly love thing to do. It hurt like hell, and I lost my balance. The security guards and whoever else put me on the stretcher with my arms and legs strapped down. Then the needle came out, and they sedated me.

When I woke up, I was in the psychiatric ward at the Grey Nuns Hospital in Edmonton — my second time as a "psych patient" in a three-year period. My psychiatrist was Dr. William Otto, and I have a vague memory of liking him. Within only a couple of days of being his patient, he asked me if I would participate in a study at the University of Alberta. Being manic, I probably thought he was asking me because I was a genius. I thought "They must want to study my brain!" Looking back, this might not have been too crazy because I was actually an outstanding example of "mania." I thought I was unique, a real phenomenon. I quickly and eagerly accepted his offer.

My mom bought me a Sony portable cassette stereo so I could listen to some music while I was in there. The psych nurses kept giving me shit for cranking up the volume way too loud!

I was in the psych ward during my birthday again (June 7), so I somehow convinced Dr. Otto to give me a day pass so I could play golf with my friends. He agreed as long as I promised to return to the psych ward that night. I promised.

I played 18 holes at the Millwoods Golf Course with my friends Rick and Larry. After being put on heavy duty psych meds (probably including antipsychotic medication) for a few days, my mania had subsided enough so that I could actually play. Having said that, I was still manic. I'm sure that Rick and Larry realized this fact immediately. My golf game was far from great, but I had a lot of fun! I had played a lot of golf with these guys, mostly at the Windermere course in Edmonton. They were both good golfers and they always played "party golf," which meant drinking and smoking joints (usually black hash). There was never a shortage of supplies, and they were always very generous with sharing their party treats. My memory of the round is a little fuzzy, but I'm sure I joined right in. Because of the medication, I shouldn't have been drinking and toking, but I didn't know any better.

I broke my promise to Dr. Otto and didn't return to the psych ward that night. I never saw him again. He must not have committed me, because the police didn't come to my mom's house to pick me up and take me back. I was a free man!

I never did take part in the study at the U of A. I've often wondered what it was about and in what aspect I would have been involved. Regardless, I don't think Dr. Otto should have asked me to participate when I was so mentally ill. I wasn't in the right state of mind to make an important decision like that. This may have caused me some embarrassment or regret that I had got involved after my manic episode had ended.

After a few days of freedom and no psychiatric medications, my mania increased. One day, I decided I was going to open up my own pro shop in my mom's house! It didn't take me long to fill the family room with as much golf "merchandise" as I could find. I hung my golf shirts up on the curtain rods and displayed golf sweaters, hats and miscellaneous golf items throughout the room. I had my golf clubs and golf bag on display as well. It was quite a sight. My entrepreneurial business endeavor ended right there — I didn't even get any customers!

A couple of days later, my mom, Rick, a family friend and I went to Rick and Gary's apartment in southeast Calgary. While there, I decided to have a bath. I was in a euphoric mood. During my bath, I was singing at the top of my lungs and having a great time! After my bath, I put on some sweatpants and a T-shirt and joined the others in the living room. They were all drinking wine, and they said a full glass on the table was for me. I immediately realized that everyone else was drinking white wine and that mine was an orange color. I found out later that my brothers had put a sleeping pill or sedative in my wine in order to help slow my mania and get me to sleep. I thought they had poisoned my wine and were trying to kill me! I guess I was having a paranoid delusion, but it scared the shit out of me!

I freaked out. I yelled at everyone, accusing them of poisoning my wine and trying to kill me. I ran out of the apartment, down the hallway and through an exit that led me to the indoor parkade. I thought for sure they would chase me, so I crawled under a car to hide. After a couple of minutes, there was no sign of them, so I left my hiding spot. I went through another exit door and was outside.

POLICE BLOCK MACLEOD TRAIL FREEWAY

I ran south beside Macleod Trail — a major thoroughfare in Calgary — for a while, then started walking. Macleod Trail has four lanes of traffic running both north and south. It is always extremely busy. I reached the outskirts of the city and was sure my family weren't following me, so I turned around and started walking back north. I ended up in Midnapore, an area

I was familiar with because I lived there when I was in high school. All of a sudden, I saw Rick, Gary and their friend approaching me from about fifty yards away and calling me to come to them. I was still spooked from the incident at their apartment, so I wasn't going anywhere near them! I took off running back towards Macleod Trail. On the way, I found a three-foot-long tree branch and carried it with me for "protection."

I was near the intersection of MacLeod and Midlake Boulevard when things got really exciting. Suddenly, there were four cops walking towards me. I didn't want to seem threatening, so I put the branch on the ground. It wasn't exactly a dangerous weapon anyway. It was obvious that they had come to pick me up and, as they approached, there was only one cop I felt I could trust. I could tell by his eyes and demeanor that he was a kind and decent man. I felt like he wanted to help me. I didn't get this feeling from the other cops, so I said I would go with the officer whom I felt more comfortable with.

There were at least five police cars blocking off traffic from all directions. Traffic was at a standstill on Macleod Trail because of me! My mom or brothers must have called the police when they found out where I was because, of course, they were concerned about me. Being mentally ill and walking where I was could have ended tragically if I had walked onto the freeway in front of oncoming traffic. The Calgary City Police did a very good job of helping prevent this from happening.

HOLY CROSS HOSPITAL IN CALGARY

The officer I thought was nice gave me a ride to the Holy Cross Hospital in Calgary. He didn't handcuff me. I was admitted into the psychiatric ward, and for about the first week, I was so drugged up I couldn't even speak. I could only give "yes" or "no" answers by nodding or shaking my head. There are some extremely powerful psych meds. In order to stop my mania, I was probably administered an antipsychotic medication such as Thorazine or Haldol. These meds knocked me flat on my ass!

Gradually, my mania began to subside. As it did, the dosage of my medication was likely decreased. After about three weeks, the sedation was gone but my mania wasn't! It was no longer "full-blown" mania, but it was still there. I was fully mobile again — probably a little too mobile. I don't know if it was a locked ward or not, but I was not allowed to leave by myself. This time I was "committed," which basically meant I was kept there involuntarily.

One day, I saw a couple of people going towards an exit. Something told me that this was a "sign" for me to escape. They went out the door, and I followed right behind them. I went down the stairs and through another door that brought me to the ambulance parking area. I saw a taxi parked right out front, which I thought must be part of my escape plan. I got in the taxi and had the driver take me to my brother's apartment.

When we arrived, I realized I didn't have any money to pay my cab fare. I told the driver to wait for a couple of minutes while I went into the apartment to get some money. My brothers weren't home at the time, but I was able to get into their apartment through an unlocked sliding glass door. I went in but couldn't find any cash. I saw a watch in one of the bedrooms and hoped the taxi driver would take it to pay for my ride. My cab fare was about $30, and the watch was worth about $50, and the driver accepted the watch as my payment.

Twenty minutes later, I was enjoying a coffee and a cigarette when two police officers arrived. My "great escape" didn't last very long! The police let me finish my cigarette and once again I wasn't handcuffed. A ride in a police car was a lot more tolerable when cuffs weren't involved.

The psych nurses kept a lot closer eye on me for the duration of my stay. Regardless, I didn't try to escape again. After another three weeks of treatment, I was well enough to be released.

My manic episode in Calgary had lasted about seven weeks, then I went back to Edmonton to live with my mother again. Almost instantly, I went into a severe depression episode that lasted for eight months. It's incredible how quickly these mood states can change from one extreme to another. Being so depressed 24/7 for that length of time is pure hell! Like my mania, my depression was caused by a chemical imbalance in my brain. My symptoms of depression were the opposite of mania. When I was depressed, I had no energy. I didn't feel like doing anything at all. Nothing interested me. I didn't care about anything. My brain shut right down. I could hardly think and couldn't concentrate. There were times I couldn't sleep. Persons who suffer from depression often have insomnia. I had no sense of humor and hardly spoke to anyone. I became very isolated, and my social life ceased to exist. It was horrible physically as well. It felt like every cell in my body was depressed. Nothing could motivate me, and there was no way I could work in that condition. All I did was lay in bed or on the couch. I had no enjoyment whatsoever, including when I watched TV or listened to music.

I thought about suicide every waking moment.

Those eight months seemed like an eternity.

CHAPTER 13

1992
CPGA Class "A" Certificate

After eight months of brutal depression, I finally started to feel better around the beginning of April 1992. I wanted to get back to work as soon as possible, but it would be extremely difficult. I was sure that many pros in Edmonton had heard about my manic episode at Silver Springs, and I was incredibly embarrassed and had absolutely no confidence. Somehow I overcame this major obstacle and landed a job teaching at Wedgewood Driving Range in Edmonton. I was employed by CPGA Head Professional Norm Claffey, who was my old roommate from the SDGA. I was really nervous at first, but my confidence grew quickly. Before long, I was right back in the groove and doing what I loved — teaching golf! Most importantly, I stayed healthy and was employed for the entire golf season!

My mom moved to Kelowna in 1992, so I moved in with my buddy Jack Thomson. We rented a duplex in Riverbend, in south Edmonton. At the time, Jack was a bartender at Club Malibu, a nightclub also located on the south side. He was a really good bartender and a great guy to party with. The two of us were a dangerous pair. I've partied with a lot of really fun guys in my life, but Jack was a classic. He was absolutely hilarious! We had a hell of a lot of fun together over the years.

I was also back to my old tricks. I had at least four relationships that year. Sometimes I was juggling two at the same time. My friends would tease me about having so many girlfriends. I would just tell them that if they tried as hard as I did, they too would be successful in this regard. I was very promiscuous back then, and I had a hard time staying in a monogamous relationship.

I taught a few lessons to a girl named Sherri-Lynn Berri, who I became quite interested in. She was good looking, tall and had a nice figure. She had beautiful, long, thick blonde hair. She was very personable and extremely intelligent. She was about my age and was just starting her career as a veterinarian. Sherri-Lynn and I had a few casual dates and started to get to know each other. There was a mutual interest, and I could see the potential of things developing further. I had the impression that she wanted a steady relationship, but I didn't want to commit because I was having too much fun "playing the field." Looking back, I don't think I was mature enough to take on the responsibility of a serious relationship at that point. As a result, nothing developed between us.

CLASS "A" PLAYING ABILITY TEST

I passed my Class "A" Playing Ability Test (PAT) at Millwoods Golf Course in 1992, which was extremely important for my career. Passing this test of golf skills was one of the main criteria I needed to achieve my Class "A" status for my CPGA card. In that era, the Class "A" PAT was 36 holes of golf in one day. You had to have a 36-hole total gross score of 152 or less to pass. Millwoods was an 18-hole, par 72 course. I shot 76-75=151. Close call, but I did it! It went down to the very last hole, which I made a par 4 on. I was playing under extreme pressure and passing with only one shot to spare was nerve-racking.

It shouldn't have been that difficult for me because I played well. I was hitting my driver and irons well, and my pitching and chipping were good. I hit twenty-seven greens in regulation. The only real problem was my putting. It was atrocious! Brutal! I had at least six 3-putts, and I missed several other putts from three feet or less. It was a nightmare on the greens for me. Had I been putting half decently my overall score would have been about ten shots lower. It could have been closer to 141. This is a perfect example of how important putting is. I could have gotten really pissed off at my putting woes, which likely would have had a negative effect on the rest of my game. Instead, I managed to keep my composure and accomplish my goal.

Passing a PAT to obtain a professional card, or to get Class "A" status, is one of the most important and difficult tasks a golf professional must face. Qualifying for a PGA Tour card (the most difficult) — or any of the tours for that matter — is usually the hardest thing a professional golfer must endure. Shooting 152 or less in a 36-hole PAT may not seem difficult for some golfers out there. Shooting two 76s is routine for the average CPGA pro. PATs are a different story because there is the pressure factor — it is very difficult. I was relieved to pass this test. I just had to pass my written Class "A" exam, which would take place in Red Deer later that year. If I passed, I would achieve my Class "A" status.

One day on the Wedgewood range, I was talking with a guy who turned out to be an Edmonton sportswriter. He told me about a course named Terrae Pines whose owner was thinking of hiring a CPGA Head Golf Professional for the 1993 golf season. He said the 9-hole course was located a little north of Edmonton, and there was a driving range and RV park on site. He encouraged me to talk with the owner, Matt Cassidy. I thanked him and said I would follow up.

By this time, it was late fall and the golf season was almost over, but I called Matt and arranged for an interview. Matt was in his late 30s, and I was twenty-eight. He was relatively new to the golf industry, and his course had only been open for two seasons. Matt hadn't employed any pros yet but was considering hiring one. I could have been a head pro with my "B1" status, but I wouldn't have been allowed to have any assistant pros or associate pros (Class "A") work/apprentice for me. I told Matt that I realized it would be my first year as a head pro, but I also talked about how his course was still in it's infancy. I said, "We could all grow together." I told him I was a hard worker, a quick study and eager to learn.

I was nervous at first, but I became more relaxed as we went along and felt pretty good at the end of the interview. Matt seemed to be a pretty decent guy. I left my resume and references with him, hoping he would be impressed with my credentials and professionalism. More importantly, I hoped he liked me personally. He said he would think about it and call within the following couple of weeks.

Two weeks later, we had another meeting at Terrae Pines, and he offered me the job of head golf professional, so I accepted. Officially, I was still a Class "B1" until I wrote my Class "A" exam in six weeks. Matt wasn't concerned about these technicalities; he mainly wanted a certified pro who could help with golf operations. It seemed he wasn't interested in hiring an assistant pro as well, and I was OK with that. I would start my new job at the beginning of March 1993. I was quite excited!

I don't know if he talked with any of my references, but I was extremely lucky that my mental illness didn't come up. I didn't say anything either because I didn't think he would hire me if I told him.

The Class "A" exam was the most important test in my life. Dave Lambert came with me to Red Deer that winter when I took the test, and we stayed at a hotel the night before my exam. I should have taken it easy and had a good sleep, but I didn't. We found out that Kim Mitchell was performing in Red Deer that night and decided to go. We had a little too much fun and didn't get back to our hotel until around 3 a.m. Then we ordered a pizza. I'm not sure about Dave, but I was really drunk. I had to get up at 7 a.m., which meant I only had a few hours of sleep. Not too smart.

I arrived for my exam at 8:30, right on time, with about thirty others. It was a six-hour exam. I was still half cut for the first hour or so, then my hangover and lack of sleep kicked in. I was a hurtin' unit. It was a long and grueling day. Despite feeling a little rough, I managed to pull off a 91%, the third-highest mark in our class. However, my advice to anyone who will someday take this exam is to avoid drinking the night before. The exam itself is hard enough!

In January 1993, I was issued my official CPGA Class "A" certificate. I have this document framed and hanging on my little "Wall of Fame" in my home.

CHAPTER 14

1993
A GOOD YEAR

HEAD GOLF PROFESSIONAL

Don Walin — Head Golf Professional. Having this title was my number one goal and was a dream come true. I had worked hard and overcome some major obstacles to get that far. I was a head pro at the relatively young age of twenty-eight, and I was proud of my accomplishment. Looking back, I'm even more proud of the fact that I didn't give up before I reached that point. Having to battle a major mental illness would have made it easy to quit.

The first thing I did was buy a 1976 sixteen-foot trailer for $1600 cash to live in for the season. It was small but was all I needed and could afford. I just used it to sleep in. Matt let me keep it in the RV park at the golf course for free. I even had free power, so it was very cheap accommodation! A lot less than having to rent an apartment. I always liked living close to wherever I was working, so this setup was perfect! I had an extremely short walk from my trailer to the clubhouse where the pro shop was located. The trailer served its purpose beautifully, and using it saved me a lot of money. Another huge plus was that there were washrooms, showers and laundry facilities on the premises. This made my living arrangement very convenient.

The greatest aspect of my job was that I wasn't working for an arrogant head pro. Now, I was the head pro! And I don't think I became arrogant along the way. One time, Matt and I were having a coffee with one of his friends, and Matt told him that I was "the most humble golf pro you will ever meet." His words, not mine.

Matt was my only boss at Terrae Pines, and we got along great. What a relief! We had good communication between us, and we were on the same page. Mainly, he stayed out of my way and let me do my job. I respected Matt for various reasons, but mostly because he treated me well. It was extremely important to me to have a good relationship with my employer. He had a great sense of humor as well. He really made me laugh a lot! There were several times (after everyone else had left), that Matt and I stayed at the clubhouse and had a few beers. It was just the two of us, and we had some good conversations. Sometimes we would talk until 2:00 a.m.

Matt had a really nice family. His wife's name was Dorothy, and they had two young boys and a girl. Gordie was nine, Curtis was seven and Dollar was four. I thought "Dollar" was a strange name, but that's what they called her. I don't know if this was her real name or a nickname, but I never heard her called anything else. She was a little sweetheart. Curtis was a good boy, although he could be a little devilish at times. The oldest boy, Gordie, was a good kid too. Gordie had been playing golf for a couple of years and was doing pretty well. I helped him with his swing a bit, which was starting to develop nicely. Sometimes I wonder if he is still playing golf, and if he is, I wonder how good he got. Matt played golf too. He was a "southpaw," (left handed) and was about a 20 handicap. Dorothy was down-to-earth, extremely humble and very intelligent. She was also a hard worker. She purchased the food and beverages for the golf course and helped out in various ways while also looking after their kids.

Matt was a smart guy. He had some help with the design and layout, but he actually operated the machinery and equipment, moved dirt and constructed his course himself. He employed some people to help him, but he didn't have a large workforce. From what I could tell, he kept all his building costs as low as possible. He owned some property that was farmland and turned it into a golf course.

Having said this, Terrae Pines was not a great golf course — it was below average. It was a very basic, regulation-length, par 36, 9-hole public course. It was almost totally flat, and there were only a few sand traps. There were a few small creeks and a pond on the 9th hole. There were many pine trees planted, but at the time they were still small — no real "tree trouble" to get into. It wasn't a difficult golf course. This description might sound somewhat negative, especially to an avid golfer. It was a good course for beginners and intermediates. A golf course that has all par 3s (or a "mid-length" course) is ideal for beginners to learn the game. Golfers can really get beat up if they play a course that is too difficult for them. Playing an easier course will lower their scores and boost their confidence.

I liked the way Matt thought when it came to the marketing and promotion of Terrae Pines. Mainly, he made it extremely affordable for the average person to play golf. During the week, he only charged $10 for 9 holes and $15 for 18 holes. On the weekend, he charged $12 for 9 holes and $18 for 18 holes. These rates were among the lowest in Edmonton area courses. But that wasn't all. Matt also did a lot of advertising in local newspapers and magazines for "2 for 1" green fees that were valid on weekdays only. This was very successful, and a lot of golfers used them on a regular basis. Because of these cheap rates, I thought Terrae Pines was like the "McDonald's" of golf courses.

By the time I came on board, Matt was well on his way to expanding his operations. He was building another 9 holes that were scheduled to open in 1995 or 1996. The design and layout of the second 9 holes was much different than the front 9. It was much better and a lot more challenging. I was really looking forward to playing it.

As a head professional, I had more responsibilities than I had when I was an assistant pro. I had to keep the pro shop stocked with merchandise, so I dealt with sales representatives on a regular basis. We had a lot of company golf tournaments, which I helped coordinate. I always talked directly with Matt in regards to the most important golf operation matters. Basically, it was the two of us who were making the most important decisions. I was the only pro working there. Matt hired a few young girls to work in the clubhouse and help in the pro shop when needed. I often felt like we were a little short staffed. Often, I had to rush from the pro shop to the kitchen to serve someone a hotdog, smokie or some other item from the confection. Several times, I had to cook hamburgers and French fries for customers. I even had to be a bartender! I served countless beers and drinks. At the same time, I had to look after the pro shop duties. I ran my ass off! It could get very hectic and stressful.

I really liked working in the pro shop, but I liked teaching golf even better. I was also the only teaching pro, so I kept busy giving lessons at the range. I really enjoyed being outside, especially on a warm sunny day, doing what I loved to do. I found teaching golf both challenging and rewarding. Some people were more challenging than others! I had to have a lot of patience. The rewarding part was watching my students learn, develop and improve their game. Matt didn't pay me to teach golf, so I taught on my own time to supplement my income.

I don't know if it's still the case, but there used to be a major discrepancy when it came to the salaries of CPGA Assistant Professionals and Head Professionals. Especially for the head pros. The pay rate wasn't very consistent, and there were some dramatic differences with regard to incomes. Basically, we had to fend for ourselves, with or without a contract. I always thought there should have been better guidelines in place between the CPGA and golf course owners, which would have made the pay structure more fair, reasonable and consistent across Canada.

My job at Terrae Pines was a perfect example of this. I was only getting paid $2,000 per month. I may have been the lowest paid head pro in the region. I was employed eight months per year, making my yearly salary approximately $16,000. Some head pros were making $100,000 a year and employed all year round. Even if I was able to work all year, my annual salary would have only been $24,000. Salaries ranged anywhere between these two figures. I knew a head pro who was working in the same region I was whose salary was $60,000/year. This guy was also a first-year head pro, and he was less qualified than I was.

I'm not complaining about how much I was getting paid at Terrae Pines. I accepted Matt's offer, and I was making more money than I ever did as an assistant pro. Most importantly, I had some good benefits. I mentioned free rent for the trailer (saving me over $700/month), but I also didn't have to pay for food I ate at the clubhouse. It was a very limited menu, but it still saved me a lot of money because I ate most of my meals there. I didn't buy any groceries. Also, I could keep 100% of my lesson revenue. Often, pros only get fifty percent from their lessons. Because of these facts, I thought Matt was being fair and I was satisfied. By the end of the season, I had easily saved $5,000. If I hadn't spent so much money in lounges and nightclubs, I would have had $10,000 saved.

As the head pro, I was only being paid the equivalent of $12.50/hour. For teaching golf, I offered several lesson packages and made an average of approximately $90/hour. Obviously, this was a huge difference! One of my goals was to cut back on the number of hours I worked in the pro shop and increase my teaching hours, which would increase my income substantially. The future was starting to look very promising.

Matt hired his buddy Howard Wilhelm, and it quickly became apparent that they were close friends. Howard was on the grounds crew, and he worked out on the golf course. I don't know specifically what his duties were, and I really didn't care. As long as he was working on the course, things were fine. The minute he came into the clubhouse, the atmosphere changed for me. It would go from very relaxed to quite tense. Howard got on my nerves very quickly. He made my blood boil! I'm a pretty easygoing guy and get along with most people just fine, but Howard was an exception. I tried really hard to get along with him, but nothing I said or did helped. We were very different people. I ended up dealing with Howard and his piss-poor attitude for the entire golf season, which was extremely difficult and stressful. The main reason I put up with him as much as I did was because he was Matt's good buddy.

Howard had never worked at a golf course before and didn't play golf. I don't know if he had even seen a golf ball before! Yet, right from the beginning he tried to boss me around when in no way was he my boss. On only our second day of working together, he left me a note in the pro shop telling me to pick up the broken tees from all of the tee boxes on the course. I was kind of shocked. It wasn't that I was above doing such a task, but I had more important things to do. Things I was hired to do. Picking up broken tees would have been part of his job description, not mine! He tried to boss me around and act superior countless times, so we butted heads a lot. He didn't like me, and I didn't like him — not a healthy working relationship.

I could never figure out why Matt and Howard were such good friends. When it came to their character and qualities, they seemed so different. Looking back, I think of the old saying, "Birds of a feather, flock together." I am a firm believer in this saying. Maybe Matt and Howard had more in common than I thought?

I told Matt a few times how disgruntled I was with Howard. Matt said he would talk with him, but I don't know if he ever did. Nothing changed. Meanwhile, I decided to hang in there and focus on doing my job to the best of my abilities. Most importantly, Matt and I got along, and he was the one who signed my pay check. He was also smart enough to try to keep me happy. He knew he had a pretty good head pro at a very low salary.

Matt and Dorothy went on a vacation for ten days, and Matt brought back a nice pewter business card holder for me. The attached note said, "Good job Don." Those three words meant a lot to me. Matt wasn't a big talker, so I knew this was a sincere gesture. I still have the business card holder.

As far as personal relationships, I had a few flings in 1993. Nothing out of the ordinary back then. "Par for the course," you might say. I saw a girl named Sandy on a regular basis. We met in 1992 and ended up seeing each other for about a year. I knew from the beginning of our relationship that she didn't have the qualities I was looking for in a serious relationship, so I never called her "my girlfriend." She was hot though! Easygoing, down-to-earth, and she had a good sense of humor. Sandy was a kind person. We enjoyed hanging out together, and she came out to the golf course many evenings to spend the night in my humble little trailer. After thinking about ending our relationship for several months, I finally did. I knew this was the right decision, but it was still tough. Even though I knew all along that she wasn't the right one for me, I had become attached to her.

Matt and I played in a golf tournament put on by the Edmonton Firefighters Department at the Ranch Golf & Country Club. It was a Texas Scramble — a fun team event with men and women participating. A bunch of us guys (including some of the firefighters) rented a large condo in south Edmonton the night before the tournament, and it turned into a big party! We had a great time! Matt was there with me and really enjoyed it too. Knowing it was just a fun event the next morning, I wasn't worried about behaving myself and going to bed early. We partied hard all night. I got drunk and only had a few hours of sleep. I was still drunk when I woke up around 7 a.m. for an early tee-off!

Matt and two ladies we didn't know were on my team. A lot of people were drinking on the course, including myself. I still had a lot of booze in my system from the previous night, so it was stupid of me to start drinking again the next morning. I was drunk for the entire 18-hole tournament. Many of my friends and associates did the same thing, but Matt was wiser. He stayed sober for his game. As a team, we didn't win any prizes. I wasn't drunk to the point where my game was a total disaster, but I definitely would have played better if I was sober! Afterward, I felt stupid about my drinking. I was embarrassed for behaving this way around my boss. Basically, I had a guilt trip about the whole situation. Matt didn't seem to have an issue with it, so I was lucky. He knew I was a hard worker, and he thought I was just blowing off some steam.

THE ALBERTA PGA CHAMPIONSHIP

The next golf tournament I played in was a lot more important and serious. It was the APGA Championship held at Country Hills Golf Club in Calgary. This was a 36-hole (two-day) event. I didn't drink when I was playing in CPGA tournaments. I always acted professionally and tried to play my best.

I was extremely nervous for two reasons. I hadn't been playing or practicing much, which meant I hadn't been playing very well and didn't have much confidence in my game. Secondly, I was worried about my reputation regarding my mental-health issues. I hadn't played golf in Calgary since 1991 when I went manic and got fired from Silver Springs. I wondered how many pros in this region had heard about the crazy golf pro. How many of these guys would be there? How would they react when they saw me and talked with me? Thinking about these things was even more nerve-racking than my worries about my golf game. It was a very tense situation.

I knew I would be a nervous wreck on the 1ˢᵗ tee box, but when I got there, I escalated right into a state of panic because there were TV cameras! I wasn't expecting that and instantly became terrified. I had never had a TV crew film me on the golf course before. This took the "1ˢᵗ tee jitters" to a whole new level. Fortunately, they were only on that 1ˢᵗ tee box. I would have been a real mess if the crew had filmed our group for all 18 holes. Way too much pressure for me.

The 1ˢᵗ hole was a short par 4, downhill. I didn't have the confidence to hit my driver or fairway woods off the tee, so I decided to tee-off with my 4 iron. I just wanted to keep my ball in the fairway, and I didn't need a lot of distance off the tee. I knew if I hit a decent 4 iron, my second shot to the green would only be from about 150 yards. When it was my turn to tee-off, I walked onto the tee box fully aware of the TV cameras. My hands were shaking. I thought I would have trouble just trying to balance my ball on a tee, so I decided to hit it right off the ground instead of using a tee. I proceeded to take the fastest and probably worst golf swing in my life. I hit this fat, huge pull hook. My ball ended up in an adjacent fairway to the left of the 1ˢᵗ hole at least 50 yards left of the 1st fairway. My ball only went about 150 yards. I was so embarrassed that I grabbed my clubs and hightailed it out of there.

I ended up being about 220 yards away from the green for my second shot, so I decided to hit my 4 iron again. This time, I hit it much better, my ball coming to rest just 5 yards short of the green. I chipped my third shot to within four feet of the hole. I had a great chance to save my par but missed my putt and had to settle for a bogey. I was still satisfied with this result. It could have been a lot worse.

It was fall, and it was windy and extremely cold. After the first few holes, it started snowing! The snow wasn't really accumulating on the ground, but it still made things more difficult. I was hoping the officials would cancel the tournament because of these conditions, but they didn't. We had to endure. I heard they were selling toques and gloves in the pro shop, so after the front nine I bought both. I was trying to keep as warm as I could, but it was just a bitterly cold and extremely long day on the course. My game was like the weather: really shitty. I shot a 92. There would have been a lot of high scores that day, and I'm sure there were others who also had a miserable day.

I decided to withdraw from the tournament after the first round because my back was very sore. I saw Dave Mayes, the executive director of the Alberta PGA, in the clubhouse and informed him about my decision. He had no problem with my "W/D." There were a couple of other reasons why I didn't want to play the second round that I didn't tell Dave. My 92 in the first round pretty much determined I wouldn't make any money. Also, the weather was supposed to be much the same the next day for the second round, and I didn't want to spend another miserable day on the golf course.

Once my "W/D" was official, it was time to party! Several of us pros ended up at the Rocking Horse Saloon in Calgary and had a great time that night. I didn't detect any negative repercussions regarding my illness while amongst my peers, and no one said anything to me about it. We just carried on like we normally would. It's still quite possible that there was some talk going on behind my back because I'm sure the news about my mental illness would have spread like wildfire among many of the Alberta PGA pros.

Overall, my first year as a head golf professional at Terrae Pines went very well. The only real negative thing was having to deal with Howard as a fellow employee. Most importantly, Matt was happy with me. He wanted me back for the 1994 season, and we often talked about long-range plans together.

For the off-season, I was lucky enough to live with my mom in Kelowna without having to pay rent. I did give her $300/month for groceries. The majority of Alberta PGA pros, including myself, got laid off after the golf season was over, which meant we would have to find another job for the winter or collect UI. At the time, UI only paid sixty percent of an individual's gross monthly earnings, so my $2,000/month salary meant I received about $1,200/month. Since I didn't have another job for the winter, the $1,200/month was my only income for the four months that I was laid off so there is no way I could have afforded to rent an apartment on a year-round basis in the area where I was working, and I couldn't live in my little trailer at the golf course during the extremely cold Alberta winter. Many head pros had their own businesses established at the golf course they were working at and were ineligible to receive UI.

From what I could tell, Matt was doing pretty well financially. I had a pretty good idea of how much revenue the course was generating, and I knew he kept his expenses as low as he could. He was also spending some of his money. I only know two examples of this, but both represent large sums of money. First, he was in the process of having a new home for his family built on the golf course. They were living in a mobile home on the property until their new home was completed. Anyway, it was probably a good investment. Matt also bought into a yacht along with his lawyer friend and two other associates. The four of them would share the use of the yacht, which they kept at the Semi-Ah-Moo Marina on the west coast of Washington State in the US.

During the off-season, Matt and Dorothy were kind enough to invite me to stay on their yacht with them for a few days. I gratefully accepted their offer, made the six-hour drive from West Kelowna to Washington and joined up with them at the marina. Their yacht was thirty-eight feet long and quite luxurious. I spent four nights with them. We made a trip to Friday Harbor (one of the San Juan Islands) and had a lot of fun together there. This trip reminded me of the early 1980s when I spent a lot of time on my parents' yacht. Dad also took us to Friday Harbor one time. I always enjoyed being in a boat out on the open waters. Cruising the vast waters on the Pacific Ocean in a yacht is an awesome experience. The scenery is breathtaking. Occasionally, we would see a whale or some dolphins that would play alongside the boat. We also saw a lot of seals. I really enjoyed the trip with Matt and Dorothy. I felt comfortable with them, and it was a great experience. I really liked having this type of relationship with my boss!

HOUSTON, TEXAS

Shortly after this, I flew down to Houston, Texas, for the first time to stay at my brother Jim's place for four weeks. Houston is one of the largest cities in the United States, with a population of about six million people. It is in the far south on the Gulf of Mexico. Jim lived in an area called "Clear Lake."

He took me to the Clear Lake Beach Club, which was incredible. I fell in love with it immediately. It was an indoor and outdoor bar located right on the

Gulf of Mexico. We went outside to a large area with nice white sand, which was where most of the action was. People were playing beach volleyball, and there was a hot tub and a stage for live music. Tables and chairs surrounded the area. There were several "cigarette boats" (thirty-foot-long speed boats) lined up side by side at the dock right in front. One of these boats would cost around $400,000 (US!) to own. The best part about the Clear Lake Beach Club was the dress code. There were a lot of bikinis and a lot of women who looked spectacular in those bikinis! Overall, it was just a great atmosphere. I enjoyed being there so much that I went back a few more times.

On the subject of females, Jim took me to a strip club called The Gentleman's Club. I have been to a lot of strip clubs in my life, but nothing compared to this place. If you could call a strip club "classy," then The Gentleman's Club would fit the description. It was a first-class facility. The furniture, décor, etc. was of high quality, and there were several stages and podiums where many dancers performed at the same time. The entertainment was non-stop, and the talent was quite impressive. There were a lot of businessmen there wearing their suits and ties. The food was good, and it was a good time.

Jim and I had a game of golf at the Greatwood Golf Club with my buddy Steve "Tex" Parker, a PGA professional from Houston. We became good friends in 1989 when he qualified to play on the Canadian Tour. He stayed at my place in Sidney, and we have kept in touch since then. It was a pretty nice golf course. An assistant pro from Greatwood (who was a friend of Steve's) joined Steve, Jim and me. It was another great day on the golf course.

I especially liked playing with Tex. He is my favorite pro. He's an excellent golfer, but much more than that, he's a good person, a class act. He is very professional. He is also very humble. He has known that I have manic depression since my first diagnosis in 1989. Unlike most of my golf pro friends and associates, Steve has remained loyal to me. Despite my illness, our friendship has remained intact for many years.

Tex introduced me to some really good Houston nightlife. One night we went to a really cool nightclub called Dave and Buster's. It was one of many times that we had a few beers together. We always had a lot of laughs and a lot of fun. We also spent some time at the driving range. We videotaped our golf swings, then analyzed them together afterward. It was great to see Tex and spend some quality time with him.

Jim and I took a couple of road trips. The first one was to Austin, then to San Antonio. I enjoyed going to these places that I had previously only heard about. On our second road trip, Jim took me to New Orleans, Louisiana. It was fantastic! We roamed up and down the very famous Bourbon Street. There were a lot of people there, and it was party central! We explored many of the countless bars. The whole place was full of excellent music and great food. I really had a good time there.

There was a good pub close to Jim's place in Clear Lake called The Cross-Eyed Seagull that we went to several times. Near the end of my vacation, I was there one night and met a girl with whom I had a brief relationship before I had to go back to Canada. She was good looking, smart, and she worked at NASA. She wasn't a rocket scientist, but she was smart enough to work with rocket scientists!

TORONTO MAPLE LEAFS

After a month of great times in Texas, I had to fly back to Calgary to attend Jim's wedding. As one of Jim's best men, I wore a tuxedo. After the wedding ceremony, there was the usual dinner and reception. By about 11 p.m., I was well oiled, and I was getting bored. I wanted more action! I decided to leave the reception and go party at some clubs on Electric Avenue. I grabbed a taxi and off I went.

I ended up at a nightclub that was full of people partying, and I joined right in. Now I was really having some fun! After I was there for a couple of hours, I started talking with some guys who were sitting at a table. It turns out they were members of the Toronto Maple Leafs. There were several of them, and we hit it off right away. They had just played a game against the hometown Calgary Flames earlier that evening.

The bar closed around 2:30 a.m., and the staff was getting everyone to leave the club. Everyone except the hockey players and myself. The manager let us stay there longer, and we kept on drinking. The guys found out I was a golf pro, so the next thing I knew, I was giving a lesson to a few of them on the dance floor. There was a large mirror that I used to demonstrate the proper golf swing. The guys were quite pleased with me. What I find even more amusing is that I was still wearing my tuxedo from the wedding. Teaching golf lessons to Toronto Maple Leafs hockey players on the dance floor of a Calgary nightclub ... while I was wearing a tux! Too funny.

I spent the rest of the winter in West Kelowna. 1993 was a good year for me. I was looking forward to going back to work at the Terrae Pines Golf Course for the 1994 season, my mental-health status was very good, and I had made it through two consecutive years without any manic or depressed episodes. And no psych wards. I hadn't seen a psychiatrist and wasn't taking any psychiatric medications during this whole time. Was I cured?

Carl Walin - Grandpa - 1900-1966
Professional Photographer owned "Walin Studio of Fine
Portrait Photography" in Wetaskiwin, Alberta 1919-1956

Dagne Walin nee Billsten
Grandma 1894-1943

Howard Clark - Grandpa

Evelyn Clark nee Merrick
Grandma

Dale Walin - Dad

Muriel Walin nee Clark - Mom

Mom and Dad's wedding day - 1954

Mom and Don - 1965

Don, 11 years old, accepting trophy for
first-flight in Wetaskiwin Junior Tournament - 1975

Don's Graduation - 1982
Lord Beaverbrook High School
Calgary, Alberta

Don's 21st Birthday with Mom
June 7, 1985 - Edmonton, Alberta

Don - "The Rock Star" - California - 1985

Don - "Ocean Driving Range"
Southern California - 1985

Indiana Jack on the left - Don on the right - with
"California Girl" in the middle - 1985

Don's car wreck from drunk driving accident
in Encinitas, California - 1986

San Diego Golf Academy Graduation Ceremony August 1986. Left to
right - Joe Novis, Kosuke Takahashi, Trevor Maywood and Don Walin

Don at the San Diego Golf Academy - 1986

Pro Am at Glen Meadows Golf & Country Club, Sidney, BC
Don is third from the left - 1988

Jack Nicklaus Jr. on the left, Don on the right - during Canadian
Tour Qualifying at Glen Meadows Golf & Country Club - 1989

Don on the cover of a magazine advertising a Canadian Tour Event - 1990

Don and Terri Comrie - picture taken by Grandma
Clark at her house in Wetaskiwin - 1990

Walin brothers and Mom at brother Jim's wedding.
Left to right - Gary, Doug, Jim, Don and Rick - 1994

"Tex" - Steve Parker, a long time friend and former Canadian Tour
Player on the left and Don at a pub in Clear Lake, Texas - 1996

Ellen Bachmann aka Elli, working as a Community
Health Worker the year Don and Elli met - 1997

Don and Captain Johnny Morris of the Edmonton Fire Department with his wife Mary behind the bar, in their home in Edmonton, Alberta - 2001

Elli's siblings celebrating after her first Lake Country
Art Walk Exhibition. Left to right - Erich, Lilli,
Elli and Walter Bachmann. Kelowna, BC - 2010

Dave Lambert and Don

Don on the left (with writer's beard) and friend Dave Lambert on
a fishing trip, holding a Red Snapper - Haida Gwaii, BC - 2011

Thao, Leo and John Kenny at the Dublin Zoo - 2018

A candid photo taken by niece Andrea Bachmann of Don and
Elli at a party at nephew Darrell Bachmann's home - 2008

CHAPTER 15

1994
PSYCHOSIS

THE DEVIL & ALIENS

The 1994 golf season started out very well for me, and I was doing a good job. Matt was happy with me, and I was happy with him too. Even Howard and I were getting along better because his attitude seemed to have improved. Perhaps Matt had a talk with Howard over the winter? It was less stressful, but I still didn't like him. I was busy giving golf lessons and everything else was going well.

Matt often talked with me about long-term plans, which made me think he wanted me around for a long time. This gave me a good feeling and was reassuring. At the beginning of the season, Matt was talking about the possibility of getting me a mobile home to live in on the golf course property. I was extremely excited about this. Unfortunately, this didn't happen. I don't know why Matt decided not to go ahead with this potential plan, but I didn't get too disappointed with this outcome.

Instead, I bought a fifth wheel trailer to park at the RV park. Looking back, I was very hasty and rushed into it. I didn't take my time to look around — I wanted to buy the first one I looked at! The one I wanted was a beautiful 1993 thirty-footer that was a hell of a lot nicer than my 1976 trailer. Matt said he would help me buy it, so for the next month, I pressured him about it. Every few days I asked him when we were going to make this deal. I was uncharacteristically demanding, and he was getting irritated. Finally, my persistence paid off. With Matt helping me with financing, I got my new RV, and I was a very "happy camper." It cost $23,000, and the monthly payments were only $200. Even better, Matt told me that he would pay $100/ month himself.

Shortly after I got my new RV, I was interviewed by Jerry Prince, a sportswriter at the *Edmonton Sun*, and I thought it went well. Jerry wrote a fairly extensive article about me, which I thought was good at the time as well. A few years later, I read the article again and felt embarrassed. I liked most of it, but there were some parts I wished weren't in there, which wasn't Jerry's fault. He wrote based on things I told him. The article stated that I had a new fifth wheel trailer and my plans for the following winter were to go down south with my RV and play some golf. I was going to go to North and South Carolina, Florida and Texas. I wished these comments weren't published. I felt stupid when I read it because these "plans" weren't feasible. For one thing, I didn't even have a truck to tow my RV, and I wasn't in a position to buy one. Even if I had a truck, I wouldn't be able to afford to go on a trip like this. Furthermore, I've never towed anything behind a vehicle in my life. Towing a thirty-foot fifth wheel for thousands of miles across Canada and down the east coast of the United States would be extremely challenging.

In hindsight, there was a reason I was pressuring Matt so much to get my fifth wheel and why I was overly optimistic regarding my winter vacation down south: I was starting to go manic again.

I was in the clubhouse one day in May when I started to see the devil in some people and aliens in others. I felt that some of the aliens were friendly and some weren't. I've only experienced the presence of aliens a few times in my life, but each time was basically the same as my many experiences of sensing God, Satan and/or "human" spirits. I sensed the energy of these entities, which many people refer to as "paranormal." The energy I felt coming from the "unfriendly" aliens was incredibly powerful. I want to stress the fact that people look totally normal physically when I have these sensations, but I sense the energy coming from them. I believe both God and the devil exist, and I believe that as human beings, our inner core is a spirit/soul. I also believe that aliens exist. This topic has interested me for most of my life, and it has increased after some of my experiences.

Usually when I was manic and having some "spiritual experience," I felt like my mind was crystal clear and razor sharp. Not when I went manic at Terrae Pines that day. I was in a state of psychosis and was delusional as well. My perception of reality was severely distorted. In layman's terms, I was really fucked up! On that fateful day, I attempted to play 9 holes with a couple of our members. As with other golf games I played when manic, it didn't go well. I was acting totally bizarre. My behavior and etiquette were not appropriate for an average golfer, let alone for a professional. By the 3rd hole, my playing partners were so pissed off at me that they quit our game and went back to the clubhouse. I went back there too.

At one point, I had quite the encounter with a bird by the RV park. This was not a normal bird, but what I thought was my ex-girlfriend, Terri. There was a small swamp nearby where this bird was residing, and it was probably just protecting its territory. The bird chased after me, sounding really pissed off. Then it retreated, so I ran towards it. I was saying things like, "Terri! Please stop and listen to me. I still love you!" The bird and I chased each other back and forth for about fifteen minutes. The whole time I was talking to it as if it really was Terri. This may have been my all-time craziest delusion.

Shortly after this episode, Matt called me into his office.

"What's going on Donny?" he said.

I said, "I can't say."

Earlier, something inside of me told me not to talk with anyone, so for the most part I tried to say as little as possible. Matt was no exception, but he must have been shocked by this sudden change. I didn't tell him that I was seeing the devil and aliens in some people, and I didn't see either of these things in Matt. He appeared totally normal to me. Matt said I was scaring some people in the RV park. He didn't know I had manic depression, so he may have thought I was fucked up on some serious drugs. I don't think our meeting enlightened Matt very much. Mainly, our conversation would have confirmed for Matt that there was something seriously wrong with me. Shortly after our meeting, I was in my fifth wheel when Matt walked over and asked for my keys to the clubhouse and the RV. He fired me, and I didn't resist. Being delusional and in a state of psychosis, I was in another world and didn't realize the severity of the consequences.

<u>Cop Car on the Driving Range</u>

I saw a police car arrive at the golf course. Obviously, Matt had called them. Even though I hadn't done anything illegal, I had a strong feeling that they were there for me. I was right. When I saw the cop car, I walked towards the driving range. The cop kept his distance, but I could tell he was following me. I kept walking, and he kept following. Now I was in the middle of the driving range. The cop car was following me on the range! He stayed about fifty yards behind me the whole time. I started throwing range balls at him, then ran. I kept throwing range balls over my shoulder towards his car. The cop drove very slowly throughout his pursuit of me. I ran until I came close to the end of the driving range. Past that area, there was a swamp. I didn't want to go in there, so I stopped and looked back. The cop car had stopped as well. Then the cop got out and stood beside his car.

When I looked at him, I thought he was an "unfriendly" alien! Physically, he looked like a normal police officer to me. But metaphysically (beyond physical matter), I sensed an alien presence coming from him. Without thinking, I turned around and ran toward the cop (alien) as fast as I could. I went straight at him and plowed right into him. The cop pepper sprayed me, which blinded me and hurt like hell! It also immobilized me. He was able to handcuff me and get me into his police car. The cop took me to the

Morinville RCMP station. The pepper spray was washed out of my eyes, and I was locked in a jail cell by myself.

It was a beautiful day. The golf course was very busy. There would have been a lot of people around the clubhouse and on the driving range who would have witnessed this spectacle. Many of these people would have known me personally. I'm sure it gave a lot of people something to talk about. The rumors about me probably spread fast.

After monitoring my very bizarre behavior in the jail cell for a couple of hours, the police decided that I didn't belong in jail, and they realized I was mentally ill and needed treatment. Later that evening, they transported me to the Alberta Hospital, a large mental institution, on the outskirts of Edmonton. I had heard this was "a place where crazy people were kept." Now they were taking me there!

It was out of the frying pan and into the fire, really. The police handed me over to the supervision of a psychiatrist; I don't know which is worse! For one thing, they both have the ability to either handcuff you or have you strapped down. Either one can have you locked up in a very small, confined space. I have been the recipient of these things many times. It's not much fun.

Some people assessed me at the Alberta Hospital, and I think one of them was a psychiatrist. By somehow keeping my thoughts to myself and not speaking much, I was able to convince them I was OK. I guess I answered their questions well enough without "incriminating" myself too much. I didn't tell them I had been seeing the devil and aliens in people, or that my ex-girlfriend came to me as a bird. They didn't commit me, and I didn't volunteer to be admitted. I was free to go.

I ended up being charged with "assaulting a police officer." I thought the charge would get dropped because I was mentally ill when it happened, but I was wrong. I had to go to court in Morinville at the end of November — a twelve-hour drive from West Kelowna where I was living at the time. I didn't get a lawyer because I wanted to explain my side of the story to the judge. If I had that opportunity, I was quite confident the judge would rule in my favor and drop the charge against me.

While I was sitting in the courtroom waiting for my case to come up, Howard Wilhelm walked in. He sat by himself about six rows behind me. Like an idiot, I went and sat right beside him right away. It was a spontaneous action that I regretted almost immediately. I felt like I "buddied up" to him as if I liked him when I didn't like him at all. Howard wasn't there to support me. If he was, he would have sat beside me instead of six rows behind me. I think he came to see me in court to amuse himself and would have been pleased if I had lost my case. I don't know how he knew the date and time of my court case to begin with because I hadn't seen him in six months. I was a little surprised that Matt didn't come to the courtroom with Howard.

As things turned out, my case was dropped due to a "technicality." I don't know what the "technicality" was, and I never really cared. I was just happy that the assault charge against me was dropped. I have always wondered if the judge was aware of the fact that I was mentally ill at the time of the incident and just decided to throw out my case. The charge of "assaulting a police officer" was a little harsh anyway. I pushed the officer, but I didn't hit him. I didn't hurt or injure him. The officer who charged me was in the courtroom, and after my case was over, I apologized and shook his hand. Afterward, I wished I hadn't done this because he seemed like an asshole.

There was something written on my police report that I thought was kind of funny. On the day I was manic at Terrae Pines, it said I was letting golfers play for free. I'm sure that Matt didn't think this was very funny. I don't remember doing this, but I'm not surprised if I did. This is a good example of manic behavior. The more I think about this, the more I laugh about that situation. Can you imagine going to pay for your green fees when the head pro spontaneously says, "It's OK, put away your wallet. Golf is free today!"

HOMELESS SHELTER

Anyway, a staff member at the Alberta Hospital arranged for a taxi to drive me all the way to downtown Edmonton. I didn't know where I was going, and I didn't have a destination in mind. The driver let me out in front of a homeless shelter, so I walked in. It was around midnight and I had a brief conversation with a guy working there. He got me a pillow and some blankets and led me to a dormitory. The room was pitch black, and I could hear a bunch of people snoring. Something about this situation spooked me, and I decided I wasn't going to sleep in that room. I walked down the hallway and found a smoking room. I was exhausted. I had a couple of cigarettes and fell asleep right there.

When I woke up, there was a middle-aged Indian man sitting on the bench beside me having a cigarette. I don't know how long he had been there, but I immediately felt like something was very special about this person. Almost instantly, I sensed the presence of God in him. This gave me a very safe and comforting feeling. The Indian man and I didn't talk to each other. We didn't have to. We seemed to have a certain understanding of each other without saying anything. I also had a cigarette as we sat in peace and quiet. Shortly after, he left. I felt like God himself had been in the smoking room with me and was watching over me. I could sense His love and spirit through the Indian man.

It was around 6:00 a.m., so I decided to leave. I walked through a door that read "Exit" and the fire alarm went off, scaring the shit out of me! I ran as fast as I could for a few blocks, making sure that no one was chasing after me. Nobody was. Once again, I found myself walking the streets of Edmonton in my own little world. In the downtown core, I came to The Brick Warehouse. The Brick Warehouse! Suddenly, it all made sense. This was where I was supposed to be! I mentioned earlier that my ex-girlfriend, Terri, was related to the owner of the The Brick, Bill Comrie. I thought I was just supposed to wait beside The Brick Warehouse sign outside the store because Terri would arrive very soon so we could reunite and get married. Bill Comrie would be there too. By becoming a member of Bill's "family" I would become extremely wealthy. This was better than winning the lottery! I waited there for a while, but nobody showed up. I was disappointed and a little confused. However, I decided to move on and continued to walk around the downtown area.

I saw a lady in her 50s on the sidewalk about half a block away and thought it was Terri. This made no sense considering Terri was still in her 20s and looked nothing like this lady. It brought "being crazy over a girl" to a whole new level! I started to follow the lady and kept yelling, "Terri! Terri! Please stop! I just want to talk with you! Terri, please wait!" As I got a little closer to her, the lady discovered I was talking to her, so she ran away. I ran after her, but I knew enough to keep my distance. I made sure I didn't get too close. This poor lady was obviously frightened, and understandably so. I had no intention of harming her, but she didn't know that. She ran across the street into an office building, so I followed her. She went into a large office where there were a lot of people — maybe where she worked? I stayed in the hallway outside the office.

Within about ten minutes, the police were there. Obviously, they had received a call regarding some lunatic harassing a lady. The two police officers were good to me and knew how to handle the situation. As a result, I totally complied with them. They didn't handcuff me, and I went with them willingly. No charges were pressed against me, and the police took me straight to the hospital.

The next thing I knew I was strapped, face down, on a stretcher. My arms and legs were tied down. I couldn't move anything. It was a terrible feeling, but it got worse. A lot worse! It felt like my entire body had become saturated with some type of substance that was making me feel extremely ill. From my head down to my feet, I had the most awful feeling I had ever experienced. I was completely disorientated, didn't know where I was, or what was happening to me. I just knew I was tied to a stretcher in a room by myself. I kept yelling, "Help me! Please, help me!" But nobody did. No one came into the room. I really thought I was dying and that the people keeping me captive were trying to kill me. I thought I had been poisoned or something. It got to the point where I was desperately hoping that I really would die.

Turns out I had been injected with extremely powerful psychiatric medications in order to treat my manic episode. They probably gave me Thorazine, Haldol or Risperdal. These drugs will help stop the mania, but they also produce severe side effects, such as I was feeling. It was torture. No one in my situation should have to experience such agony and misery. I have also experienced severe muscle tightness from these drugs and have been so sedated I couldn't talk or function normally for prolonged periods of time. When I was put on Thorazine, I could barely walk at all. All I could do was shuffle my feet as if I was 100 years old.

Psychiatrists are quick to administer these drugs, and sometimes the dose is too high. This has happened to me several times. In order to get a better understanding of the effects of these drugs and the dosage, psychiatrists should have to take them. It would be "a taste of their own medicine" so to speak.

It's hard for me to describe the feeling that consumed my body when I was tied down to the stretcher. I felt incredibly ill and was awake for a long time after they gave me this drug. As a result, I suffered for a long time. I wish they would have given me something that would have put me to sleep. That would have been so much better!

Finally, I did go to sleep. When I woke up, I was in the psych ward at the Charles Camsell Hospital in Edmonton.

Charles Camsell Hospital Psych Ward

I was trying to walk down the hallway one day, which took a long time because I could only shuffle my feet. A girl walked by me and said, "Oh, the old Thorazine shuffle, eh?" Obviously, she was familiar with this drug and knew the side effect it produces.

On another occasion, I met this guy in the smoke room. Literally, half of his face was missing. It was a shocking and horrific sight — quite grotesque. He had tried to commit suicide by shooting himself in the face. I was surprised that he even survived this tragedy, and I felt so bad for him. It must have been incredibly difficult for this fellow to go on living after this happened. I can't even imagine what the poor guy has been through. It made me think about my own suicide attempt in 1990. It's a miracle I wasn't killed or severely disfigured like this guy was. Looking at him, I realized the same thing could have happened to me.

ALCOHOLISM

The psychiatrist treating me at the psychiatric unit was Dr. Ben Segal. He asked me if I drank alcohol, how much and how often, so I was totally honest with him. I had never been in denial about my drinking, and this was certainly no time to start. I had known for many years that I drank too much, too often. Once I started, I would usually end up getting drunk. The booze controlled me. I couldn't control it. I had a lot of fun when I was drinking, but overall it did me more harm than good. I was a "self-diagnosed" alcoholic. More than anything, I was honest with myself about drinking. I have never been labeled as an "alcoholic" by a doctor (including psychiatrists), or any other kind of health-care professional. However, Dr. Segal strongly advised me to quit drinking. It didn't mix well with my bipolar disorder, so I decided to take his advice. I quit drinking, and it was the smartest thing I've ever done!

I was able to stop drinking on my own without assistance from AA or anyone else. I haven't tasted alcohol for over twenty-five years, since May 20, 1994 — with two exceptions that I'll explain later. I love being sober all the time, and I don't miss the hangovers! Despite this, I haven't become a "reformer." I don't try to change other people's drinking habits, and I always make sure that we have beer in our fridge to offer our guests. We always have an assortment of liquor to offer as well, and I'm usually the first one to ask others if they want a beer or other alcoholic beverage when they come to our home.

I ended up staying in the psychiatric unit for about six weeks. By this time, my mania had subsided, and I was well enough to go home. Not having my own place, I had to rely on my mom again. I stayed at her home in West Kelowna, which was very fortunate. Many people with a mental illness have to live in some kind of group home, and many become homeless altogether and end up living on the streets.

Once again, my manic episode was replaced with a depressed episode. I went from one extreme to another without a period of normalcy in between. As always, my depression lasted a lot longer than my mania. I was debilitatingly depressed for seven months. I lay in bed or on the couch most of the time and constantly thought about suicide.

CHAPTER 16

1995

BAD LUCK

Around the end of January 1995, I came out of my depression. As always, this was a very sudden and welcome relief. All of those months of severe depression, then within a day or two, I feel like a new person. This "metamorphosis" happened earlier than usual this time. My "transformation" didn't usually occur until spring or early summer.

Back in the winter of 1992, I was in a minor car accident in Edmonton. I was stopped at a stop sign when I was rear-ended by another vehicle. I suffered from whiplash as a result and consulted a lawyer, and he agreed that this was a case for a lawsuit. He said he would represent me on a "contingency fee" basis, meaning that I didn't have to pay him any money up front. We would sue the guy who rear-ended me, and his insurance company would be responsible for any compensation paid out. If my lawyer was successful, he would get thirty percent of the money that was awarded. This arrangement sounded pretty good to me, so my lawyer went ahead with the lawsuit process on my behalf.

From that point on, I had to keep records of things associated with my injury. I had to record my physiotherapy appointments, including what kind of treatment I had each time I went. I also recorded my doctors' appointments and all the medications prescribed to treat my injury, such as pain killers and anti-inflammatory medication. I did this for close to three years. Looking back, I'm a little surprised that I could even accomplish this task given my mental health. In January 1995, my lawyer informed me that my case had been settled, and I was awarded $26,000. My lawyer's share was $7,000, and within two weeks I received a check in the mail for $19,000.

The CPGA annual dues I paid gave me some insurance coverage, including Long Term Disability (LTD). About six months after I became mentally ill while working at Terrae Pines, I was approved to receive LTD benefits, which paid me $1,000/month, and my claim was backdated to the end of May 1994. I received a check from the insurance company for $7,000 in January 1995, the same week I was awarded $19,000 for my car accident lawsuit. $26,000 in one week! I was far from rich, but it was the most money I had ever had at one time, and I didn't have any debts. It was a good feeling to have a little bit of money.

I received LTD benefits for the next five months before I was cut off. At the time, LTD coverage expired after one year. A few months after my policy was terminated, the insurance program was changed from Long Term Disability to Lifetime Disability — a massive difference. Being on LTD for one year paid me $12,000. If I was on Lifetime Disability, which I would have qualified for, I would have been paid $12,000/year for the last twenty-five years. I have "lost" $300,000 (and counting) because of this.

I got totally screwed in this regard and have considered fighting for my rights or appealing my case with the CPGA and the insurance company. I really wish I had talked to a lawyer about this matter a lot closer to the time it happened. Now, twenty-five years later, it's probably way too late. But sometimes I still think "What if there is a chance?" If there was, I could be back paid for all these years and receive $1,000/month for the rest of my life. This is a real long shot, but I'm an eternal optimist. Where there's hope, there's hope. Anyone know of a good lawyer who might have good news for me on this matter?

Later in 1995, I was put on a Canada Pension Plan (CPP) Lifetime Disability program. I only received $550/month from this, and twenty-five years later, I'm still on this plan. With an increase of about $5.00/year (which is ridiculous), I now receive $700/month. For Canada, this is literally below poverty-level income.

My Own Driving Range! Almost...

When I received my insurance money in January 1995, I looked into the possibility of owning and operating my own driving range. The Green Bay Driving Range on Kelowna's west side had been closed for the previous year or two. One day, I went there and met the owner of the property, a gentleman in his 80s, named Arnie Wiigs. Arnie and his wife, Blanche, lived on the property, which included an RV park. Mr. and Mrs. Wiigs were very nice people.

The driving range had been closed because some of the netting needed repairs and some new netting needed to be installed. This wasn't a priority for Arnie. The Wiigs main moneymaker was their RV park, and the driving range was just a small operation. It was close to 300 yards long and a little less than average wide. There were only a dozen hitting stations, but I figured there was room to add a few more. All the AstroTurf matts were just like new. Apparently, there was a golf pro who gave lessons now and then in the past, but not on a regular basis. This place had potential!

Arnie told me that if I did the necessary repairs and got the range operating, I only had to pay him $400/year to pay the property taxes on the land. I couldn't believe it! Between selling range balls and giving a few lessons, I could easily generate that much revenue in one day! I wanted our deal to be in writing, so I wrote a contract. Arnie was quite pleased with this and said it was "very professional." We all signed the document.

There was an old shack on the property that was used to sell the range balls. Part of my plan was to tear it down and build a golf shop fully stocked with equipment, clothing and accessories. I could sell range balls and book golf lessons from there as well. I also planned on building a practice green and a practice sand trap.

My dream was coming true. I would be the owner and operator of my own golf facility! I would be able to hire my own staff. I wouldn't have to work for or with any arrogant golf pros and have to deal with their egos. I was so excited!

At the time, there was one other driving range on Kelowna's west side. It was a pretty good facility, but I knew they would be closing their business within the next year or two because the property was being turned into a housing development. This meant I would have the only driving range in this region. In 1995, the population of West Kelowna was about 30,000, so I think my range would have done reasonably well financially. I wouldn't become rich, but I thought I would do OK. The Green Bay Driving Range (I was going to change the name) was in a good location near several RV resorts and was very close to Okanagan Lake. It was just off Boucherie Road, a main road in the area. It was a five-minute (or less) drive from most regions of West Kelowna, including the very busy Hwy. 97.

Arnie said another problem with the driving range was some of the balls had been going into the neighbors' property on both sides of the range, and they were complaining. I wasn't surprised because the netting was in poor condition. There were several large holes and some areas where there was no netting at all. The netting didn't cover the top perimeter of the range as it should, and there were smaller gaps and holes all over the place. No wonder the balls were escaping! Arnie gave me the impression that if I did the repairs, the neighbors would be OK with the driving range reopening.

The Green Bay Bible Camp was on one side, so I went over there to explain the situation before I started doing any work. The guy I talked with didn't have any problem with the range opening up again. What a relief! The neighbor on the other side was another RV resort. There was also an open field on their property, which I didn't really give much thought to in the beginning. I may have seen a couple of horses, but it wasn't full of farm animals that could get injured by golf balls! I thought about going over there to talk with the owner, but for some reason I decided not to. I guess I took it for granted that he wouldn't be a problem for me after I did these repairs.

I started right away and worked on the range almost every day. For several hours each day I mended the netting. Mainly, I just sewed up the holes with string. It was a very tedious job, but it had to be done. After a month of this, I was making good progress.

One day, I was driving home from the range when a lady drove into me. It was a minor accident, and there were no injuries, but my Accord suffered about $2,000 damage. My insurance company classified this as a write-off, towed my car to the junkyard and mailed me a check for about $2,000. I was very disappointed because I really liked this car. It was in very good condition, and it was paid off. I could have driven it for a long time. I wished they would have done the repairs so I could have kept it. I also thought it was worth more than $2,000.

So, I needed a vehicle. Since I now had my own driving range, I thought I would get a truck because I knew it would come in handy. Having a truck would also be a nice change, as I had never owned one before. I thought I could save quite a bit of money on taxes if I purchased the vehicle in Alberta, so I went to Calgary to look for one. It didn't take long to find a small, dark blue 1993 Toyota with low mileage in excellent condition. It was a 5-speed manual and had some zip to it. Fun to drive. It came with a canopy, which was useful. After taking it for a test drive, I convinced them to knock off $2,000 by paying right away. We agreed on $12,400, and I wrote them a check. No financing, no payments because of the insurance money I had received. What a great feeling!

I took my truck to A&B Sound in Calgary and had a Pioneer CD stereo system and box speakers installed. While they were installing it, I went shopping for CDs. I was like a kid in a candy store. So much to choose from! It's a good thing I wasn't manic. If I was, I probably would have bought at least fifty and spent about $1,000. As it was, I dropped about $200 on fifteen CDs and an organizer. I hadn't owned a CD player or CDs before, so I was tremendously excited! I have always loved music. Listening to my favorite songs puts me in a better mood than anything else. When I popped the first CD in the deck, I was more than happy. It sounded awesome! CDs were an amazing invention at the time. Press a button and in a split second you can listen to your favorite songs. So much better than the cassettes of the 1980s and 8 tracks of the 1970s.

My eight-hour drive back to Kelowna was most enjoyable. I took the Trans-Canada Highway #1 that goes through the Rockies. Rogers Pass is the breathtaking summit, and I never got tired of it no matter how many times I drove through. I strongly recommend making this drive when the weather is good and the roads are in good condition. It can be very stressful if the roads are all snowy and icy. I had my new CD system cranked for the majority of the trip back home. I was having a blast, but I did have a bit of a headache by the time I arrived home. I was in Rock Star mode, singing at the top of my lungs most of the way.

My plan of saving money on taxes by buying my truck in Alberta didn't work out. When I had my truck registered and licensed for BC, I didn't save any money at all. I should have researched this and got my facts straight before I did this. Oh well, live and learn.

I had a manual sunroof installed in my truck and installed custom-made seat covers that matched the color of my truck perfectly. It wasn't a fancy or elaborate vehicle, but I really liked it.

My truck came in handy right away. I bought a bunch of netting for $800 from a golf course in Kelowna that had closed their driving range. It was still in good condition and was more than enough for what I needed. I loaded a huge amount of this netting into the back of my truck and brought it over to my new driving range. I was one step closer to making my dream a reality.

I repaired all the holes in the netting that I could reach from the ground, then I rented a crane to repair the areas that were higher up. I was paying a guy to help me with this, and we were making good progress.

After we had been working on this project for a couple of months, the neighbor from the RV resort came over to talk with me. He wasted no time telling me he would sue Arnie and me if we reopened the driving range. He thought some of his farm animals might get hit by stray golf balls. I tried to assure him that I was making all the necessary repairs to avoid such a thing happening, but he didn't care about what I had to say or what my intentions were. I couldn't reason with this man. He owned a few llamas and alpacas, which are fairly large animals. Once I had all of the netting repaired, it would have been very unlikely that any of them would be struck by golf balls. If they did, I really don't think they would get injured. By the time a golf ball traveled the distance to reach one of these animals, it would lose most of its velocity and wouldn't be going fast enough to do any harm. The netting for my range would have met the height requirements for any standard driving range, and I didn't anticipate having this problem with the neighbor.

I couldn't believe that this guy watched me work on the range for two months before he decided to talk to me. Not only had I put a lot of time and effort into this project, I had also invested close to $5,000 of my own money. I wish he would have expressed his feelings as soon as he saw me fixing it. I also wish I had gone over and talked with him before I even started doing any work. I later found out that there seemed to be a vendetta between Arnie and this guy. Had I known this from the beginning, I would have talked with this guy first! When he threatened to sue, I pretty much knew my dream had been squashed. Arnie was in his 80s, and there was no way I was going to ask him to get involved in a lawsuit on my behalf. Arnie was a good man, and he really tried to help me out, but I knew he didn't want a lawsuit. If I owned the property the driving range was on, I would have hired a good lawyer and fought hard for my rights. There was an excellent chance of winning my case if it went to court.

As it was, Arnie and I mutually agreed that I couldn't continue with my quest. Having come so close then losing the opportunity to own and operate my own golf facility was a crushing blow.

HEAD GOLF PRO AGAIN

After my driving range plans were kyboshed, I had to move on. Almost immediately, I was hired as the head golf professional at the Michaelbrook Ranch Golf Club in Kelowna, an 18-hole mid-length course. It mainly has short par 3s and 4s. It was well-suited for beginners and high-handicap golfers. I didn't really care about this because I was a head pro again, which was very important to me at the time.

Dennis, the owner, interviewed me twice for the job. The first interview went well, and I left my resume and references with him. About a week later, he wanted to see me again. The first time we talked, I didn't say anything about my mental illness or what happened at Terrae Pines. Matt Cassidy was good enough to write a nice reference for me that didn't mention my manic episode at his golf course.

To start my second interview, Dennis said, "I talked to your last employer, Matt Cassidy."

My heart sank.

"He told me about your mental illness," he said.

My heart dropped to the floor. I thought I was totally screwed, but Dennis surprised me and said he was familiar with bipolar disorder. His wife was present during this meeting and as we talked, it seemed they were kind and caring. Most importantly to me, it seemed as if they both had empathy and an understanding toward people who were living with a mental illness. Dennis hired me as the head pro at their golf course, and I was very pleased and extremely fortunate. I had a new chance to get my career back on track. Another good thing was that I was to be paid $2,500/month, which was more than I got at Terrae Pines.

I started my new job around the middle of March when the course opened for the season. It wasn't very busy, but there were still several golfers who came and went during the day. I was familiarizing myself with my new surroundings and the other staff members. Dennis would come and go, but he didn't talk with me much. I was the only one working in the pro shop at the time, and it was totally bare. Dennis told me the remaining inventory from the previous season was in storage, and I was responsible for getting all of it out and stocking the pro shop.

On my second day of work, Chris Turton, the owner of the McCulloch Orchard Greens Golf Club, came into the pro shop. Chris's course was a mid-length, 9-hole course. He was looking for a head golf professional and asked me if I could recommend someone, but I didn't know anyone. I liked Chris right away. My first impression was that he was a lot more friendly and personable than Dennis was. I thought to myself, "Shit! I think I would rather work for this guy." But I quickly reminded myself that Dennis had hired me despite the fact that I had bipolar disorder, which I thought was monumental.

I ended up working overtime for the first three days and thought things were going fairly well. Unfortunately, I was making little progress with stocking the pro shop. Obviously, this was a top priority for me, but I felt I didn't have much of an opportunity to get this done. I had to collect green fees and help people. I didn't have a chance to get any inventory out of the storage room because I was on my own. There were a lot of things I had to do, and I had a lot of responsibility in general. I felt like I was under enormous pressure right from the beginning.

Halfway through my fourth day of work, Dennis came into the pro shop and fired me. I was shocked and didn't see this coming — it blindsided me. I could sense that Dennis was somewhat annoyed on a couple of occasions due to my lack of progress with stocking the pro shop, however, he didn't talk to me about it. Firing me after four days? I felt like he didn't give me much of a chance to prove myself. I may have set a record for the shortest term of employment for a CPGA pro! After Dennis fired me, I went into the small pro shop office to gather my composure. I sat down and put my head on the desk on the verge of tears. I couldn't believe it.

Amidst my devastation, I had a sudden jolt of inspiration. I would go straight to the McCulloch Orchard Greens Golf Club and talk with Chris about a job. Unfortunately, he had already hired someone, but another idea popped into my head. Maybe I could go around the Kelowna area trying to sell memberships and golf tournament packages for Chris' course. He didn't have to pay me a wage or salary, just ten percent of the revenue I generated. I made this proposal to Chris, and he accepted my offer. We hopped into a power cart and he gave me a tour of his golf course. I told him I had an upcoming trip to Alberta, and that I could get started as soon as I got back to Kelowna. He was just fine with this. We hit it off, and I was looking forward to this arrangement.

Looking back, my proposal — a spontaneous decision I didn't think through — was a little too optimistic. It was a good deal for Chris, but not for me. It didn't matter anyway. Due to circumstances surrounding my trip to Alberta, I was unable to work for Chris when I returned to Kelowna. I never saw him or talked with him again. He probably thought I was an irresponsible idiot. Unlike Dennis, Chris didn't know I had a mental illness.

So, another job bites the dust. In less than three months, I suffered three major career setbacks. I always wanted to work, and it wasn't for a lack of trying. I tried extremely hard to stay employed over the years, but things just didn't go my way.

My mom and I drove ten hours to Wetaskiwin to celebrate my Grandma Clark's ninety-second birthday with her. I'm so glad we did this because it would end up being her last birthday. She was doing very well and still living in her own home. I thought she had a good chance to make it to 100 years of age. Unfortunately, later that year Grandma fell and broke her hip. She was hospitalized, and she stopped eating. Grandma went downhill from there and passed away in the hospital. I loved her so much and miss her dearly.

A couple of days after the party I went manic again. At one point, I was in my grandma's basement by myself looking at pictures of all these people on the walls. Some pictures were of my grandpa, who had died in 1980. Grandpa Clark was a bank manager for CIBC for thirty-five years. There were pictures of his friends and associates, relatives and many others I didn't know. Like my grandpa, many of these people would have been deceased. After looking at these pictures for a while, something very strange happened. All of a sudden I wasn't alone anymore. I could sense the presence of other spirits/souls. I could feel their very powerful energy. It seemed like some of the people in the pictures had "come to life." I was sure one of these spirits would have "belonged" to Grandpa Clark, especially since he used to live in this house. I had no idea who the other spirits might be. I had seen TV programs where people declare that pictures can contain trace elements of a person's energy or spirit. I wonder if this supposed phenomenon is related to what I experienced. Regardless, the physical sensation I felt from this energy was undeniable.

At first, I was freaked out! But I soon realized that the spirits were friendly and would cause me no harm. In a sense, I was having some fun with this. I would take a few steps forward then collide with an invisible wall of energy that would cause me to stumble and fall backwards. I would go in a different direction and hit another wall of energy. Again, this force rocked my body and caused me to stumble around. I continued to try and walk around the basement and kept running into these spirits. I went from being scared to a state of amusement. I went back and forth, then side to side. It felt like I was doing a "jig" or some kind of crazy dance; it's hard to describe. It was extremely bizarre to say the least. This went on for about twenty minutes, then I went back upstairs.

My grandma, Mom and Auntie Joyce were sitting at the kitchen table. I didn't tell them about my experience in the basement and just joined in on their conversation. At first, everything was normal, but then I sensed the presence of the devil coming through Auntie Joyce. A couple of minutes later, she returned to normal, and the presence of the devil shifted to my mom. After another very brief period the devil left my mom and went into my grandma. The spirit of the devil kept transferring back and forth between these three ladies whom I loved very much. The sequence wasn't always the same, and the devil spirit didn't get into me. It was intense, and I didn't know what to do. Finally, I decided I had to get out of there, so I went for a walk by myself.

After a few blocks, I went into a convenience store. I heard some loud thumping noises coming from above the store. I was curious what it was, so I went to check it out. I left the store and found an entrance that led to the upper level of the building. I walked up the stairs and ended up in a large room. No wonder I heard those thumping noises from below, there was a large dance class practicing up there. The instructors were teaching their students — girls between the ages of 10-14. The parents, mostly the mothers, were sitting in chairs all around the perimeter of the dance floor proudly and anxiously watching their children. There was loud music playing and the room was full of people. I walked right in and sat in a vacant chair beside one of the mothers.

The lady I sat beside smiled at me right away. She seemed to be friendly. I noticed she had braces on her teeth. When she looked at me again a couple of minutes later, I sensed the presence of the devil coming from her. I thought to myself, "You son of a bitch, leave me alone!" But he didn't. He stayed right there beside me. It was like he was mocking me, teasing me. I didn't talk with this lady, but I decided to stay until everyone left so I could "protect" everyone from the devil. After some time, the staff were trying to get me to leave. I refused to go because the lady (and devil) were still there, and there were still several people in the room.

The next thing I knew, the cops were there. Someone had called them to get me out of there. I hadn't told anyone that I was sensing the presence of the devil in this lady, but my behavior was probably strange. I hadn't caused a big scene or anything. During the class, I just blended in with the parents and sat quietly in my chair watching the dancers.

The cops quickly figured out I was mentally ill. Anyway, I hadn't broken a law and there wasn't a psychiatric ward in Wetaskiwin, so they ended up driving me back to my grandma's house. One of the officers went inside the house to talk with my mom and make sure things were OK before they let me go.

Everything was OK for a while. Everyone was just "themselves" and there wasn't any "spirit" stuff going on.

Later, I had another strange experience. I was at the kitchen table again with my mom, Auntie Joyce and Grandma. We were having — what seemed to me — a telepathic conversation. At first, we were just talking with each other as normal. Then I could sense the spirits, not the devil, coming from within them. We communicated without talking. I felt like their spirits were testing me, and I sensed there was a hierarchy among the spirits. Some seemed to have a higher power (or ranking) than others. I don't know if these spirits were those of my mom, grandma and aunt, but it seemed as if more powerful and "higher up" spirits were "channeling" themselves through these ladies to communicate with me telepathically. Somehow, we understood each other on a non-verbal basis — an intense and amazing experience. In the end, I felt like I had passed their "tests." Mainly, I think they wanted to know if I was truly authentic. I think they concluded that I was. I hope so anyway!

I didn't see/sense spirits all the time during these manic episodes. They seemed to appear and disappear at their own will. It was very mysterious to say the least. Impossible to understand or explain.

At one point, I was in my grandma's garage and saw some tin foil on the shelf. This gave me a great idea. Tin foil is a conductor, and I could use it to try and make contact with the universe or maybe even aliens! I found an old baseball cap, wrapped some of the foil around it and went outside into the darkening evening. With my tin foil apparatus secured to my head I walked along the sidewalk, back and forth in front of my grandma's house for about fifteen minutes. I was quite excited about the potential possibilities. Unfortunately, I made no contact.

I didn't detect any paranormal activity at my grandma's house the next day, but things changed that evening when Satan made another appearance. Once again, I could sense his evil spirit coming through my mom, Grandma and Auntie Joyce. As usual, I could only sense his spirit in or through one person at a time. Then he would transfer from one individual to another. It always seemed to turn into a major battle between Satan and myself. After a very lengthy and difficult "duel," I'd had enough. I didn't know what to do, so I called the police to come over. I couldn't wait for the police to get there — I had to get out of that house immediately — so I took off running east on 47th Avenue. After just a few minutes, I saw a police car traveling west towards my grandma's house. It didn't have the siren or lights on, but it was moving very fast. I knew they were probably responding to my call. I stepped off the sidewalk onto the side of the road and waved my arms frantically to flag them down. They saw me and pulled over to where I was immediately. Two officers got out of the car. After talking with them for a while, I got into their car. The police didn't know what to do with me, so I asked them to take me to the local hospital. Then I changed my mind because I knew Satan would find me there too.

"TAKE ME TO JAIL"

Then I had another idea.

"I know! I think there's a warrant out for my arrest for assaulting a police officer. Maybe you could take me to jail!"

Obviously, I wasn't in my right state of mind at the time. Who "asks" to be taken to jail? Anyway, they checked, and sure enough there was a warrant for me. Off to jail I went. The warrant was issued because I missed my court date regarding my incident at Terrae Pines Golf Course the year before. There was a method to my madness: jail was the only place I thought I would feel safe from Satan. I thought the devil could harm me by using other people to get at me. So, I asked the police if they would put me in a cell by myself. They were nice enough to do so.

I don't know if these small-town cops had any prior experience with a full-blown manic, manic-depressive individual or not. If not, they were about to get initiated. I paced back and forth in my cell for hours at a time. I felt like a 2,000-pound raging bull. It turned out that being locked behind bars didn't make me very happy. There were five First Nations men in another cell. As it turned out, I didn't sense the presence of the devil in anyone while I was in jail, which was good. It was bad enough just being in there in the first place.

Later, I started thinking about Terri and how she broke my heart. I started singing Rod Stewart's "The First Cut is the Deepest" over and over — countless times — at the top of my lungs. It was about 2 a.m., and the First Nations guys kept yelling at me to shut up. They were trying to get some sleep. Being manic, I couldn't sleep at all. Every time they yelled at me, I yelled right back at them. I had an incredible amount of adrenalin surging through me, and my yelling was a great deal louder than theirs. As the "Dragon" (my Chinese astrology sign), I basically slayed them with my verbal assault. As I've said elsewhere, don't get a Dragon pissed off at you — especially a Gemini Dragon. To piss off a manic Gemini Dragon is asking for trouble.

They kept me in jail over the weekend while Mom contacted Rob Wachowich, a lawyer we knew in Edmonton. He came to Wetaskiwin on Monday morning to represent me in court. While taking me to the courthouse, the police handcuffed me to one of the First Nations prisoners, and the two of us were put in a small waiting room. Soon, a door opened and Rob was right there. I was so happy to see him! Rob talked to the judge on my behalf, and the judge set a court date in Morinville, Alberta, that fall to deal with my "assaulting a police officer" charge. For the time being, I was free to go.

It was a forty-five minute drive from Edmonton to Wetaskiwin, and Rob talked to the judge for less than five minutes. This cost me $500. I should have been a lawyer!

THE ALBERTA HOSPITAL

A day or two later, I ended up at the Wetaskiwin Hospital, and a doctor decided to send me to the Alberta Hospital by ambulance. I didn't really know what was going on as I was in a state of psychosis. I remember looking out the back window of the ambulance as we traveled down the highway. There were many vehicles behind us. It was daytime, but I noticed that almost all of them had their headlights on. This was normal, but I didn't think so at the time. I thought all the people driving these vehicles knew I was in the ambulance and put their lights on especially for me! I was like their leader, and they were all following me. What an incredible feeling! I don't remember if I thought I was Jesus Christ at the time or not. It's quite possible, as this happened many times over the years when I was in a manic episode.

Regardless, I was back at the Alberta Hospital — a huge psychiatric institution. Being a patient there was the worst experience of any of the times I spent in many different hospitals and psych wards. It was a nightmare. I was put in a co-ed, locked ICU ward. There were about fifteen of us in there, and most of these patients definitely belonged in this unit. They were extremely ill and/or quite aggressive. I was very ill as well, at least in the beginning. There was no doubt that I was put in there for a reason.

With the help of psychiatric medications, I had improved significantly after about the first ten days. I stopped being delusional. While I was doing better, it was still extremely difficult for me in that unit. Quite frankly, I didn't belong there. Once I had settled down and returned to my easygoing self again, I should have been moved to a different unit where the patients were less ill and less aggressive. I didn't feel safe in my unit. I was scared and worried about the other patients most of the time. It seemed like an eternity!

One time, this First Nations guy kneed me in the groin. On another occasion, his buddy narrowly missed my head when he threw an apple with a lot of force at me. The apple smashed into the wall and broke into several pieces. These guys were a constant threat. They were always looking at me like they hated me. For the six weeks I was there, I was worried they were going to attack me at any time. It didn't take long for them to find out that my mom was bringing me cigarettes, so they were constantly demanding that I give them my smokes. I usually did so they wouldn't beat me up over it.

These guys were the worst patients on my unit, but I didn't feel comfortable around the others either. While my mental health kept improving, it seemed the other patients basically stayed the same. I don't know what all their different mental illnesses were, but I think some of them had serious schizophrenia.

There was only one patient in there who I could associate with. He had bipolar disorder as well. Like me, I thought he was doing quite well, and he seemed to have a good temperament. He kept to himself, away from the others. I noticed that he spent a lot of time walking up and down the long hallway by himself. We met and got along well, so I often joined him on these walks. The two of us paced up and down that hallway, back and forth, back and forth, over and over countless times for several hours every day. We talked a bit. Mostly, I think we felt safe with each other. I also did a lot of walking in there by myself. There were only two ways to occupy my time: smoking and pacing. The time went by very slowly.

After I was in there for about two weeks, I was allowed to go on a few supervised walks on the grounds of the hospital. It was great to get outside and get some fresh air!

There was a lady in my unit who was very scraggly and unattractive. She appeared to be extremely mentally ill. One day, she walked right up to me and lifted up her dress. She wasn't wearing any undergarments. She totally exposed herself to me. It was disgusting! Her face came very close to mine as she did this. My automatic reaction was to push her away from me. As I did this, one of the male psych nurses ran over, put me in a choke hold and threw me to the floor. I could hardly breathe when he was choking me, and I got a bloody nose in the process. He clearly overreacted. I didn't deserve to be treated that way.

On another occasion, this same guy monitored me while I was having a shower. He sat on a stool right outside my shower stall while I showered. I thought this was strange and an invasion of my privacy. Patients may have been on "close observation" in the ICU, but this was going a little too far. I wasn't a threat to harm myself and didn't need to be watched that closely. How could I harm myself by having a shower even if I wanted to? As I got to know this nurse better, I discovered he was a real asshole. He shouldn't have been allowed to work in this profession.

Another time, I was watching TV with a big First Nations man sitting beside me. (What's with all these First Nations? Like I already said, I'm not prejudiced towards them.) This guy was friendlier than the other First Nations guys in my unit and didn't pose a threat to me. While we were watching TV, he turned to me and said, "They can see us, you know?"

I looked at him and said, "I know."

MY MOM'S UNCONDITIONAL LOVE

As always, my mom was right there for me. I ended up in that shit hole for six very long and excruciating weeks. She stayed at my grandma's house and made the hour-long drive to the hospital to visit me four or five times a week. She was the epitome of unconditional love. This never wavered with her. She was always steadfast and true. Mom was completely loyal, faithful and reliable.

It must have been extremely difficult for her to deal with me and my bipolar disorder. Having to see me when I was so ill and coming to see me in psychiatric wards so many times must have been very hard for her. Despite this, she never complained about it. Never! She had a tremendous amount of compassion and love for me. I was incredibly lucky to always have her support, and to have her as my mom.

I was always happy to get discharged from a psych ward, but the Alberta Hospital took first place. Being locked up in an ICU psych ward for six weeks is bad enough, but to feel threatened and in fear of other patients the whole time was a nightmare. I was so relieved to get out of there!

I went back to West Kelowna with my mom. I was extremely lucky that we had such a good relationship, and that I was able to live with her.

CHAPTER 17
1996
KELOWNA, BC

My manic episode was followed by a lengthy bout of depression, as usual. This time, I was depressed for about nine months. It was the same as always. Severely depressed 24/7 and thinking about suicide constantly. Not much fun.

I started feeling better around the beginning of March 1996. I purchased a membership at the Johnson Bentley Pool in West Kelowna, a nice facility. I got into a good routine of going there four times a week. I usually arrived about 7 a.m. and stayed until 8:30. I would start my morning with a Jacuzzi. There were usually other people in there at the same time, so I met a lot of people and had some interesting conversations. When I was depressed, I was very isolated and hardly socialized at all, so I really enjoyed being able to talk with people again. After a nice hot Jacuzzi, I would jump into the pool to cool off. I stayed in there for a while, then I would spend some time in the steam room. Then back into the pool to cool off again. I also liked spending time in what I called "the relaxing pool." This was a small, shallow pool where the water temperature was perfect to just lay in and relax! After this, I would go back into the Jacuzzi. I repeated this cycle a few times, had a shower and went home.

At home, mom would have breakfast ready for us. It was usually bacon or sausage and eggs, with hash browns or potatoes and toast. This always hit the spot after all my "exercise" at the pool.

This was my routine. It was really good for me, and I loved it! I did this for about 2½ months and things were going well for me. I think I may have even played a couple rounds of golf.

A few days before my birthday, I was feeling a little "too good," and I started to go manic. I was home with my mom and Gary on my birthday, and I was sensing the presence of the devil in my mom. I didn't see the devil in Gary at all, which is somewhat ironic because he should have been the one with the devil in him! My mom spent most of her time at the kitchen table, so I tried to avoid Satan as much as possible by staying in the TV room at the other end of the house.

For my first four manic episodes, I was picked up by the police and brought to hospitals whereby I ended up being "committed" as an involuntary patient to a psychiatric ward. After that, I think I became a little wiser. For most of the manic episodes since then, I knew when I needed to go to the psych ward, and I went voluntarily. There were even times when my family members didn't think I needed to be hospitalized just yet, but I insisted. I knew the psych ward would be the best place for me when I was in that state of mind.

This was one of those times. I knew I was destined for the McNair Unit (the psychiatric ward) at the Kelowna General Hospital, but I wanted to celebrate my thirty-second birthday first. I wanted to get all dressed up and go to Rose's Pub, one of the best in Kelowna, that night. There are usually a lot of really good-looking women there. I was single, and I wanted to look impressive, so I went on a bit of a "manic spending spree."

A "Manic Spending Spree"

My first stop at Orchard Park Mall was a jewelry store. I bought a gold bracelet and a gold chain that cost about $800. I paid cash out of about $2,000 I had in my pocket. I tipped the manager $60 to buy some drinks for her and the other female employees after work. She shouldn't have accepted this money, but she did. I was acting like a high roller, flashing around this big wad of cash for them to see.

After that, I wanted to buy a new suit and tie. The jewelry store manager recommended someone in the mall, so I asked her to call this guy and let him know I was on my way. My demeanor was like a VIP or some kind of big shot. However, an extremely friendly one! At the suit store, two guys looked after me. They treated me as if I was really someone important. They measured me, fitted me and equipped me with everything I needed. What great service! My new suit, tie, shirt, belt and dress socks cost about $500. Again, I paid with cash. I tried to tip the manager $20, but he was very adamant that he wouldn't accept this money from me. He obviously had better morals than the jewelry store manager.

My last stop at the mall was at a florist. I bought a dozen long-stemmed red roses and a nice glass vase to keep them in for $60 cash. I didn't offer a tip this time. My plan was to take these roses to Rose's Pub that night and give them out to the ladies.

Mom was in the kitchen getting dinner ready when I got home. I could still sense the presence of the devil in her, but Gary seemed normal. I decided to stay in the TV room away from Mom. An NHL playoff game was on, and the camera panned to famous golf icon Jack Nicklaus in the crowd. The broadcaster said it was the first hockey game he had ever attended. At the same time, I thought I was Jesus Christ and that everyone I was watching on TV could literally see me! Incredible! It became clear that Jack Nicklaus was there because of me. He could see me (along with all the others at the hockey game) and be a part of witnessing the return of Christ! What a great feeling this was!

I have had this sensation many times, but not always about being Jesus Christ. My experiences of this type have resulted in a diagnosis of "delusional, psychotic and/or relating to a state of psychosis" from psychiatrists. Most people would agree with this. Looking at this phenomenon more objectively, I think it might not be so crazy after all. There may be some logic to it. I don't think anyone on TV could actually see me with their own eyes as I was watching them from my own living room — that is delusional. But people like myself "sense" that people on TV can "see us," which likely means we are sensing their energy — "invisible energy" that is part of the collective consciousness of human beings and the universe as a whole. This "transfer" of energy might correlate with a higher dimension and/or realm of existence. It was very clear to me that when I was having these experiences, I was always watching live TV.

In July 2015, I had a discussion with my psychiatrist, Dr. Diaz, about this topic. When I told him my experiences were with "live TV," he said, "real time!" It was like this made sense to him, and he had experienced an "ah-ha" moment. Maybe there is a scientific link with quantum physics? Could people's "energy" from live TV programs be transmitted through TVs by electromagnetic waves of energy? Many psychics can do readings from thousands of miles away and over the telephone. If this is possible, why couldn't someone's energy come through a TV?

When I was in a state of mania, I had increased sensitivity and enhanced "psychic" awareness. I may have been tuned into a higher "frequency" or vibration of this energy. I think I was in an altered state of consciousness. It felt like my mind was crystal clear every time I had this experience.

While I was watching the hockey game, I changed the channel to a live basketball game, and I received the same sensation. It seemed like some of the players and others at the game could "see" me. Then something new happened. I had a very strong sense of the devil's spirit come through Dennis Rodman and right to me. I actually felt this energy. It really startled me! I thought it was interesting that this particular person was involved. Dennis was a superstar and notorious "bad boy" for the Chicago Bulls at the time. I'm not saying he was evil, but he had a "devilish" side to him. I put the hockey game back on again and enjoyed a BBQ steak dinner while I watched the game and watched them watching me.

Then it was time to get ready for my big night out, so I showered and got dressed. I looked pretty dapper in my new outfit, and Gary helped with my tie. To this day, I still don't know how to tie a tie. I only wore one on very rare occasions, and just never learned how to do it.

Gary drove me to Rose's Pub in my truck and dropped me off about 9 p.m. I had the dozen long-stemmed roses with me so I could give them to the best looking women there — hand out "roses at Rose's." Before I went in, I changed my mind and told Gary that most of the best looking women are bitches and don't deserve a rose. I told him to keep the roses in my truck so I could give them to the nicest nurses at the hospital when he took me there later. The nurses looks wouldn't be a factor. I told Gary to pick me up right in front of the pub at exactly 12:01 a.m., immediately after my birthday was officially over. I promised him I would be outside and would meet him there at this exact time. From there, he would drive me straight to the Kelowna General Hospital.

Rose's was packed, but I was able to get a seat at the bar and order a club soda and orange juice. Each one cost $2.50, and I gave the bartender $5 and said keep the change — generous tips for such a low-cost beverage. When I ordered my last one for the night, I gave the bartender a $100 bill and told him to keep the change. He gave me an odd look and said, "Are you sure?" I told him I was sure. There was a large tip jar on the bar counter, and I assumed all the bartenders (and possibly the waitresses) would be dividing the money amongst themselves at the end of the night. I told the bartender who was serving me to put my $100 bill into the tip jar so it could be shared with the others, so he did. I was far from being a wealthy person. Giving a $100 tip was stupid of me, but I was totally manic at the time and had lost my insight and common sense.

I had about $2,000 on me at Rose's. Every time I paid for my drink I pulled this big wad of cash out of my pocket and made sure that some of the $100 bills were visible — it was my "flash" money. I was also flashing my diamond rings and new gold bracelet to impress the ladies. I wanted them to notice me and think I was a high roller or someone important.

My strategy wasn't working, so I decided to go to the pool tables where some guys and girls were playing pool. I watched them for a while. A girl playfully tugged on my tie and told me to loosen it and "relax." I said, "I am relaxed!" and kept my tie secured. Nothing developed out of this scenario. I didn't even have a conversation with her or any other females there. My big night turned out to be uneventful with the ladies.

I did see an acquaintance named Brian there. I had met him at Rose's on a couple of previous occasions, and he seemed like a pretty good guy. I told Brian I would let him in on a secret. I told him that I was Jesus. He didn't say anything. He just looked at me with a sad look in his eyes. I could sense his compassion. He must have realized I was mentally ill, and he handled this situation very well. He didn't try to discredit my claim and didn't argue against it.

Dealing with someone who is mentally ill (and perhaps delusional) is like dealing with someone who is really drunk and is very difficult to communicate with or to reason with. It's best not to argue with them or go against what they're saying because it may antagonize them. A good response in these situations from the "sane" person is to simply say, "oh yeah" and leave it at that. Silence is good too — just don't say anything. Listen to what they're saying, then let it slide.

I was mainly chain-smoking menthols and hanging out with Brian. Each time I had one, I offered one to him saying they were like candies. He couldn't quite keep up with my pace. Brian was the only person there whom I told I was Jesus Christ. I wasn't acting strange or mentally ill, so I just blended in with the other patrons. Overall, I had a pretty good time.

At exactly 12:01 a.m., I left the pub. As planned, Gary was parked right in front of Rose's and had my roses with him. He drove me straight to the hospital. We parked and went in. I was carrying my vase containing the dozen long-stemmed red roses. I went to the registration desk at the emergency ward, and Gary stayed in the waiting room. The lady at the desk asked if she could help me and, pointing at Gary, I said my brother was acting very strange and that he was mentally ill. I figured he should be admitted to the psychiatric ward. Gary couldn't hear everything I was saying, but he knew I was up to something. Plus, he could be a little paranoid as well. He looked like he was going to hightail it out of there! I was very convincing, and I looked credible in my suit and tie. Gary was wearing cut-off jeans and a T-shirt.

I told her I was just joking, and that I was there for myself. I told her I needed a shot.

"A shot of what?" she asked.

"Tequila!" I said with a grin. I thought that was kind of funny at the time, but she didn't laugh at my remark.

It was time to get serious with her. I informed her that I had manic depression, and that I needed to get a shot of Haldol and Cogentin. I made it very clear that I had to be admitted into the McNair Unit. I was assessed in the emergency ward while giving roses to the nurses. It didn't matter to me what they looked like — older, younger, attractive, unattractive, or whatever — I gave one to the nurses who seemed friendly. This was the vast majority of them. The nurses seemed quite surprised and very appreciative.

My assessment concluded with the fact that I needed to be admitted into McNair. Luckily there was a bed available, and I was taken straight there by the hospital staff. I still had a few roses with me, and I gave them to the female psych nurses who treated me well. A psych nurse talked with me for a while and asked me some questions. One of her questions was, "Are you hearing voices?" My answer was "Yes, yours and mine."

After this, she escorted me to my room. As it was about 2:00 a.m., my roommates and everyone else on the ward were sleeping. It had been a long and busy day, but I wasn't tired. I usually only slept for a few hours a night when I was manic. The psych nurses wanted me to go to bed right away, but I didn't want to. Why would I? I was wide awake! All I wanted to do was to go to the smoke room and stay there until I was ready for bed. I wouldn't disturb any of the patients or the staff. I would be so quiet. Despite this, the nurses were adamant, so I proposed a compromise. I said if they gave me some Ativan to help me sleep, I would go to bed soon, so they did. I had a couple of cigarettes and within thirty minutes I was in bed sound asleep.

"HELLO, *KELOWNA DAILY COURIER?* THIS IS JESUS CHRIST"

A few days later, I made an interesting phone call to the *Kelowna Daily Courier*, one of Kelowna's main newspapers. A girl answered, and I told her I had the most incredible story. I said I needed to speak with the top person at their newspaper, and I wouldn't discuss this with anyone else. She put me on hold.

A couple of minutes later, a man got on the phone. I forget his name, but I think he was the head honcho. I told him to "Stop the presses!" because I had the greatest story his newspaper would ever print.

"I know this is really hard to believe," I said, "but you are talking with Jesus Christ right now. I have returned. I am calling you from the McNair Unit at the Kelowna General Hospital. This is the psychiatric ward, but I'm not crazy. Far from it. In this lifetime, my name is Donald Clark Walin. I was born on June 7, 1964. I am thirty-two years old. In my past life, I was Jesus Christ. I understand how crazy this must sound to you."

I spoke with this gentleman for at least twenty minutes. He was great and listened to everything I said. He didn't tell me I was insane or say anything derogatory. He handled this situation extremely well. Nearing the end of our conversation, he very politely told me that they couldn't do any stories from the hospital. Looking back, I think it may have been more accurate to say that they couldn't report on stories from psychiatric patients on psych wards. Regardless, I told the man that I really appreciated him listening to my story. I didn't pursue the matter any further.

One night I was looking for something to watch on TV after midnight when I tuned into *David Letterman*. When I was channel surfing, all of the TV programs were normal, but Letterman's was different. Dave and his guests could "see" me! It was just like what I had experienced at my mom's house when I was watching the hockey and basketball games. Over the years, I had this sensation many times from several locations. The TV programs that gave me this feeling were always live broadcasts — sporting events, talk shows and the news. I learned which programs this would happen on and tune in. Instantly, whoever was on TV could "see" me. Often it also seemed like they were talking about me. This is even harder for me to describe. After giving this a lot of thought, I will try to explain what this "experience" was like for me.

First of all, it was never a "paranoid" delusion, meaning I didn't get into a state of paranoia when this happened. It always gave me a good, positive feeling. The people on the TV "talked about me" in an indirect way, and I kind of had to "read between the lines." It was like they were acknowledging my presence. I think the only people who could really understand what this sensation is like are those who have experienced it. Many people who have bipolar disorder and schizophrenia have these experiences, which makes me think there's something to it. It always happened when I was manic and in an altered state of consciousness. Does this interconnect the realms of quantum physics and metaphysics? When it happens, it seems so real! If it is just a delusion, I would like to know what the commonalities are in the others who have experienced this. What I can say for sure is that it's very cool when it happens! Anytime I tuned into *Letterman*, I knew I would be an integral part of his program. I made a "guest appearance" on his show many times. One time when I was watching, I saw one of the funniest things I have ever seen. I was manic at the time, so my sense of humor was tenfold. I still think it's absolutely hilarious whenever I think about it in my "normal" state of mind.

It was in the mid 1990s, and it was Letterman's birthday. He had the famous actress Drew Barrymore as a guest on his show. Very suddenly, Drew jumped up onto Dave's desk in front of him, lifted her shirt and flashed her breasts at him. I don't think she was wearing a bra. The perfect birthday present! The funniest thing was Dave's reaction. The look on his face was priceless. He clearly wasn't expecting it. Drew was younger then and was maybe a bit of a free spirit at the time. From what I could tell, Dave would have been the only one who saw her breasts. I think that anyone who doesn't think this is funny may be a prude. It was a harmless act. Dave was quite surprised at her gesture, but I think he also found it to be very humorous.

Prior to going manic, I made plans for another trip to Houston, Texas. My flight was booked and paid for, and I was really looking forward to going there again. My psychiatrist at the time was Dr. Catherine McKercher in Kelowna. My usual five- to six-week stay in the psych ward would have forced me to cancel my trip. After only ten days in McNair, I was no longer delusional. I stopped thinking I was Jesus Christ and was no longer seeing the devil in people. I could watch TV without thinking that the people could see me or were talking about me. I had been administered an extremely powerful antipsychotic medication called Haldol. Due to my apparent quick recovery and some smooth talking, I convinced Dr. McKercher to discharge me after ten days. It was a hasty decision. In the meantime, it was "Houston, here I come!"

In Houston, my brother, Jim, was a member at a private golf course named Baywood Country Club, an 18-hole track we played one day. He introduced me to Donnie St. Germain, the PGA Head Golf Professional there at the time. Donnie and I hit it off immediately. He was personable, outgoing, hospitable and generous. He didn't charge me anything for my round of golf or for range balls (probably because I had my CPGA pro card). He made me feel very welcome and told me I could play or practice there as much as I wanted to.

COLONEL BLAINE HAMMOND - ASTRONAUT

A week or so later, I had one of the greatest thrills and honors of my life. I had the good fortune to meet and play golf with a real astronaut! Holy shit! Jim was playing in the Men's Club Championship at Baywood, a 36-hole, two-day event. I didn't watch him play the first day, but he shot a 75 — good enough to put him in one of the final groups in the Championship Flight for the final round. I went with him on the final day of the tournament as his "caddy." It was a beautiful day for golf. I didn't have to carry his clubs because everyone in his group used power carts, so I became more of a chauffeur, which was fine with me. Obviously, Jim knew his course much better than I did. As a result, I didn't get too involved with club selection or reading greens. I couldn't help a lot with "course management" and strategy, as I had only played this course one time. More than anything, I was there for moral support.

Unfortunately, Jim didn't play well in the final round. He had one really bad hole — a 185 yard, par 3 — on the back nine that really hurt his score. There was water between the tee box and the green, and Jim hit four balls into the water from the tee and ended up with a 12 on the hole. He was totally out of contention after that.

The wife of one of the guys in Jim's group was riding around on a power cart with her husband. She was friendly, and we started talking after the first few holes. She told me her husband was an astronaut! I was quite excited about this, but I had to contain myself. I wanted to talk with him and ask him all kinds of questions, but I knew I shouldn't while he was competing for the championship. I wanted to let him focus and concentrate on his game and hope I might get a chance to talk with him for a little while afterward. I don't know what he shot in the first round, but I think his score must have been the same or close to Jim's since they were paired together for the final round. He shot significantly lower than Jim in the final round. He was friendly, and we chatted a bit throughout the 18 holes.

His name was Colonel Blaine Hammond, and he was affiliated with the United States Air Force (USAF) and the National Aeronautics and Space Administration (NASA). He went by "Blaine." After the guys finished their round, Blaine decided to play another 9 holes with his wife, so Jim and I joined them. Luckily, I had my clubs in the trunk of Jim's car at the golf course. I only remember two things about those 9 holes. The first thing is that I "cold topped" my drive on the 1st hole and it only went about 125 yards. I was so embarrassed! They gave me a "mulligan." I also made a putt from about twenty-five feet on the 9th hole for a birdie, which was a good way to finish. I really enjoyed playing golf with Blaine and his wife. He was a good player. He had a good temperament for the game and was a real gentleman.

After our round, we went into the clubhouse and had a couple of drinks. Jim and I took the opportunity to ask Blaine about being an astronaut, and he was fantastic about sharing some of his knowledge and expertise with us. It was incredibly interesting and fascinating. Blaine told us that his shuttle traveled through space at 124,000 miles per hour. I think he said it only took about six hours to orbit the Earth. What a trip that would be!

I have been fortunate to meet a lot of very nice and interesting people through the great game of golf, but Blaine takes the cake! Playing golf and socializing with Colonel Hammond was a tremendous honor for me, and I have great respect for this man. I only met him once, but we spent most of the day together, and I will cherish the memories of that day forever. He was an extremely intelligent and likeable guy. Pardon the pun, but for an astronaut, he was a real "down-to-earth" guy. I have one of his business cards with the NASA logo on it. Blaine autographed the back of it for me, and he wrote his space shuttle number on it. I have a vast array of business cards, but this one is my favorite.

When I was back home in Canada, Jim brought two of Blaine's "mission patches" to me as souvenirs. One has two astronauts holding on to the outside of a shuttle in space. Blaine's last name is on there along with the last names of five other astronauts (Helms, Lee, Linenger, Meade and Richards). The other one has a shuttle in space. This one has Blaine's name on it and the last names of six other astronauts (Bluford, Coats, Harbaugh, Hieb, McMonagle and Veach). They're replicas that Colonel Hammond and the other astronauts may have had sewn on their spacesuits, hats or other types of clothing. I believe these two mission patches represent two of Colonel Hammond's space missions. It was incredibly kind of him to give these items to me, especially since we only knew each other for that one day! I really hope I can see or talk with him again someday so I can express my gratitude for his generosity and thoughtfulness. I also have some good pictures of the Colonel and I on the golf course that day.

MY DAD VISITED ME — THIRTEEN YEARS AFTER HE DIED!

One afternoon around two, I was at Jim's place by myself. I had a shower and started to shave when I suddenly sensed an intense presence. It startled me so much that I cut myself shaving. Whatever it was had my full attention. When I left the bathroom, I could still sense it coming from upstairs — I could feel it. It was very powerful. Before long, I was communicating with this presence (energy). I was completely shocked when I found out that the "presence" was my dad, who had died thirteen years earlier. I know it was my dad. Somehow, I was able to have a telepathic conversation with him. I didn't see him or hear his voice. As a matter of fact, I was really hoping he wouldn't appear to me physically. I was literally saying out loud, "Dad, I know you are here, but you are freaking me out right now. Please don't show yourself to me, and please don't talk to me!" By using telepathy, my dad told me the following: "I love you, son. And I am proud of you. I'm still with you and watching out over you."

It was an incredible experience. I thought my dad's choice of words was remarkable as well. Unfortunately, we didn't have a very good relationship when he was alive because he was moody and had a bad temper, but he was a good man. We were very different people. I have always been a communicator whereas Dad was not. It was hard for him to express his feelings. He wasn't an "I love you" kind of guy. I never heard him say these words even to my mom, whom I know he loved very much. It was quite profound when he said, "I love you, son."

This "spiritual" communication between my dad and I lasted for about ten minutes. By this time, I was bawling and weeping uncontrollably. It was by far the hardest I had ever cried in my life. It had a huge impact on me. I went downstairs and called Jim at work. I was so emotional that I could barely talk. I tried to tell him what had just happened, but he probably thought I was going manic or losing my mind. He told me to stay there and that he would come home right away.

"Forget it!" I said. "I'm out of here! I will meet you at The Cross-Eyed Seagull."

It was a short walk, and I arrived at the pub first. Up to that point, I hadn't drunk any alcohol for about two years. After what I had been through at Jim's place, it would have been easy for me to end that streak and start drinking again, but I didn't. Somehow, I stayed strong enough to stay away from the booze at a time when I was really tested. Instead, I ordered a large glass of club soda and orange juice and smoked a couple of cigarettes. I was just trying to collect myself. I was there for about ten minutes when Jim arrived. We left the pub right away, and I spent the rest of the afternoon with him while he did some work errands. The remainder of that day and the evening was uneventful, which was just fine with me. I'd had enough excitement for one day.

A couple of days later, I played golf with my buddy Tex. He took me to a private club in Houston called Bay Oaks Country Club and introduced me to the head pro, Ken MacDonald. Ken told us that if we wanted a beer or anything to eat to just put it on his tab. He must have really liked Steve. Maybe part of it was good old Southern hospitality. Regardless, I was impressed with Ken's kindness and generosity. As much as we appreciated his offer, we didn't put anything on his tab. Ken didn't charge me to play golf, and he gave me a good deal on a golf shirt in his pro shop. I enjoyed playing with Tex, the former Canadian Tour player. We played about fifteen holes but didn't finish the rest of our round due to rain.

Donnie St. Germain was involved with a magnet network marketing program. These magnets were for therapeutic use and were supposed to improve circulation in the body and alleviate pain. I already had a previous interest in magnets but had never tried one. I bought one from Donnie and started using it for my bad back right away. The one I had was fairly large — about 7" x 4" and 1/8" thick. I placed it in the middle of my lower back and held it in place with a tensor bandage. The pain in my back seemed to diminish a bit when I was using it, so it didn't take much convincing for Donnie to get me interested in the program he was involved with; I pretty much jumped on board right away. I was familiar with network marketing and liked its concept. I also thought the magnets had great potential to help a lot of people. There are millions of golfers with bad backs and other ailments who could use this product, and that's just the golfers; any athlete could benefit from them!

Donnie took me to a magnet network marketing conference at a Hilton Hotel. There were about three hundred people there. At the beginning of the conference, he told the main speaker (a lady) that I had a bad back. This lady asked if she could put a magnet on my back (I wasn't wearing the one I had recently bought). She said she would check with me in about an hour to see how things were going. After an hour, she asked me from the stage, "How does it feel?"

"It feels like I have to fart!" I said.

"Do you want to go outside to do that?" she asked.

I didn't say anything else. I just sat in my seat until the presentation was over. Gas was building up inside of me. I thought the magnet I was wearing was responsible for this feeling, and I was just being honest. Maybe a little too honest. The worst thing was that I must have totally embarrassed Donnie. The poor guy was sitting right beside me. A lot of people there would have heard what I said. Sorry Donnie! Normally, I wouldn't say something stupid like that in front of three hundred people. I didn't know that I was back in the early stages of mania again. My "filter" was becoming less filtered.

After the presentation was over, a lady involved with the conference wanted to use me for a demonstration with another magnet. I eagerly complied. She had me lay down on my stomach on a type of massage table. She had a magnetic device that was shaped like a baker's rolling pin, and she rolled this magnet up and down my back for a while. After just a couple of minutes, I started getting back spasms that rapidly got worse. The pain was intense. It hurt like hell. Every time I had a spasm, my whole body lifted about six inches off the table. The lady asked me if I wanted her to stop, and I said, "No, keep going." There were a lot of people watching this. Donnie was right beside me and kept asking me if I was OK. I tried to assure him I was, but it probably looked like I was in serious distress. This demonstration didn't bode well for magnets, but I don't think they were responsible for my back spasms. The pressure being applied from the rolling pin triggered the spasms. I've had back spasms (especially when I was manic) when nothing was touching me at all.

After this spectacle, I was talking with another lady and told her I had bipolar disorder. She told me she was a "healer" and asked if she could check something with me. I gave her my permission. She felt around my head with her hands. After she examined me, she told me that I was "low on salt."

One beautiful day, I was at my favorite place in Houston, the Clear Lake Beach Club. As always, the place was packed, and the women flounced around in their bikinis — there was "eye candy" all over the place. Normally, I would have been in there like a dirty shirt, but I wasn't on this day. I had put on some weight in my stomach because of certain psychiatric medications I was taking, and I had a big belly. I was pretty trim for my whole life before this, so my new body was shocking, and I had zero confidence with the ladies, especially the hot ones. I didn't even bother trying. I just sat on the patio watching the action. This was very frustrating and humbling, but I was still enjoying myself.

I was talking with James, a guy I'd met a couple of times at the Beach Club, and we decided to go to The Turtle Club. It was packed, and we shared a table with a few girls on the upper deck. After a couple of hours at this pub, I'd had enough and was ready to go home. James was drunk and wanted me to stay there with him and these girls. If I was drinking, I'm sure I would have stayed, but I was completely sober, which is a different story — kinda boring. James said that if I waited awhile, he would give me a ride home. He almost got us into a car accident on the way to The Turtle Club, so there was no way in hell I was going to be a passenger after another two hours of steady drinking. I went downstairs to the main bar and asked them to call a cab for me and said goodbye to the group of people I was with. The waitress who came to get me for my taxi escorted me arm in arm from the upper level, down the stairs, through the extremely busy main level bar area, right to the main entrance. I thought "Wow, how's that for service!" When we were going through the crowd of people, I felt like everyone was watching me — more like "the spirits" of all these people were watching me. I felt like I was very special, and that they all knew who I was. It was a great feeling!

I went outside and saw an elderly man walking towards me using a cane. He was my taxi driver, and there was something unique about him. As he was driving me home, I realized why he was so unique. He wasn't an ordinary taxi driver. He was God! God was giving me a ride home! I must have sensed God's presence coming through the old man. As always, it was a great feeling to experience this sensation. We stopped at Burger King on the way home, and I bought some onion rings for God and a burger for myself.

Within the next couple of days, I started to see the devil in people again. Jim called Dr. McKercher in Kelowna for some advice, and she told him to take me to the hospital and get a shot of Haldol and Cogentin. I was fully cooperative, and it seemed to settle me down, so I went back to Jim's place and slept for a while. Most importantly, I stopped seeing the devil.

I was very lucky I didn't get hospitalized in Houston. I could have ended up in a psychiatric facility there, which would have been a financial catastrophe. I had basic travel insurance for my trip to the United States, but I don't think my insurance would have covered any hospitalization concerning my bipolar disorder. For one thing, it was a "pre-existing" condition. As it was, the one needle I had as an outpatient cost me $80 US. Being hospitalized and receiving further treatment probably would have cost me a fortune.

Because of the state I was in, my return flight to Kelowna was changed to get me back there as soon as possible. On the first leg of my flight from Houston to Calgary, I started thinking about the "healer" lady who told me I was "low on salt." The flight attendants were giving salty peanuts to passengers. I had some, and I wanted more and more. Being manic, I got a little carried away. I had it in my head that I needed to increase the amount of salt in my body. I kept asking the flight attendants for "More peanuts, please!"

On my flight from Calgary to Kelowna, which only takes about fifty minutes, I sat beside a nice senior lady. I talked her ear off the whole way.

She probably couldn't wait to get off that plane! Fortunately, I made it home safe and sound.

I kept in touch with Donnie St. Germain and thought I was going to become very wealthy from the magnet network marketing deal. At first, I was going to be the Kelowna representative. Then I wanted to be in charge of western Canada. After that, I would be the top guy for all of Canada! My mania caused my grandiose thinking. I told Donnie I wanted to talk with the very top guy of this program, and he was reluctant at first. I was persistent, and he finally relented and gave me the name and phone number of a man in Florida. By the time I called this guy, my mania had escalated and I thought I was Jesus again, which is who I introduced myself as. The poor guy must have thought I was a complete lunatic! He must have also wondered why in the hell Donnie gave me his name and phone number. Needless to say, the man didn't offer me any kind of business proposal. My main concern is for any embarrassment I caused Donnie. Sorry again Donnie!

Thinking I was Jesus and seeing the devil in people meant I had to go back to the psych ward. I was starting to figure this out, so I voluntarily admitted myself again.

For the first few weeks, I was promoting magnets and letting other patients try using the magnet I had. In general, most people were quite receptive, and I was getting a lot of positive feedback. Gradually, my mania — and my enthusiasm regarding magnets and the whole magnet network marketing program — diminished. Donnie must have been a pretty good guy. Somehow, (probably from Jim) he found out I was in the psychiatric ward. He phoned me when I was in there because he was so concerned about me. I couldn't believe it! It meant a lot because we only met each other a few times.

I was in McNair for about five weeks, stabilized for a brief period, then went back into a state of severe depression for about eight months. I could barely function. In the end, I didn't do anything with the magnets.

CHAPTER 18
1997
COMMUNITY HEALTH

"PEPTALK" PEER SUPPORT GROUP

I started to feel better in May 1997 and became involved with a volunteer organization in Kelowna called "Peptalk" — people with a mental illness helping others with a mental illness. I ended up as one of Peptalk's volunteers over the course of several years when I was well enough to do so. There was usually a group of about ten volunteers. We had a program coordinator, and we all had to have special training in order to do our jobs properly. The active volunteers were all doing well and were stable when working with others. The coordinator tried to match us up with someone who had the same mental illness as we did and/or with someone they thought would be the best match for each other. We would get together with someone once or twice a week for an hour or two each time. Each individual was allowed up to ten visits with us. Usually, we only had a couple of "clients" at a time. A volunteer and their client would decide between themselves which activity they wanted to do during these sessions. One of the most common things was to simply get together at a coffee shop for a visit.

Anyone can acquire a mental illness. One of my clients was a doctor who owned his own practice in Kelowna. He had been diagnosed with bipolar disorder, had recently been in a severely depressed episode and had tried to commit suicide. He was in the psychiatric ward in a nearby city and was ready to be discharged. The Peptalk coordinator thought that the doctor and I would be a good match, so she asked if I could pick him up and give him a ride home. She also thought we could get to know each other and spend some time together afterward. I was more than happy to do so. I felt like this was a privilege, and I was grateful for this opportunity.

I met him at the psychiatric ward and drove him home. We had lunch and talked for a couple of hours about our bipolar commonality. He showed me several boxes of wine he had purchased when he was on a manic high. He expressed concerns about being off work indefinitely and how he was going to be able to pay his mortgage and other bills. I tried to assure him that everything would be OK.

Over the next two weeks we talked a lot. He would say he wanted to get together, then would come up with an excuse as to why he couldn't. He did this a few times, and each time he called, he sounded worse. He was upset and on the verge of crying at times. He seemed quite unstable to me. I was very concerned about him and felt the need to intervene somewhat. I couldn't discuss this with my Peptalk program coordinator, as this happened on a weekend. I didn't know if he had been seeing a psychiatrist, so I couldn't express my concerns to him or her. I decided to call the psychiatric emergency phone number at the hospital — supposedly a 24/7 service. No one answered! I had to leave a message on the answering machine. I couldn't believe it! I kept trying with the same result every time.

About two hours later, someone finally returned my call. It was one of the psych nurses on the McNair Unit whom I knew quite well. I told him about my client and that the matter needed to be taken very seriously. He just blew me off and said not to worry about it. I had the impression he wasn't even going to look into this. I thought he was much too nonchalant and didn't seem to care. What the hell was this guy doing working a 24/7 Emergency Crisis Line?

I informed the Peptalk coordinator about it on Monday and left a few messages for the doctor after that, but he didn't return my calls. We have had no contact since. I have checked our local directory for his name, and it's not listed there. I have thought about him many times over the years, always hoping that he was OK.

The coordinator called me one time to see if I would go to McNair and spend some time with an elderly lady who was very depressed. I agreed. The lady was in her 70s and was really nice, but it was obvious that she was withdrawn and quiet. She didn't talk much. I could tell she was depressed. Her husband had died two years earlier, which likely had a lot to do with her mental state. The poor lady had a broken heart. It turned out I had met her husband several times at the pool. I didn't know him well, but he was always friendly when I ran into him there. He was an avid golfer.

This couple had a famous son, but I won't say their names because of confidentiality reasons. He was a retired NHL hockey player. His mom didn't say much about her son, if anything at all. She didn't tell me about this connection, but I figured this out by myself when I found out what her name was. She did show me a Stanley cup ring of her son's, which she had on her neck chain.

I went to the McNair Unit twice to do my small part in helping her.

HOME SUPPORT WORKERS

In 1996, I started seeing a "home support worker" who was working in the mental-health field. I was becoming very isolated when I was depressed and didn't have a social life at all. My nurse and case worker, Helen Barnick, at the Canadian Mental Health Association (CMHA) in Kelowna, thought this would be good for me and made the necessary arrangements. I didn't want to do this at first, then I decided to give it a try. I'm really glad I did! Some of the home support worker's duties were similar to the duties of the Peptalk volunteers. They visited their clients at home or went for a coffee or a walk together. These are just a few examples.

I ended up having a few different home support workers. I thought the first one was nice, but for some reason I didn't have her for very long. The second one's name was Rene. She was an Austrian lady. She had a good sense of humor and was a good person. Around the end of May 1997, Rene and I were sitting at a picnic table by the lake. It was a beautiful, warm and sunny day. We were having a good conversation and enjoying some laughs. Everything was "normal," including my mood state. In a split second, things changed dramatically. Something came from or through Rene and zapped me. It felt like I had been struck by a mini lightning bolt. This sensation I had was very powerful and extremely intense. It jolted me. It seemed to come through Rene's eyes, and I instantly recognized what it was: the fucking devil again! As usual, I wasn't expecting his arrival, so it scared the shit out of me!

I said, "Sorry, Rene, I got to go!"

I ran to my truck and took off without looking back. She had no idea why I acted like that, but I explained it to her later.

A few days later, I was visiting my friend Mary in West Kelowna. It was about 8 p.m., and I was going manic. I was acting strange, and I sensed the presence of the devil coming from the other end of her home. Mary called her friend Ursula, who also had bipolar disorder, to come over. I didn't sense the devil in either of them, so I wanted to protect them. They stayed in the kitchen while I stayed in the living room by myself. Without my knowing it, Mary called the police. I was sitting on the couch with my feet up on the coffee table, and the next thing I knew there were two cops standing in front of me. One male and one female. The male cop looked young to me. At this point, I was extremely intense. The female cop started tickling my feet to get me to relax a bit. She was nice and seemed to know how to handle the situation properly. While she talked with me, the male cop didn't say anything. She was older than him and probably had more experience dealing with people who are mentally ill. She told me her name was "Buzz."

The officers came to Mary's house in two cop cars. I agreed to go to the hospital if I could go with Buzz in her car. My wish was granted. I was fully cooperative and wasn't handcuffed during this episode. Sitting in the back seat of the cop car, I told Buzz I needed to have a cigarette. Much to my surprise, she told me to go ahead and have one. I said, "There's no ash tray back here. How am I going to put it out?" She told me to just butt it out on the floor when I was done. I thought Buzz was really cool to let me do this, and I really appreciated her kindness towards me.

Buzz stayed with me at the emergency ward until I saw a doctor. While we were waiting, we went outside so I could have another cigarette. We had a good conversation, and she treated me so well! I was taken to the McNair Unit, and Buzz went on her way. Early the next morning, Buzz came to the hospital to see how I was doing. I couldn't believe it! Talk about going above and beyond the call of duty! I never saw her again, but I will always remember the super nice cop named Buzz.

When I became manic and ended up in McNair, Rene also came there to see me. I didn't detect the presence of the devil in her at all. We had a nice visit, and she even gave me a reflexology treatment. She was a kind and caring individual. I had Rene for about six months until another change was made.

After a couple of weeks in McNair, I was allowed to have two-hour passes, which was soon increased to four. My mom would pick me up at the hospital, and we would go to a park or home for a few hours. I always enjoyed these outings, but I also looked forward to going back to the psych ward. I thought I was in there for the special purpose of helping some of the other patients. It felt like it was my job, and I loved it. When it was time for me to return to the unit, I would often say to my mom, "Well, I have to go back to work!"

My psychiatrist from 1997-2000 was Dr. Linda Loewen. I liked her, and we had a pretty good relationship. Having said this, I could also be quite a challenge, especially when I was manic. There were many times when I was too much for her to handle, and she literally didn't know what to do with me. On a few occasions, Dr. Loewen had Dr. Latimer (former head of psychiatry at the McNair Unit) take over my case because of this.

Two of my psychiatrists told me they believed the devil exists, but I wasn't able to get Dr. Loewen's opinion on this matter. When I asked her if she believed God exists, all she said was that she believed in a "higher power."

In 1997, I spent about five weeks in the McNair Unit. I continued to live with my mom after that.

ELLEN BACHMANN A.K.A. ELLI

My final home support worker working in the mental-health field was Elli, a Licensed Practical Nurse (LPN) and very good at her job. Elli was, by far, the best one of all. I was one of her clients from 1997-2000. During this time, we became good friends. Elli knew me when I was well and had seen me when I was manic and depressed. She had other clients who were bipolar, and she knew this mental illness well.

The first time Elli and I met was at Tim Hortons coffee shop in West Kelowna. It was spring, and I was doing well. We got along right away. When the weather was nice and I was feeling up to it, we went for long walks along Okanagan Lake. We did this a lot. If Elli had some time to spare before her next client, we would often sit down and talk at the Rotary Beach Park right beside the lake. On my way to meeting her, I would often go to Tim Hortons to get us a coffee and donut or a muffin.

In the beginning, I saw Elli for about an hour per day, three times a week. Then it got increased to two hours per day, five times a week. I was happy about this. When the weather was poor and during the winter months, she would usually come over to my mom's place to see me. My mom really liked Elli, and they established a good relationship.

When I was depressed, I didn't want to see or talk to anyone. Except Elli. For some reason, I always looked forward to seeing her. There was something very special about her, and our friendship kept growing. There was nothing more to it. We just became good friends.

CPGA "RETIRED" PRO

In 1997, the CPGA put me into the "retired" category. I had informed them I had bipolar disorder and gave them some of my medical information. It was very clear I couldn't work. I still paid my annual dues and was still considered a member of the association. If I ever got well enough to work again, I could come out of the retired category and resume my status as an "active" pro. I thought this was a fair arrangement.

Around the same time, I was put on a Canada Pension Plan Lifetime Disability government plan. I only received $520/month for this. I was also eligible to receive BC (British Columbia) benefits, which paid me an additional $250/month. In total, my only income was $770/month. Ridiculous. However, my BC benefits covered the cost of most of my medications, including my psychiatric meds. These medications would have cost at least $800/month. Without my BC benefits, I wouldn't have been able to pay for my medications.

UBC MOOD DISORDER CLINIC

As usual, my manic episode was followed by a depressed episode. After about three months of severe depression, Dr. Loewen decided to send me to the University of British Columbia (UBC) Mood Disorder Clinic in Vancouver. She had tried many combinations of psych meds with me, but nothing was working. She wasn't able to get my chemical imbalance "balanced." Dr. McKercher and Dr. Loewen could have had me admitted into McNair for depression because I told them many times that I constantly thought about suicide when I was depressed. The only reason I wasn't hospitalized on these occasions was because I always assured them I wouldn't commit suicide. There is "thinking" about suicide, and then there is "acting" on those thoughts. It can be a fine line. I came extremely close, but I never crossed that line.

In the winter of 1997, I spent six weeks in the UBC Mood Disorder Clinic. It seemed like forever. Each day I was depressed seemed like a year to me. I was in there for all of November and half of December. They tried some "cognitive therapy" on me, which didn't help at all. No surprise. I already knew my depression was caused by a chemical imbalance. It wasn't psychological. I was administered different psychiatric medications as well, but this didn't work either. For a while, they had me using a SAD light — a special light that simulates sunshine — for about twenty minutes each morning. It didn't help me at the time, but it sure did when I started using it on a regular basis during the winter months a few years later.

SEASONAL AFFECTIVE DISORDER (SAD)

Seasonal Affective Disorder (SAD) is another mental illness of which I have suffered from since I moved to the Okanagan Valley from Alberta in 1994. The Alberta winters are a lot colder than here, but at least they get a lot of sunshine to go with the cold and snow. The Okanagan Valley gets snow, too, but our winters here are milder in comparison, and there is a lack of sunshine. Many people living in this area, including myself, suffer from winter depression because of this lack of sunshine. Hence, we have "SAD." In 2000, I began using a SAD light every morning for about thirty minutes from November 1 to March 31. I still do this, and it has helped me immensely! It cost $230 and is the best investment I have ever made. After using it for twenty years, I haven't even had to change the original light tubes yet. It still works great! It means this light has only cost me about $12/year — a small price to pay when it is so helpful in deterring winter depression.

The very first day I tried my new SAD light, I got a little carried away. Instead of using it for the recommended 20-30 minutes, I used it for about six hours! I started the day feeling quite depressed. After using my new light for such a long time, my mood improved significantly. I went from feeling depressed to almost a hypomanic state. In the morning, I had very little energy. After using the light, I went shopping at Extra Foods. I almost felt like running up and down the aisles! Quite a transformation.

Vancouver gets a lot of rain during the winter months, which is exactly what happened when I was there in the winter of 1997. During the six weeks I was at UBC, it rained almost every day. It was brutal. I hated it, and it certainly didn't help my depression. For something to do, I often walked in the rain a few blocks to a hockey arena and watched guys play hockey for a while, but I was too depressed to get any enjoyment from it. Mainly, I was just trying to kill some time. The time went by so slowly when I was out there. It was painful. During my walks to the arena and back to the clinic, I saw a lot of big city buses driving down the road. I seriously thought about jumping in front of one of them many times. It would have been so easy. I had no hope that things would get better for me, and the only way I thought I could end this misery was to commit suicide.

At the clinic/psychiatric ward, I tried watching TV at times, but I couldn't even concentrate or focus enough to do that. I certainly didn't feel like talking with anyone, so I avoided contact with the other patients as much as possible. I went to my room and laid on my bed a lot. I usually didn't sleep. I would just lay there. I reluctantly attended some group classes, which didn't do a thing for me. I told the psych nurses that all I could think about was suicide, and that it was driving me crazy.

There were two psychiatrists treating me, and I didn't need any "talk therapy" from them. They didn't try to treat me in a psychological manner because they knew my mental illness, including my depression, was primarily a result of a chemical imbalance. Unfortunately, the psychiatric medications they were using on me didn't help.

The amazing thing was that my mom and Doug came to see me four or five times during those six weeks. They drove all the way from West Kelowna to Vancouver (and back), which is a 4.5-hour drive each way over the mountainous Coquihalla Highway. When the weather and roads are good, it's an absolutely beautiful drive, but the winter months can be treacherous. On two trips they drove through a lot of snow, and parts of the highway were extremely icy. This makes for very stressful driving and can be quite dangerous, but it didn't stop them. Wow, that's devotion. This meant a great deal to me.

I was able to get weekend passes every time they came there. The three of us stayed at a motel on these occasions. I always looked forward to their arrival and was anxious to get away from the psych ward for a couple of days. My mom was far from rich, but she didn't hesitate when it came to paying for all of the expenses for these trips, which was a lot of money. Mom's main concern was me, so the money didn't matter.

With no improvement in my depression after six weeks at the UBC Mood Disorder Clinic, I was discharged and home for Christmas. Back in Kelowna, Dr. Loewen continued to search for the solution for my chemical imbalance. We kept trying different combinations and doses of meds, but nothing was working. I felt completely helpless and hopeless. I stayed depressed for another brutally long four months.

CHAPTER 19
1998
"REGULAR" AT THE MCNAIR UNIT

LOVE OF MUSIC

It was like someone flipped a switch in my brain again. After several months of depression, I woke up one morning feeling better. Something in my brain must have started working properly again while I was sleeping. How can that happen? How can a person be so depressed for such a long time, then feel so much better that suddenly? How can one's prolonged chemical imbalance become balanced again during only one night's sleep? There was no change in my medication or anything else during this time.

As usual, I didn't enjoy listening to music when I was depressed. It was also the first thing I felt like doing when I started to feel better. The first morning I was feeling better, I woke up earlier than usual after eight solid hours of sleep. Mom wasn't up yet, but I really wanted to listen to some music. Luckily, I had a set of headphones for my stereo with a twenty-five-foot cord. I was all set!

I quietly paced in the living room listening to my favorite CDs for an hour. When my mom woke up, I played music we both really enjoyed. I was singing and in a fantastic mood, which went on for a few hours. Out of the blue, I was a totally different person than I had been for the previous eight months. I was my happy self again, and it was a huge relief! This became my morning routine for a while.

Halfway through May, the weather was warming up, so I changed my routine to the outdoors. Almost every morning was incredibly gorgeous, so at 6:00 a.m. each day, I drove to Rotary Beach Park and went for hour-long walks beside Okanagan Lake while listening to my favorite music on my Sony Walkman. I walked quite briskly and would be singing along to my tunes for most of the way. I was in ecstasy!

Around this time, Elli got married. She invited me to her wedding, which took place on a hot day in her brother's backyard. The wedding ceremony was nice, and I met Elli's mom, her brothers, Erich and Walter, and sister, Lilli. And, of course, I met her new husband, Jake. It was a fun day and, ironically, I caught Elli's garter!

I ended up getting to know Jake quite well. He and Elli came over to have coffee with Mom and me many times. When Elli was working, he would often come to visit by himself. We didn't become good friends, but I thought he was an OK guy. He just wasn't someone I really clicked with.

On Father's Day, I drove down to Rotary Beach Park. It was another perfect, beautiful morning. There were a couple of men there flying remote control airplanes. It was really cool to watch, and it reminded me of my dad. Being a pilot, I knew he would have enjoyed watching all the amazing maneuvers of these airplanes over Okanagan Lake.

I decided to go for a drive and ended up in Summerland, a small town about a thirty-minute drive south of West Kelowna. Once there, I turned around and drove back home. Being Father's Day, I wanted to play a dedication song for my dad, so I chose "Old Man" by Neil Young. I was really into it and listened to it a couple of times. Then, I got the "tingles," a.k.a "spirit contact." My dad had joined me for my drive! I knew it was him. Usually when I get this sensation, I know it comes from "spirit," but I don't usually know whose spirit it comes from. His previous contact with me in Houston was like a telepathic conversation. This time was different. We didn't have any kind of conversation, but I just felt his energy. There was no doubt in my mind that my dad was there with me. I kept pressing "repeat" every time "Old Man" ended. I listened to that same song over and over, probably about ten times. I had the tingles from my dad the entire time. It was incredible!

Having Dad connect with me in spirit on those two occasions makes this situation even more profound to me. These encounters are totally authentic to me, and I don't believe I was delusional when I had these experiences.

"SEND ME A FUCKING AMBULANCE RIGHT NOW!"

Along with various other psych meds, I was taking lithium, a common mood stabilizer for bipolar disorder, but one of the side effects is tremors. I was on a pretty high dose of this drug, and I had major tremors. My hands were almost always shaking. It was terrible. I could barely hold onto a cup of coffee. My tremors affected me with other tasks as well. I kept a number of journals for my book, but I could barely write because my hands shook so bad from the lithium!

Someone gave me the idea to buy a tape recorder, so this became my method for "writing" for a while. Within a short period of time, I recorded ten 90-minute cassette tapes. It worked really well for me. When I started this process, I was in a "normal" state of mind, but about a week later, I started to go manic. During this phase, I talked into my tape recorder a lot!

As usual, the devil showed up. I have written about this happening to me many times, and I hope this topic hasn't become mundane. In my experiences, there is nothing "mundane" about this evil spirit. His presence always made things exciting, to say the least. He has scared the shit out of me several times, but this time takes the cake.

I went into the kitchen where Mom was one evening and instantly sensed the devil's presence in her. My "alarm bells" went off immediately. I tried talking with my mom as if things were normal, but this didn't work very well. The devil's spirit/energy was dominating her. I wasn't sensing my mom's usual loving and easygoing demeanor. I was dealing with pure evil. After a couple of hours of this, I couldn't take it anymore. I had to get out of there. I called McNair, gave them my name and talked with one of the psych nurses.

"Lucifer is here," I said.

She said, "You mean the devil?"

"Yep. I need to be admitted right away. Could you please send an ambulance to my mom's place?"

She didn't want to cooperate. She wasn't very understanding and wasn't helping me at all. After talking with her for ten minutes, I became very frustrated. I was getting nowhere with her, and she wasn't going to send an ambulance for me. Finally, I got really pissed off at her and yelled into the phone as loud as I could, "Just send me A FUCKING AMBULANCE right now!" Then I slammed the phone down on the receiver. End of conversation.

Fifteen minutes later, the paramedics knocked on the front door. I checked them out as soon as they entered the house, and they both seemed "normal" to me — no devil spirit. However, "Lucifer" was still channeling his evil spirit through my mom. It was a very intense situation for me. One of the paramedics asked if she could take my blood pressure, so I sat down at the kitchen table so she could do this.

"What does it feel like to take Jesus Christ's blood pressure?" I light-heartedly asked her.

She didn't answer, she just focused on doing her job. I suppose they experience all kinds of strange things on the job.

My blood pressure was 220/? (I forget the bottom number). It felt like my heart was going to pound right out of my chest because of my encounter with the devil. They put me in the ambulance and took me to the Kelowna General Hospital, so I calmed right down. The devil was no longer present. I talked with the paramedics all the way to the hospital, and really enjoyed the ride.

I was back in McNair for the fourth time in three years. I was starting to feel like a bit of a "regular." I knew most of the psych nurses and many of the psychiatrists.

My favorite psych nurse was Doug. He was a great guy! I saw Doug every time I was in there, and we often talked about golf, hockey and many other things. Doug was very compassionate and treated patients with kindness and respect, so I always looked forward to seeing him. He was very intelligent and had a good sense of humor. He was very good at his job. There were a few other psych nurses working there whom I liked as well, and some whom I really disliked. I felt that some of them just didn't have the right qualities for this profession. We need more people like Doug working in the mental-health industry! I have the same viewpoint with psychiatrists. I like some of them I have gotten to know, but I wonder how others even got their license to practice!

During the summer of '98, Elli and Jake visited me in McNair a few times. Elli was getting to know me (and my illness) very well by this time. She knew my "normal" self and had spent considerable time with me when I was manic and when I was depressed. I had gotten to know Elli quite well too. She had many qualities that I liked and admired. Overall, she was just a great person. During these first two years that I was one of her clients, our friendship kept growing and getting stronger. There was nothing more to our relationship than that. It was strictly platonic. Elli and I got along extremely well and always enjoyed each other's company. It was as simple as that!

Dr. Loewen treated me with a cocktail of psych medications that included an antipsychotic medication until I was no longer manic. The drug of choice was Clozapine, which I could handle better than Thorazine, Haldol and Risperdal. These meds are extremely powerful. They are like a major sedative or tranquilizer and will knock you flat on your ass!

I was discharged after about six weeks. I had stopped thinking I was Jesus, and I wasn't seeing the devil in people anymore. I was sleeping a lot better as well. I felt well for a very short time, then became severely depressed again. I hated this roller coaster ride.

SHOCK TREATMENTS (ECT)

Dr. Loewen tried using many different combinations of psychiatric medications with me, including antidepressants. Nothing we tried could get me balanced. After being depressed for a few months, I decided to try Electro Convulsive Therapy (ECT), known by many people as "shock treatments." Dr. Loewen had suggested this in the past, but I didn't want to try it. For whatever reason, I was leery of it. I learned that ECT can be used to combat both mania and depression. For people with bipolar disorder, it's more commonly used for depression. I also learned that it is a lot safer than it used to be. What really sold me was the eighty percent success rate helping an individual overcome depression. That's all I needed to hear and agreed to give it a try. Besides, I was totally desperate and had nothing to lose.

I had my ECT treatments done at the Kelowna General Hospital as an outpatient. I went there three times a week for a total of nine treatments. I had to be at the hospital by 6:30 a.m. every time, and I couldn't drive myself home after, so Gary drove me there and picked me up afterward. Having to get going so early in the morning was made even more difficult by my insomnia. I was in the middle of a three-month period where I was only getting a couple of hours of sleep each night. Having insomnia was bad enough, but to have it when I was depressed was even worse. When I was getting eight hours of sleep, I thought about committing suicide constantly during the sixteen hours I was awake each day. When I had insomnia, my suicidal thoughts tormented my mind almost 24/7.

The doctors put me out for the ECT procedure, which was my favorite part. Being administered the anesthetic felt like dying and going to heaven. The sensation only lasted for a couple of seconds before I was totally out, but it was the greatest feeling I have ever experienced. I wished this feeling would have lasted longer. It was incredible!

Around 10:30 a.m., Gary picked me up and drove me home. After each "shock" treatment, I noticed a slight improvement with my mood for only about an hour or two, then I went back to being 100% depressed, so that was quite disappointing. I felt like this was a last resort, and it didn't work.

I remained depressed for another four months. Finally, I started feeling better in the early summer of 1999.

CHAPTER 20
1999
MY LAST MANIC EPISODE

RIVERVIEW PSYCHIATRIC HOSPITAL

I didn't want to end up at the Riverview Psychiatric Hospital, but I did. It would turn out to be my longest period of hospitalization, and I hope the last one for the rest of my life. Between Kelowna's McNair Unit and Riverview, I spent three months in the psych ward in 1999.

Within two days of voluntarily checking myself into McNair, my status was changed to "committed" by Dr. Paul Latimer, the director of psychiatry at the Kelowna General Hospital at the time. This was not unusual, as it had happened a few times in the previous three years. Dr. Latimer wanted to send me to Riverview in Port Coquitlam, British Columbia, a suburb of Vancouver about five hours west of Kelowna. Riverview is a huge place and more of a long-term care psychiatric facility. There are several large buildings located on approximately six hundred acres of land. There are several different psychiatric wards located on these premises, and Riverview accommodates approximately six hundred patients in total. Some of these people have been living there for many years.

Dr. Latimer had threatened to send me to Riverview a few times, but my family and I always managed to talk him out of it. Riverview had a bad reputation. During my many hospitalizations in McNair, I talked with several people who had either been patients there or were familiar with it. All I heard were very negative comments from these people. I can't remember all the issues they had against Riverview, but I distinctly recall countless remarks that gave me the impression that it was a hellhole and I should avoid being sent there.

Before Dr. Latimer sent me to Riverview in August 1999, I was one of his patients on a few occasions. Between 1997 and 1999 when Dr. Loewen was my psychiatrist, I went manic every summer. Each time, I voluntarily admitted myself to McNair and was under her care. On some of these occasions, Dr. Loewen didn't know what to do with me. Basically, I was too much of a handful. When I was manic, I could pretty much out talk anyone, and I especially wouldn't hesitate to challenge a psychiatrist if given the opportunity. A few times when Dr. Loewen reached her wit's end, she passed me on to Latimer. I call him Latimer because I don't have the respect to call him "Dr."

When Dr. Loewen passed me on to Latimer in 1999, he seemed determined to send me to Riverview. This isn't a "paranoid delusion" on my behalf. His intentions were obvious. I have always been a very good judge of character, and even when I was mentally ill and in a manic state, I still knew who treated me well and in a respectful manner and who didn't. Latimer didn't. At the same time, I'm sure he must have known that I disliked him. As soon as he could, Latimer arranged to transfer me to Riverview. When he told me, I blew up at him. I really let him have it!

In Chinese astrology my sign is "The Dragon." My wife sometimes tells others, "Don't piss off the Dragon or he will breathe fire and scorch the ground you walk on!" I suppose this is true. It doesn't happen very often, but if someone does get me mad enough, I definitely will say what's on my mind. I am also a Gemini, and one of the Gemini's main characteristics is that of a communicator. We are known to be extremely talkative. When you combine a Gemini with a pissed off Dragon, there is very likely to be a verbal onslaught you do not want to be the recipient of. People who know me well, and who have known me long enough, have witnessed this side of me.

When Latimer told me he was sending me to Riverview, I unleashed a barrage of words — most of them vulgar — like a rapid-fire machine gun. Then he left his office in a hell of a hurry! The next thing I knew, I was surrounded by hospital security guards, Latimer, and some of the psych nurses. I cooperatively let them take me into the ICU where they injected me with a very powerful tranquilizer. I was out immediately. When I was unconscious, I was taken by ambulance from the Kelowna Hospital to the Kelowna Airport, then I was flown by air ambulance to Vancouver. When I woke up, I was in the ICU (E-4) at the Riverview Psychiatric Hospital in Port Coquitlam. Latimer had sent me there without notifying my mom or any of my family members. We were angry.

The ICU at Riverview was actually a lot better than McNair's ICU in a few regards. It was a lot larger than Kelowna's, and it was a co-ed unit. There was a shared common area where patients could watch TV, socialize, read or just relax. Most importantly, there was a smoking room! If you are a smoker, you really appreciate a smoking room, especially if you are locked up in the ICU and you can't go outside! Your activities are extremely limited when you are held captive. You can only watch TV during certain hours, and being locked up in one small area for several days or weeks results in very long days.

People with a mental illness, like myself, need to be hospitalized in a psychiatric unit at certain times when we are going through a particularly rough time. There are several types of mental illnesses, and a person's admission into a psychiatric facility might be their very first time experiencing what this is like, and they will probably get their first diagnosis from a psychiatrist. Regardless of what illness a person has, they are going through a very stressful time. Too much stress in one's life often triggers relapses of a mental illness or may even be the main cause in the first place, as it was in my case. Usually, people who are put into ICU require closer observation than those in the general population. They may be suicidal or pose a serious threat to harm others. I have met several people in ICU wards who were very aggressive and threatening towards me — even violent. At Riverview, a guy named Tony burned me under my eye with his cigarette.

My best guess as to why I was put in ICU was that my attending psychiatrist decided I "may become" violent or be a physical threat towards others. There were times when I was manic that I became extremely intense and got really pissed off! The times I got extremely agitated were usually triggered by an altercation between myself and the staff — a psych nurse or one of my attending psychiatrists — at the psych ward I was in. Someone would really have to rub me the wrong way to get me this angry. For the most part, when I was manic I was like my normal self. I was usually in a pretty good mood. I was a fun-loving guy, full of love, and I got along with almost everyone. During the time I spent in E-4, Dorothy was the only patient with whom I made friends. This might sound funny, but she seemed like the most normal person in there. Dorothy and I had a lot of good conversations. The other patients were either too ill, or I just simply did not hit it off with them.

It is a well-known fact that having a cigarette can help relax a person when they are stressed out. Many people with a mental illness smoke because it calms their nerves to some extent, so there is some serious smoking going on in a psych ward smoking room! Over the course of my ten trips to psych wards, I spent most of my time in the smoking rooms. My time at Riverview was no different. Not only could you smoke in there, but it was also a good place to socialize with the other inmates. There was almost always someone in there I could talk with.

One of Riverview's rules, which I and many others thought was very stupid, was that they closed the smoking room from 10 p.m. to 6 a.m. If someone who smokes is having trouble sleeping because they are manic, have insomnia or for any other reason, they should have the option of going for a cigarette. If it is 3 a.m. and you can't go outside, the smoking room is the only place you could go to have one. There isn't a good reason I know of to close the smoke room at all. They have security cameras in every psych ward smoking room I have been in, so it is very easy for the nurses and other staff to monitor these small rooms. When it is closed at night, ninety-five percent of the patients are sleeping. If a few patients get up in the middle of the night, go have a cigarette and go back to bed, I just don't see a problem with this. I am not a proponent of smoking in general and do not condone it. It has been scientifically proven that smoking cigarettes can cause cancer, heart disease and can be extremely detrimental to one's health in several ways. Smoking cigarettes is also extremely addictive.

I had the impression that Riverview was a hellhole before I was sent there. The first day I was a patient at Riverview, I got a blow job! I thought that I was in heaven! Not hell! This incident started out quite innocently. I was in the smoke room with some of my inmates and, as I mentioned, E-4 was co-ed. There was one woman who was extremely flirtatious with some of us men. I think she may have been bipolar and was exhibiting signs of manic promiscuity. I was also in a manic promiscuous state and hadn't had any sex for like four years. Because of my illness, I was severely depressed ninety percent of the time and was unable to have any kind of relationship. I guess I was ready for a little fling!

Things escalated very quickly between us two horny and revved up manic patients. One minute we were doing a little kissing and touching in the smoke room, and a couple minutes later the two of us were in her room in the female dormitory. Then all of a sudden, she's giving me a blow job! I could hardly believe my good fortune! Luckily, the two of us didn't get caught performing this brazen act. She was in her late twenties or early thirties and was fairly good looking. Within a day or two after our encounter, she was either released or transferred from E-4, and I never saw her again. During my ten hospitalizations in psychiatric wards, this was my only sexual encounter.

Immediately upon my arrival at the E-4 ICU unit at Riverview, I filled out a "review panel" form. This is a type of legal application in which a patient who is committed to a psychiatric ward by a psychiatrist can fill out and apply for assistance from a mental health advocate lawyer and be discharged from that psychiatric ward. I had filled out a review panel form once or twice before, but I think I was talked out of going through with the process by the psychiatrist who was treating me at the time.

The head psychiatrist at my Riverview unit was Dr. Phil Severy. Having been treated by around twenty psychiatrists over the years, he was the best I had ever met. He told me that this process took about three weeks, and that Latimer should not have sent me there in the first place! Dr. Severy told me he would discharge me from Riverview himself in a week. True to his word, he made the necessary arrangements and within one week I was sent by air ambulance back to Kelowna.

Unfortunately, I was sent back to McNair and was once again forced to be in the care of the infamous Latimer. Within a week, Latimer sent me back to Riverview again! Another free air ambulance ride for me, but not so cheap for the taxpayers. Within a few hours, I was back at Riverview. Looking on the bright side, at least I wasn't put in the E-4 ICU this time. Instead, I was put in the D-3 unit, a co-ed unit where patients were allowed more freedom and given more opportunities than E-4.

I was still a "committed" patient, so I was being kept there against my free will, but D-3 was a lot better. Being a new patient to D-3 meant I also had a new psychiatrist assigned to me. His name was Dr. Scott, and he was very different from Dr. Severy. I ended up staying in D-3 for about eight weeks with Dr. Scott as my psychiatrist. I didn't like him, but I just dealt with him as best I could.

Soon after I arrived in D-3, I decided to fill out another review panel form because I felt that if I didn't I would be committed to Riverview for a very long time. I certainly felt that this was Latimer's wish for me, and it appeared that Dr. Scott wanted to keep me there for a long time as well. I really had to fight for my rights. I couldn't personally do anything because I was committed, so I needed a mental health advocate lawyer to get me out of there. It was like I was in jail and needed a lawyer to bail me out! My situation had become dire, and it was clear I would have to go through a court-like proceeding to get out of Riverview and regain my freedom.

I contacted a lawyer named Brett and liked him right away. When I first spoke with him on the phone, he was very friendly and personable. I briefly explained my situation and got the impression that he really wanted to help me. Within a week of our phone call, we met and got along very well right away. Brett was intelligent, enthusiastic and a determined go-getter. I felt he had the determination and tenacity to get me out of my predicament.

He explained that my review panel hearing would happen within three to four weeks and there would be five people in the room with three psychiatrists, including Dr. Scott. This was a concern because, as I mentioned earlier, I had the impression that he wanted to keep me at Riverview for an extended period of time. I was certain he would vote against my release at the hearing. I was desperately hoping and praying that Brett would convince these people to let me be a free man!

Patients in D-3 were given much more freedom than in E-4. If you were doing well enough and abiding by the rules, you were given privileges to leave the ward. The doors giving access into and out of E-4 were locked, and one of the staff had to press a control button to let someone in or out. The doors in D-3 were always unlocked. I was given quite a bit of freedom because I was doing well. After being locked inside 24/7 in E-4, it was a huge relief and extremely enjoyable for me to be able to go outside by myself when I wanted and have a cigarette or go for a walk.

I liked the patients in D-3 a lot more than the ones in E-4 as well, and I became friends with several of my D-3 comrades. My new buddies included Steven, Kurt, Kevin, Dennis, Allan and Marty. Steven had obsessive-compulsive disorder (OCD). I'm not sure what his obsession or compulsion was, but he was extremely intelligent and had a terrific sense of humor. I enjoyed many conversations with him, and he always made me laugh a lot. Steven intrigued me, and I was somewhat fascinated by him.

Kurt had schizophrenia. He must have been doing quite well when I knew him because he seemed very normal to me. He wasn't having any delusions or displaying any paranoid or psychotic behavior when I was with him. He was also very intelligent and had a good sense of humor. I always enjoyed Kurt's company.

Kevin was twenty-one and had bipolar disorder. He was a patient at Riverview because of some of his manic behavior. He had just returned from Norway where he was working as a commercial fisherman with his uncle. Kevin's mom and dad came to visit him every weekend and were very nice people. They lived on Vancouver Island, where Kevin's dad owned and operated a salmon fish farm. On a few occasions, he would bring fresh smoked salmon for us patients in D-3. Delicious! When I had a pass to go home to West Kelowna for the Thanksgiving weekend, he gave me some smoked salmon to share with my family. Kevin's dad and I got along great. He too had a good sense of humor.

Dennis was from Kelowna and was about forty. I don't know what his mental illness was, but as with all my buddies, Dennis had a great sense of humor. To cut down on the cost of cigarettes, my mom had sent me a tub of tobacco, papers and a machine to roll my own cigarettes. I didn't like this idea at all because I didn't have the patience to make cigarettes with this machine even when my mood was normal. At the time, I was manic and was an extremely busy guy, so I spent most of my time visiting with people. I had no time or interest in rolling my own smokes, so I made a deal with Dennis. If he rolled my cigarettes for me, he could also roll them for himself. This way, he would get free cigarettes and I would not have to roll them myself. Just prior to negotiating this deal, I had been noticing that Dennis was constantly picking butts out of the ashtrays and off the ground and putting them into a plastic bag. When he had enough, he would take what little tobacco he could get from each butt, use some rolling paper and roll his own cigarette. He happily accepted my offer. Using new tobacco and a rolling machine was quicker, more efficient and more sanitary. Dennis did a great job and kept us both fully supplied. He rolled, we both had lots of smokes, and we were both happy!

My friend Dorothy, whom I met when we were both patients in E-4, was transferred to an all-female ICU ward. We kept in touch by phone from our respective wards (D-3 & D-4), and her sister, Lynn, came to visit me on a regular basis in D-3. I liked Dorothy as a friend, but I had become quite intrigued with Lynn. She was very attractive. She was close to my age, intelligent and had a great sense of humor. We hit it off right from the day we met. We had many good conversations and a lot of great laughs together. I really appreciated that she came especially to see me, as Dorothy was in a completely different ward.

I brought Dennis with me a couple of times when I visited Dorothy, and it didn't take him long to take a shining to one of the ladies in Dorothy's ward. It brought a smile to my face and made me happy when I saw them walking together holding hands. Dennis ended up going to the ladies' ward a lot to spend time with his new girlfriend.

Lynn was good to Dorothy. During the week she would work all day then come to Riverview to visit her. She came almost every single day, even on the weekends. Lynn was extremely loyal, loving and supportive toward her sister. Dorothy was under close observation because she had apparently tried to commit suicide when she was in ICU. Lynn usually visited Dorothy around the same time every evening, and I would often go to Dorothy's ward when I thought Lynn might be there. Basically, I would flirt with her every chance I had.

September '99 was sunny and warm in the Vancouver region. The weather was so nice that Lynn almost always wore shorts — short shorts! I loved that! As good as she looked, and as well as we got along, I never made a sexual pass at her. I wanted to kiss her so bad, but I refrained for two reasons. The main reason was she had a fiancée and was living in a common-law relationship. Being in a manic state, I did have some lack of insight and some impaired judgement, but I still respected the fact that Lynn was in a serious relationship. Wisely, I chose not to get involved. The other reason was that I had gained fifty pounds in the last few years, mostly in my stomach. It was a side effect from psych medication. I was pretty fit and trim for most of my life, but I went from a flat belly to a huge gut! I had ballooned to 230 lb. It was humbling to say the least. I never thought I was "hot" or extremely good looking, but I used to have some confidence when it came to the opposite sex. My new 230 lb. physique shot my self-confidence to hell, and making a pass on Lynn, or any other good-looking female, was out of the question.

One thing I liked about Riverview was Penn Hall, a clubhouse of sorts for the patients to hang out at. It had a cafeteria where we could buy hamburgers, hot dogs, French fries and a variety of other food items. The prices were very reasonable. There was also an old bowling alley there. It wasn't functioning properly, as it wasn't computerized, so the pins didn't reset themselves, but at least we could throw the bowling balls down the lanes and knock the pins over. I enjoyed doing this by myself and didn't keep score.

Once a week they had karaoke at Penn Hall, and I participated in it one night. I had never done karaoke in my entire life, and it was always out of the question for me, even when I was extremely drunk. Now here I was, "Mr. Shy Guy," bellowing into a microphone in front of a crowd of about 100 people. My first song choice was "Daniel" by Elton John. As I sang, I walked confidently back and forth across the stage like I owned it! I was so into it! I really felt like I was living up to my old nickname "The Rock Star." I wasn't exactly dressed like a Rock Star though. Like most of my days spent at Riverview, I was wearing a long sleeve nylon golf jacket with no shirt underneath, blue jean shorts and my cobra-skin cowboy boots with no socks. My mania caused me to brim with exuberance and confidence. I thought I was such a great singer! To top it off, I got a standing ovation from the crowd when I finished. What a rush!

Whoever wanted to sing karaoke had to write their name on a blackboard beside the stage so the event organizer would know who was up next. Thinking I was Jesus Christ at the time, that was exactly what I wrote down for my name. I ended up singing three songs, and I received a standing ovation each time! No one ever questioned the fact that I signed up as Jesus Christ.

THE GREAT ESCAPE

The most fun I had during my two-month stay at Riverview was my "Great Escape." It all started with an innocent visit from Mom and Gary, who had driven from West Kelowna to see me for a few days. They made this trip a few times, and I really appreciated it, especially because it was an eight-hour round trip. On the day they were leaving, I was fed up with being hospitalized for such a long time, and I just wanted to go home with them. I couldn't because Dr. Scott wanted to keep me there and, since I was still committed, I had no choice in the matter.

Before they left, Mom left $60 at the nursing station for me to buy cigarettes. In 1999, cigarettes cost about $5 a package, so I was to be given $5 per day for my smokes. I did some smooth talking and convinced one of the psych nurses to give me all $60 right then. As soon as I had the money in my pocket, I decided to go drinking, which was unusual for me as I had completely quit about five years earlier. I hadn't had a drop of booze in all that time, except once in 1997 when a bartender accidentally served me real beer instead of my usual non-alcoholic beer. I asked my Riverview comrade, Marty, to come drinking with me, and he happily accepted. I used the phone in the hallway to quietly call a taxi and gave instructions for the driver to pick us up in front of our D-3 ward. We both had "grounds privileges," which meant we were allowed to go outside of our unit by ourselves as long as we stayed on the grounds at Riverview. Therefore, going outside was absolutely no problem. Catching a taxi to the bar? A definite no-no.

Luckily, the taxi arrived immediately, and we hopped right in. I asked the driver how much it would cost to take us to the nearest stripper bar, and he said about $20. I wanted to have as much money as possible to drink with, so I asked the driver to take us to the closest drinking establishment, and he dropped us off at a nearby lounge. Our fare was close to $10, so Marty and I had $50 left to drink with! I had no concern whatsoever about saving $10 for the taxi ride back to Riverview. The only thing on my mind at the time was that we were going to have some drinks and have a hell of a good time doing it!

The two of us slovenly and disheveled dudes must have been some sight as we walked into that lounge. Marty was fifty-three years old, his hair was messy, and he had a beard and mustache. He was a bit hard to understand also because he had no teeth. Like me, he had a big belly. He wore the same clothes every day: a red T-shirt and dirty blue jeans held up by a pair of suspenders. I was thirty-five, my hair was not well groomed, and I had a scraggly beard and mustache. Normally, I am clean shaven, but whenever I was manic and thought I was Jesus Christ, I would grow a beard and mustache so people could see that I did indeed look like him. I was wearing the same outfit I wore at karaoke (and every other day), so we were quite a pair.

It was about 3:00 p.m. and there were only a few people in the lounge. Despite our appearance, the staff served us, and I paid cash for our drinks. Marty had two or three screwdrivers, and I drank about six beers. I asked the bartender to put on some music for us, which he did, and by this time I was in a very good mood. Still manic, I was exuberant, confident and extremely outgoing. I even told our waitress and the bartender that we had come from Riverview!

I went to use the washroom, and while I was in there this guy comes out of one of the stalls. I greeted him enthusiastically and introduced myself as Jesus Christ. Without hesitation he says, "I was just thinking about you!" I was thrilled to hear his response. Looking back, I realize that this was just a quick and witty reply, as most people probably would have looked at me like I was crazy and given me a derogatory remark. Of all the times I have been manic and thought I was Jesus Christ — and there have been many — I never got annoyed, angry or upset if someone didn't believe me. I never tried to persuade or convince anyone either. Obviously, almost everyone I said this to did not believe I was Jesus Christ, but there have been a few people who did believe me. Of course, these people were also mentally ill. Regardless, what an awesome feeling it was when these people called me Jesus!

After I had drank the beers, I thought I was going to get sick to my stomach. Having been a non-drinker for close to five years, I went from completely sober to quite drunk in a short period of time. Once I had the first beer in me, it automatically took hold. I wanted more and more. I really wanted to tie one on! That's how alcoholism works. Once an alcoholic, always an alcoholic. Having said that, I'm very happy and proud to say I have not had any alcohol since that incident. I've been a completely "sober alcoholic" for twenty years, and I've only drank on two occasions in the last twenty-five years. I went outside to throw up in an outdoor patio area where no one was around. Not only had I not drank for several years, I was also on a combination of psychiatric medications. No wonder I felt sick! I didn't throw up outside, but I did lie down on the patio and have a little rest.

Next thing I knew, I was looking up at two police officers. One male and one female. Either the bartender or our waitress had called them to come and pick Marty and me up. We hadn't done anything illegal but because we told them we were from the Riverview Psychiatric Hospital, I guess they thought it was time for us to go back there. Our little party lasted for about three hours before the law caught up with us. We went with the police very willingly, and I asked if I could ride in the lady police officer's car and was granted permission to do so. Marty went with the male officer.

When we arrived at Riverview, two staff members from our unit were waiting outside. One of them was one of my favorites, Doug. He had a big smile on his face as he watched Marty and me get out of the police cars and walk toward him. My comrade and I were then escorted back to D-3. For being bad boys, we lost our grounds privileges for a while, which meant we were totally confined to our unit. We were also put back into our Riverview pajamas. In psychiatric wards, patients often have to wear hospital pajamas if they are confined to their unit/ward.

While Marty and I were on our "Great Escape," my mom had gotten home and called to speak with me. The psych nurse told her I was MIA. I hadn't shown up for my pre-dinner medication or for the 5 p.m. dinner. They didn't know where I was, and of course my mom was worried and concerned. I called her shortly after the police brought us back. She was obviously relieved that I was OK, but unhappy I had been given the entire $60 all at once.

One time, I had my mom and brother bring my leather briefcase to me. I used to use it for business purposes when I was working as a golf pro, but when I was manic, I would put old business cards, notebooks, pens, money, cigarettes and other miscellaneous items that I thought were important in it. Marty was like my caddy, but instead of carrying my golf clubs, I had him carry my briefcase for me. I gave him cigarettes for doing this, and he seemed quite happy with this arrangement. For a great deal of the time, wherever I went, Marty was close behind me, lugging my briefcase. I suppose it looked pretty funny to the average person, as we didn't exactly look like the standard executives.

REVIEW PANEL HEARING

The day of my long-awaited review panel hearing finally came after six weeks. I felt like I was on trial and was going to court to defend myself, but I wasn't totally on my own. Brett was there to represent me, and I was really counting on him to help me win my appeal. If we won, I would be a free man and be able to leave Riverview immediately. I was extremely excited and was hoping desperately that we would be able to convince the members on the panel to agree with our plea that it was no longer necessary to have me as a committed patient.

I walked into the meeting room with Brett and introduced myself as Don Walin to the five-man review panel. Thankfully, I was no longer in a full-blown manic state, so I didn't think I was God and/or Jesus Christ. The panel was made up of Dr. Scott, two psychiatrists I hadn't met before and two other men. I took a seat at the end of the long table at a spot that had a pencil and a writing pad. Brett took a seat to my left. It was a quiet and sullen atmosphere. No one was joking around. This was a serious matter. I had already decided beforehand to let Brett do most of the talking on my behalf. I would answer questions if asked, or I would reply to them if they wished. But, for the most part I was relying on Brett. He was an experienced mental-health advocate lawyer, and he had been down this road before. I hadn't.

I had seriously considered going through this process a few times prior to this Riverview ordeal when I had been committed. I ended up "putting my time in" until I was released, which was usually four to six weeks. Between McNair and Riverview I had been committed for three months and counting by September 1999. Dr. Scott told me on various occasions that he felt I should remain a committed patient at Riverview indefinitely.

I had been informed that many people were institutionalized at Riverview for several months and in some cases several years. My three-month term was more than enough for me. I felt I had to take this action to get out of there, or who knew how long I could end up being in there. I knew I couldn't count on Dr. Scott's vote. Just the opposite. He wanted to keep me there. Brett was my only hope.

As soon as my hearing started, I began taking notes. I listened intently to everything the men were discussing about my case and recorded a tremendous number of notes very rapidly. I didn't have to speak as Brett did the talking on my behalf. After about thirty minutes of discussion, the panel members asked Brett and me to leave the room so they could deliberate and reach a decision. Brett and I went outside to talk and have a cigarette. Within ten minutes, someone came out to inform us that a decision had been made. I couldn't believe how quickly this had happened! I was bewildered, and I anxiously walked back into the meeting room with Brett by my side. I was immediately informed that I had won my appeal. The final verdict was that it was no longer necessary to keep me at Riverview against my will. I wasn't committed anymore and could leave Riverview pronto. I was a free man again!

I was so glad I had stood up for myself and my rights by making the bold decision to go through the review process. Thankfully, the two psychiatrists and the other two men on the panel had disagreed with Dr. Scott's decision to keep me contained. Brett was a huge factor concerning my victory. His expertise helped to win my appeal and ultimate release. Thanks again Brett!

Dr. Scott asked me if I would voluntarily stay at Riverview for three more days. I'm not sure why, but I decided to be cooperative and honor his request. When that time was up, two Riverview security employees drove me to the Vancouver Airport to catch my flight back to Kelowna. Within a couple of hours, I was at my mom's house in West Kelowna. It felt so good to be back home!

Postscript: Riverview Hospital closed in July 2012. In December 2015, the provincial government announced plans to begin construction in 2017 to replace the obsolete buildings with new mental-health facilities scheduled to open in 2019.

SPIRITUALITY

I would like to point out that when I was manic and thought I was God and/or Jesus Christ, I always knew at the same time that I was Don Walin. I never denied this fact. After several years of learning about spirituality and trying to make some kind of link or connection between my mental illness and my many experiences with the spirit realm, I have formed a theory that explains some of my beliefs and opinions towards this matter. I will describe my "Mania Spirit Theory" later.

When someone is in a state of mania and think they are Jesus Christ, psychiatrists diagnose that individual as delusional, psychotic and/or being in a state of psychosis. The psychiatrist will then administer antipsychotic medications to the patient and treat them until they are no longer delusional and/or psychotic (i.e., they no longer think they are Jesus Christ). I have been hospitalized for being manic nine times. On six of these occasions, I thought

I was Jesus Christ. During my last hospitalization in 1999, I thought I was God and Jesus. I have heard of and read about other people who had manic depression and who also thought they were Jesus Christ when they were manic.

This spiritual phenomenon — not only the Jesus Christ matter, but spirituality in general — has intrigued me for many years. During my hospitalizations, I noticed a high rate of interest involving the subject of spirituality among the other mentally-ill patients. Being subjected to all of this spirituality initiated my personal quest to learn about the spirit realm in general, and especially to try to make some sense out of my experiences when I was mentally ill (manic). The more I learn, the more everything makes sense to me. I have always thought my "manic experiences" were real and genuinely associated with the spirit realm. Psychiatrists are often much too hasty with their diagnoses and treatment of people like me.

On several occasions I have tried to converse with psychiatrists regarding spirituality in order to hear their viewpoints and get them to engage in a conversation on this topic. I have attempted this when I was manic and when I was in a normal state of mind. Some of the psychiatrists would not even tell me whether they believed God exists. I hope the psychiatric establishment will eventually be more open to discussing topics of a spiritual nature instead of avoiding this subject altogether.

CHAPTER 21
2000
A NEW BEGINNING

It was great to be discharged from Riverview and be back home in West Kelowna. But soon after, I fell into a depressed episode that lasted for about four months. The winter of 1999/2000 was a rough one for me.

In April 2000, I started feeling better. This pattern was normal for me and my bipolar disorder. Once I started feeling better, I would usually become totally manic within just a few days and end up in the psych ward. This time was different. Once I began to feel well, I stayed well. It was like a miracle!

For several years, I complied by always taking my psych meds as instructed. Many psychiatrists put me on several different combinations of these meds, but nothing balanced my chemical imbalance. One spring day as I was out for a walk with Elli, she suggested I take my Clozapine all the time because it may help keep a lid on the mania. By avoiding the mania, perhaps it would also help deter the depression that followed. Manic episodes are exhausting. Your mind and body can't "shut down" without medication. Your ideas and energy are endless, and sleep is almost impossible. Exhaustion and depression seem inevitable after weeks of manic behavior. At first, I was totally opposed to this idea because Clozapine is an antipsychotic medication, which I hate! I had been administered Thorazine, Haldol, Risperdal and Clozapine many times over the years in order to stop my manic episodes. These drugs accomplished this, but they had terrible side effects. Also, I would almost immediately get majorly depressed. To me, antipsychotic meds = depression, and there was nothing worse than being severely depressed.

MAGIC COCKTAIL OF PSYCHIATRIC MEDICATIONS

At the same time Elli suggested this, Dr. Loewen decided to put me on 200 mg. of Clozapine every night around 9 p.m., and I have done so ever since. It is also a very powerful sedative, but it has kept that lid on my mania, and I have a great sleep every night. Ironically, one of the psych meds I used to hate so much turned out to be one of the most important and favorite ones I take.

Dr. Loewen put me on two kinds of antidepressants (Celexa and Desipramine), and a mood stabilizer (Topiramate) as well. Daily, the Celexa is

40 mg. The highest recommended dose for the Desipramine was 300 mg./day. Dr. Loewen prescribed me 350 mg./day. The Topiramate is 50 mg./day. That's it. That's the magic cocktail of psychiatric medications that Dr. Loewen put me on in April 2000 that caused me to start feeling better. Ever since then, I take this exact same combination of meds every day. Clozapine hasn't caused any depression, and I don't suffer from any side effects from it. Thanks to this combination of psychiatric medications, my chemical imbalance has been balanced.

Elli became a Registered Practical Nurse (Licensed Practical Nurse in British Columbia) in 1979 while living in Thunder Bay, Ontario. She started working for Interior Health as a community health worker (also known as a home support worker) when she moved to the Okanagan in 1992. Before her move to West Kelowna, she lived and worked in a medical capacity in one way or another in Humble, Texas, and previous to that in Hollywood, California. She was working in the Mental Health Department of Home Support in Kelowna when she became my worker in 1997. As I've mentioned, Elli and I became very good friends while she was my support worker. I was living with my mom at the time, and Elli would visit with me and my mom, or we would go for coffee or for a long walk along Lake Okanagan. These visits were therapeutic. People with a mental illness often become socially isolated, especially during times of severe depression, and it helps to have someone who understands your mental illness, other than family members, to talk to. A worker can also be helpful when they notice symptoms of your illness that may require medical help. The sooner we get the help the better.

As I mentioned, Elli got married in 1998, and I became somewhat of a friend with her husband. Occasionally, he would visit by himself and have coffee with my mom and I, or we would go somewhere like Tim Hortons for coffee. Elli and Jake's marriage was short-lived. By 2000, it was all over. I had no idea they were having problems, and neither of them told me what was happening. While working with me, Elli kept her personal problems to herself. Her professional role meant she was there to help me, not stress me out with her personal trials and tribulations. I had no idea that her marriage was on the rocks until she called it quits with him.

Shortly after they were married, Jake became extremely angry, controlling, jealous and possessive. Each day when she came home from work, she would be interrogated. She faced a barrage of questions about who, when, where and what she did at work. It turns out he also accused Elli of having an affair with me. This was untrue! The relationship between us had evolved into a good friendship (which Jake was a part of), but in no way whatsoever was it an affair.

Elli decided to tell me about it over coffee one day.

"Don, I thought you better know that we are having an affair," she said.

I have been delusional, but I was of a healthy mind at this time, and I knew we were not having an affair! All joking aside, she told me what she had been going through, and that her marriage with Jake was over. Her main concern was that he may suddenly show up at my mom's place ready to accuse me of something I didn't have a clue about and want to fight. This never happened. Jake returned to Ontario, and they divorced the following year.

Because I had been feeling better for a couple of months, I thought I would try and go back to work. Previously, work stress had caused me to go manic on the job a few times, so I thought I would start out slow and easy this time, beginning with a part-time job as a volunteer. There was an indoor golf facility close to my mom's house called Dave's Golf Spot. It was a retail golf store and had a computerized golf simulator that consumers could play golf on, practice or take golf lessons. There was also a practice net that golfers could hit balls into. The facility was open all year round. To be honest, it was a dive. There was an ugly old orange couch in there that looked terrible. The only other furniture was a small plastic table with four plastic chairs. The whole interior and layout was rudimentary at best. It was more like an eyesore.

In June, I took my resume to meet the owner, Dave Allewelle. He looked at my resume immediately, and I was upfront with him about my disorder. We talked about some of my history with this illness. He was impressed with my resume and references, and we got along well right from the start. I told Dave I would work for free on a part-time basis if I could teach golf there and get paid eighty percent of my lesson revenue. I wasn't concerned about making a lot of money at that point. Mainly, I wanted something to do, something I enjoyed. Also, I thought this might be a good way for me to ease back into the golf industry. If this went well, maybe I could start working at a golf course again.

A few days later, we had a second meeting where he accepted my offer, and we discussed how it would work. He didn't have any other employees because it was such a small operation. In a sense, Dave may have felt pretty lucky. Not too many Class "A" golf pros with experience working as a head pro walk into your business out of the blue offering to work for free. On the other hand, I felt lucky because Dave had some faith in me and gave me a chance when many others wouldn't have. I will always be grateful to him for this. He was a good, kindhearted person. Dave was a member of the United States Golf Teachers Federation (USGTF). I think he went to Phoenix, Arizona, for a five-day course to get this certification. I have several years of experience teaching golf, but I am the first to admit there is a lot more I could learn, so I don't know how someone can become a certified golf instructor after only five days of training. I'm not saying I was a better teacher than Dave. He was a little older than me (maybe in his mid-40s), and I don't know how much experience he had overall. I didn't see him teach much and vice versa. We didn't discuss our individual teaching methods and philosophies very much either.

Dave was quite religious, but he didn't push it on me. He was also a heavy smoker, so we spent a lot of time drinking coffee and smoking cigarettes. We shared a lot of laughs and good conversations while we did this. A few years later, Dave quit smoking.

In the summer months, Dave taught golf at Lake Okanagan Resort part-time. If he was doing this or playing golf, he would close the store. Having me around to help allowed him to have his business open more frequently, which made him more money. I ended up giving lessons to just a few people the whole time I worked there. In the end, Dave gave me 100% of my lesson revenue, but I still only made about $250.

My volunteer work schedule at Dave's Golf Spot was about three days a week, around eight to ten hours per week. Dave had quite a bit of golf merchandise for sale, and my main job was as a salesclerk. There was very little traffic coming through his business, and it was a very quiet place. In fact, I would usually only see a few customers on my three-hour shifts. As far as my mental health was concerned, this was an extremely low-stress job, and I seemed to be managing quite well.

Elli wanted her nephew, Darrell Bachmann, and I to meet each other. During that time, Darrell was the head superintendent of The Falls Golf Club in Chilliwack, BC. He is an avid golfer and has a low handicap. He was coming to Kelowna and bringing a girl named Colleen with him. Darrell and Colleen were getting together with Elli, so she asked me if I wanted to join them. I said "Sure." We had dinner at The Keg, and Darrell very generously paid the tab. As soon as Darrell and I met, he said to me, "I love you man!" It was my introduction into the very loving Bachmann family. It turned out that this was Darrell and Colleen's first date. For Elli and I, it was just a casual get together as friends. After The Keg, we all decided to go to Gotchas, a popular nightclub in Kelowna. It was packed when we got there. Darrell and Colleen had a few drinks and did some dancing. Elli had three tequila shots, and then she just started drinking water. She wasn't drunk. She loves dancing and gently tried to persuade me to dance with her. I was dead sober and way too shy, so there was no chance of that happening. No worries, she just went and danced with Darrell and Colleen. I was still having a good time.

After we were there for a couple of hours, I began to feel a little differently towards Elli. I started to feel something I had never felt with her before. I realized I was attracted to her. I was thinking, "Damn, she looks pretty good." The next thing I knew, I wanted to kiss her, which had some complications.

First of all, Elli was my home support worker and a good friend. I was also self-conscious about my huge belly. Attempting to kiss her would be a very gutsy call. I waited until Darrell and Colleen went back on the dance floor before I "made my move." I motioned for Elli to give me a kiss on my left cheek. As she went to do this, I turned my head towards her so that her kiss met my lips. It was a little sneaky, but it worked perfectly! That was our first kiss, and we ended up calling that night our first date. We use that date, July 22, 2000, as our anniversary date. Of course, we never forget that it was Darrell and Colleen's first date also. Pretty cool.

Later, Elli told me that when I kissed her, she thought "Wow, that was nice," but, "Oh no! I don't want to lose my good friend!" The irony of that statement is that we have been happily "married" for twenty years now, and we are best friends. It is the glue that bonds us together.

After our first date, things progressed between us. I called Helen Barnick, my case worker at Mental Health in Kelowna, and told her that I was doing well and didn't need Elli as my home support worker anymore. The last thing I wanted was for her to get into trouble over our situation. Obviously, it would be unethical for her to be having a relationship with one of her clients. Elli and I met with Helen and explained that we had become a couple. Helen was OK with this, as Elli was no longer my home support worker.

The next obstacle was with my mom. During the three years Elli was my home support worker, my mom loved her. They always got along great. There were no issues whatsoever. As soon as our relationship became romantic, all of that changed dramatically. My mom became a totally different person. The culprit for my mom's transformation was mainly jealousy, which can be a very ugly and nasty trait. My mom wasn't a jealous person, per se. But she did have some of it in her, as I had witnessed before.

We are all human, and I think pretty much anyone can get a little jealous, for many reasons, from time to time. But it can also get very serious and destroy relationships. Mom felt like Elli was taking me away from her, which I thought was ridiculous. I was still living with her and spent more time with her than Elli. When Elli and I would go to the park by the lake, we would bring Mom with us. She should have been happy for us. Instead, she was trying to control and possess me, and she was treating me like a child. I was thirty-six years old!

Elli worked during the day five days a week, and I would spend the whole day with my mom. Around 7 p.m., I would go over to Elli's place. Because my mom was the way she was, I always made sure I was home by midnight and slept in my own bed. Elli and I would end up making out, and I would fall asleep. She would wake me up so I could go home by midnight. We both wished I could just stay for the whole night. Instead of Cinderella, Elli started calling me "Cinderfella."

Elli and I have a lot in common. One thing is that we're both dog lovers. At the time, she had a basset hound named Arlo, and we quickly became best buddies. Elli has told me many times that around 7 p.m. every evening, Arlo would be sitting at the front door waiting for my arrival. Arlo was funny and was quite a character. Everyone loved him. He was like a celebrity in our neighborhood. It seemed like everyone knew his name, but they didn't know ours. When we were out walking him in the park, people would say "Hi Arlo! Hi Arlo's mom and dad." Elli gave me a key for her place so I could go over and walk Arlo when she was working. I really enjoyed this because I hadn't spent much time around dogs since we had our three German shepherds in Wetaskiwin.

On Elli's days off, I spent time with her at her place, and then went back to my mom's to spend time with her. When I got home, Mom would be ranting and raging about Elli. It was unbelievable how angry and nasty she became. I would try to reason with her, but I couldn't. It was like she lost her mind. Some days I couldn't take it anymore and went back to Elli's.

Elli tried to talk with my mom over the phone and in person. As always, she was nothing but kind, loving, patient and reasonable. She tried extremely hard to reason with Mom. In turn, Mom would swear at Elli and call her nasty names. She was so cruel. All of this was totally unfair, and Elli didn't deserve any of it. It was a very difficult time.

This kind of situation could damage or end someone's relationship, but thank God Elli hung in there with me — and my mom. Over time, things got better. Happily, this issue got resolved before it was too late. Mom finally came around and returned to her normal self again. At last, she accepted the fact that Elli and I were a couple. During the last several years of mom's life, she and Elli got along extremely well.

Despite the stress I endured from my mom's behavior, I managed to stay healthy for the rest of the year. For the first year since 1993, I didn't go manic and end up in a psych ward.

CHAPTER 22

2001

A NEW HOME

I was still working part-time at Dave's Golf Spot. It gave me something to do over the winter months, and I stayed there well into the golf season. A major factor was that I liked Dave, and we got along so well.

Elli and I didn't plan to move in together, but it happened naturally during my mom's incessant jealousy. The first time I spent the whole night at Elli's was on Christmas Eve of 2000. It was nice to wake up beside her and spend Christmas day together. After that, my overnight stays became more common. Then, I began to bring some of my personal possessions over there, little by little. It just evolved from there. The only other woman I have ever lived with was Linda, back in 1987. The first thing I brought over to Elli's was the computer I had recently purchased because she was going to teach me how to use it. I had taken a computer course at the SDGA for a whole semester, but it didn't go well. I received a "D" — my worst grade out of all the courses I took there.

I signed up for an adult beginners' computer course at Mount Boucherie High School in West Kelowna in the first part of 2001. There were to be four, two-hour classes. During the first class, I was having a really hard time and not getting it. The instructor was good, but I didn't understand what he was trying to teach us. I couldn't follow his commands. I got extremely frustrated and felt like a complete idiot. I didn't go back for the other three classes.

Elli was a good teacher. She spent a lot of time with me and was very patient. She taught me the very basics, like how to use the internet and how to Google for information, so I started to use my computer quite a bit. For about a year, I was researching real estate properties for my friend Dave Lambert, and I started to enjoy using Google to get the information I was looking for.

A new golf course opened in West Kelowna called Vintage Hills Golf Course & Academy. It was owned by John MacKay. (Years later, under new ownership, the name of this facility was changed to Two Eagles Golf Course & Academy.) I got involved right away because I could see its potential. There is a practice facility there with a regulation-size driving range and a 15,000 square foot practice green where golfers can work on their putting, chipping and sand trap shots. From a teaching pro's standpoint, this facility is also very good for giving lessons. I wanted to become one of their teaching professionals, so I dropped off my resume. I thought there may have been a lot of competition in the Kelowna region, but I wanted to give it a shot anyway.

I got to know Chris Hinton, the head pro, and John, the owner. They brought me on board, and I started teaching. This was still a confidence-building time for me. Besides a few lessons at Dave's Golf Spot, I hadn't taught since Terrae Pines in 1994. The lesson programs were still in their infancy, and I taught sporadically.

In the summer of 2001, I took over from Dave Allewelle and became the golf instructor at Lake Okanagan Resort. This was a part-time job, two days a week. Unlike Vintage Hills, this teaching facility was feeble. Totally inadequate. My students had to hit golf balls off of a dilapidated matt into a net. The balls could only travel about fifteen feet. I liked to evaluate the "ball flight," which was a crucial part of my lessons, so hitting a golf ball only fifteen feet isn't far enough to determine this. It didn't matter that much though because most of my lessons were for children from 3-10 years old who needed to learn the basic fundamentals. I had to keep things nice and simple for them, so I wasn't too concerned about "ball flight."

There were usually about a dozen children per group, so I often felt like I was babysitting rather than teaching golf. I really had to keep a close eye on them all the time because they had a tendency to fool around. The youngest ones had a very short attention span, so I couldn't teach a lot to them. One little Asian girl, about four years old, walked over to me and held my hand for a few minutes. She was adorable! I tried to keep the lessons interesting and fun for the kids. I was getting paid an average of $50-$60/hour, and I worked for every cent of it!

One day, Chris Hinton invited me to play golf with him and two of his CPGA pro friends at the Okanagan Golf Club on the Bear Course. I hadn't played in a group of pros like this for seven years, and I was only playing a handful of times a year. I was quite nervous, and I didn't play very well — I think I shot 81. But I still enjoyed the day.

ALMOST WENT MANIC AGAIN

In the fall of 2001, I was finished teaching golf at both places and just doing my volunteer job at Dave's Golf Spot. One afternoon when I was there, I began to feel strange. People coming in there seemed "different." Physically, they looked normal, but I was sensing their "spirit." I didn't sense the presence of God or the devil, just "regular" spirit coming through people. Nonetheless, this was a major concern — red flags, for sure. Whether this phenomenon was real or delusional, I knew it happened when I was starting to go manic or was already manic. It always happened in a split second, out of the blue. I have never received any "notice" for spirit showing up, it just does. Welcome or not.

Regardless, I had to get out of the shop and away from these people ASAP. It was too much stimulation for me. Dave was in Ontario, so I called his son, Paxton, and told him I wasn't feeling well. I asked him if he could come over to the shop because I had to leave right away. Thankfully, he did. Then I called Elli, and she came to the shop immediately. We went straight home. Luckily, Elli had a little bit of extra Clozapine put aside for emergencies. She gave me about 25 mg., and I laid on the couch and fell asleep. When I woke up, I was OK. It's amazing how powerful Clozapine is and what it can do. This episode was a close call. My "mini-mania" only lasted for about an hour and, luckily, I avoided another trip to the psych ward. This is a perfect example of how there can be such a fine line between a normal mood state and a manic one. Nurse Elli knew exactly what to do. She saved me!

Dave called me that night from Ontario because he had been talking with Paxton and was concerned about me. He was genuine and sincere.

For my health and well-being, I decided to end my arrangement with Dave. Even though I wasn't working a lot of hours, apparently it was causing me enough stress, which resulted in a near relapse. I took a break from things until the end of December, but I started going to the pool again. I loved to go there during the winter months and use their hot tub, steam room and swimming pool. It was relaxing and rejuvenating. With a renewed sense of vigor, I felt good going into 2002. I had been well for one year and nine months — but who's counting?

CHAPTER 23

2002-2005
THREE MILLION DOLLAR BUSINESS PLAN

In the spring of 2002, Christopher Bosky, the recreation director at Lake Okanagan Resort called me a few times. He really wanted me to come back in the summer and teach golf again, but I told him I had already made other plans and that I couldn't do it. I had started a new project in January that basically turned into a full-time job for the next four years. I was developing a business plan. I spent at least forty hours per week working on this detailed and extensive plan. I did the whole thing on paper, including several pages of financial statements. Elli typed everything up and did a tremendous job of designing the plan on the computer. She worked on this for countless hours in addition to working her regular full-time job. We needed three million dollars to bring our plan to fruition.

I really did my homework on this, including an incredible amount of research. I used the computer a lot, and it was a great plan! I had extremely positive meetings with the City of Kelowna and the West Kelowna First Nations council. Along the way, Elli and I had a few meetings with Roxanne Lindley and her husband, Wayne. The Lindley family owned a lot of property in West Kelowna. Roxanne's father was the first Okanagan First Nations chief in West Kelowna, and Roxanne became the chief in 2016. We needed three acres of land for our business, and commercial real estate in Kelowna was approximately $300,000/acre at the time. We proposed that if the Lindleys allowed us to build and operate our business on her family's land, they would own a 1/3 share of the business. After talking with Elli and I, and having looked at our plan, they seemed very interested. If they agreed to this, we had to raise two million dollars.

Everything seemed to be falling into place. About two weeks after we finished our business plan in 2005, I was playing golf at Vintage Hills with my friend, Ken Nakamura. We got paired up with another couple, named Keiven and Petra Bauer. During our round of golf, I told Keiven and his wife about our plan, and they were very interested right away. Keiven was the CFO of a large company with $200 million in annual revenues. He was in his late 50s and in the process of retiring. He and Petra had recently moved to West

Kelowna Estates from the west coast. Keiven was eager to look at our business plan, so we exchanged contact information.

Less than a week later, we had our first meeting. It went very well, and I gave him a copy of our plan. From there, Keiven and I met on a regular basis. Usually, our meetings were at his home office. Sometimes, we met at Tim Hortons. I was open and honest with him regarding my bipolar disorder. I had been well for five years, and Keiven didn't have an issue with this at all. He never questioned my mental-health status in any way.

Keiven was a good guy. He was very smart and excelled when it came to business and financial matters. He told me one time that he really didn't need to work at all. He wasn't bragging, he was just being honest. He had worked incredibly hard and became extremely wealthy. He never told me what his net worth was. He was very humble in this regard.

He spent a considerable amount of time helping us with our business plan, particularly with our financial statements. I kept telling him I wanted to pay him for his help, but he wouldn't accept any money from me. He was extremely generous with his time and effort. Things moved really fast with Keiven helping us. Within a month, he had made arrangements to have two million dollars financed directly into our plan through his own personal banker in Vancouver. Right before he finalized this transaction with his banker, he asked me, "Are you sure you want to do this?"

"Yes!" I said.

I told Keiven several times that I wanted him to benefit financially from the business. This was all new to me. What I found strange, was that I never heard Keiven refer to himself as a "business partner" or "investor." Every time I said something about him being a benefactor of the business, he would say, "We'll worry about that later."

After we had the financing in place, we had an extremely important meeting that could have sealed the deal for us. Keiven, Elli and I met with Roxanne, Wayne and some members of the West Kelowna First Nations Band. Our meeting was held outdoors overlooking Lake Okanagan, right near the three acre parcel of land we wanted for our business. The meeting seemed to go well, and we thought Roxanne and her associates were seriously considering partnering with us. We just had to wait for their decision.

Elli had a Heart Attack

Elli had been working extremely hard on the business plan, but I didn't realize the toll it was taking on her health. About a week after our meeting, Elli had a heart attack. She was only forty-nine years old, and, luckily, it was a minor one. Stress was a factor, and she was hospitalized for a few days. Later, she admitted to me how much stress our plan was causing her. Elli's heart attack scared the shit out of me and was a major wake-up call to say the least. Thank God it wasn't fatal because I would be completely lost without her. She means everything to me.

After this happened, I reconsidered my own health status. I had been well for a record of five years, but I knew from experience that this could change in a heartbeat. Too much stress could tip the scales in manic depression's favor very quickly and destroy everything in its path. Many of my plans and dreams didn't work out because of my mental illness, but this time there was three million dollars involved.

Elli and I had some lengthy conversations about this whole business thing. In the end, we knew that our health must come first, so we were planning on completely backing out of the whole deal. At almost the same moment, Roxanne called us. She informed us that she and her family were negotiating with realtors and land developers over the sale of their land. Basically, they could get a lot more money for their land by selling it instead of going with our proposal. She was sorry that our deal didn't work out, but it was a relief for Elli and I.

I had to inform Keiven that we were backing out of the deal, which I was dreading. He was an incredible support system for us. I started by telling him about Elli's heart attack, and he seemed very empathetic and even asked if there was anything he could do to help. There wasn't, but it was nice of him to ask. I told him how much we appreciated his help, but Elli's heart attack made us realize that my own illness could relapse at any time — stress was a huge factor. Being "the head guy" of this operation, I would have a lot on my plate. I gave Keiven a sincere apology and thanked him for all of his time and effort. I told him about Roxanne backing out of our deal as well. We still could have pursued some property in north Kelowna that we had been looking at or could have looked for other land for our business, but we had made up our minds. We were done. This was very disappointing for me. My dream was quashed.

Throughout this process, I felt like Keiven was becoming a friend and possibly even a mentor. Unfortunately, after this last conversation, I never heard from him again. I guess he considered our relationship as strictly a business endeavor. He may have been pissed off that I didn't follow through with things after he got involved, which I understand. I was surprised that he wasn't a lot more stringent regarding the two million dollars he would have financed for our business plan. Like I said, I never heard him identify himself as an investor or business partner. I assumed this was his motive for doing this. I doubt that he was "giving" us two million just to be a nice guy.

In the end, it was a good thing for Elli and I (and for Keiven) to step away from this transaction. Fortunately, because of his goodwill, we didn't owe Keiven anything besides our gratitude. After helping us, Keiven started doing the books for Chuck Fipke, a multimillionaire who made his money in diamond mines. What a contrast to go from working for me, who had no money at all, to working for a multimillionaire!

I haven't described what this business plan actually is because I still think it's a great plan, and I want to keep it confidential. It includes golf and real estate. It is a multi-purpose, multi-revenue generating business that combines several businesses under the umbrella of one main business. These businesses are designed to network with each other in order to maximize revenues and profits. Just a reminder that Chief Financial Officer Keiven Bauer was sold on this business plan as soon as he looked at it. I haven't shown my plan to anyone else since Keiven. If I didn't have my health issues, I am quite confident this business would have been operating very successfully for a long time.

As I invested four years of my life, full-time, on this plan (plus Elli's countless hours), I would still like to be compensated for all the time and effort we put into this project. Even though it's been several years since its conception, this plan still has tremendous potential. It might even be a better time to do this now, as opposed to then. I really believe this could still work. Are there any investors out there who may be interested? I am open for offers. I thought it might be a good idea to plug this in my book!

CHAPTER 24
2006
No More Pro Card

Because of my bipolar disorder, the CPGA put me in the "retired" category for my professional status in 1996. I kept paying my annual dues and received a new "retired" pro card every year for ten years. I was hoping to someday come out of "retirement" and be an "active" CPGA professional again, but after this ten-year period, I realized the chances of this happening were very unlikely, to say the least. Aborting our business plan in 2005 was the last straw for me as far as trying to keep my pro card.

In 2006, I made the incredibly difficult decision to accept the fact that I would never be able to work again. My career as a CPGA golf professional was officially over. I decided to stop paying my annual dues, which meant I no longer received my "retired" pro card and consequently meant I was no longer considered an official CPGA professional, period. When I didn't pay my annual fees for 2006, I didn't receive my new pro card in the mail as I had since 1987. It was a sad feeling, and it took a long time for me to get over it.

The good thing about 2006 was that I stayed well for another year, my sixth with no mania, no severe depression and no psych wards!

CHAPTER 25
2007
DIAGNOSED WITH OCD

After six years of wellness, I was diagnosed with obsessive-compulsive disorder (OCD) in 2007. I diagnosed myself first because I had been experiencing what I thought were OCD symptoms for close to a year. At first, I kept this to myself because I wasn't sure if that's what it was. Over time, it got worse. One day, I told Elli I thought I had OCD, and she wasn't overly surprised. She had noticed some of my symptoms as well. Shortly after that, my psychiatrist, Dr. Diaz, confirmed the diagnosis.

OCD is an anxiety disorder that involves repetitive behaviors or compulsions. There are different types of OCD. For example, people who fear getting an infection may constantly wash their hands. Famous Canadian comedian, TV star and gameshow host Howie Mandell has OCD of this kind. He won't shake hands with anyone and goes to extremes trying to avoid any germs. My OCD means I spend an enormous amount of my time counting and checking things. Especially checking. I probably spend at least two hours every day doing this. It's normal for a person to check things two or three times, which is the way I used to be. Since having OCD I can't seem to stop there. Once I start checking something, I keep checking it. Over and over and over again. I will do this countless times. I'm aware I'm doing it, but I can't stop. The urge to keep checking is incredibly powerful. The "obsessive" is the thinking part, and the "compulsive" is the acting part. My OCD started with checking normal things, such as making sure the stove was turned off, the lights were off and the doors were locked. Over time, I kept adding things. Now it seems like I can't do anything without checking it several times. I get fixated, and my mind gets stuck. Often, I don't even realize I'm doing it and Elli will tell me to "Stop!"

Because I'm at home most of the time, that's where the vast majority of my OCD occurs. The two things I check most are that the stove is turned off and that the gate is closed and locked so our dog can't get out of our yard. With the stove, I make sure all four elements and the oven itself is off. I make sure the stove lights are off. For a normal person, this would take a few seconds. Maybe they would double-check this, taking a few more seconds. It takes me about three minutes. This may not seem like a long time, but by doing this a ridiculous number of times a day, it really adds up. I have a ritual for when I'm checking the three lights on the stove to make sure they're off. I check the left side, then the middle one, then the one on the right. As I do this, I count "1, 2, 3." I try to stop right there, but I am never able to. Instead, I try to count "1, 2, 3" three times. I usually do this a lot more than three times. Then, still focusing on the lights, I start saying "off, off, off" three times. I usually do this a lot more than three times as well. At some point, it will finally register in my mind that the stove/oven is off, and I can walk away from it.

When I say this process takes me three minutes, this is when I'm at home. Leaving the house is much more difficult for me. If I leave the house by myself, it usually takes me ten to fifteen minutes to check the stove. If I'm leaving the house when Elli is at home or if we are leaving the house together, I still check the stove but only for a few minutes. One time when I was trying to leave by myself, I checked the stove for forty-five minutes. That's a really long time to be going "1, 2, 3, off, off, off. 1, 2, 3, off, off, off. 1, 2, 3, off, off, off." Try doing this fifty times, repetitively, non-stop, while trying to focus and concentrate 100% while doing this. It's incredibly stressful and almost drives me crazy! When the stove light is on, it's so obvious to me! The bright red lights register in my mind immediately. It makes me think I should always be able to tell if the stove is on or off in a couple of seconds. This should be "obvious" and it should "register," but it doesn't. If I start my "ritual" and get the least bit distracted, I start all over again.

My OCD became so bad that I began to avoid leaving the house by myself. With Elli working thirty-two hours per week, this left me home alone a lot. I almost stopped walking our dog. I didn't want to deal with my OCD, and my solution was to not leave the house. If I was going to go out with a friend, I would have them come and pick me up so they could come in the house and assure me the stove was off. After this was done, we could go on our way.

My OCD affects me in many ways but is almost always related to checking things. One example is when I go shopping (which I don't like in the first place). When I get to the store, it takes me five to ten minutes just to get out of the car. I spend this time checking to make sure the car is in "park," the windows are all up and the doors are locked. As I do this over and over, I see other people in the parking lot and envy them for how quickly they do the same thing I'm doing. It looks so easy. It's automatic for them, like they don't even have to think about it. It only takes them a second or two, and then they go into the store. I wish I could do that.

When I start shopping, I read the label on each item several times before I'm convinced I have the right product. This is somewhat stressful, and it takes me a lot longer to shop than it would for the average person.

When I get home and park the car in the driveway, I go through the whole process again. I'm sure our neighbors have seen me checking to make sure my car is locked many times. They must think I'm crazy as they watch me tugging on the car door handle countless times. This happens wherever I go with the car. I'm sure people must see me doing this, and it's embarrassing, but I can't stop it. It's like I get possessed.

There are psychiatric medications I could take for my OCD, but Dr. Diaz and I have agreed against trying this. It took several years to get me balanced on the right psych meds for my bipolar disorder, so we don't want to take the chance of putting me on more psych meds that might have a detrimental effect on my brain chemistry and possibly cause an imbalance again.

My personality and character is pretty easygoing, and I am not a moody person, per se. Then I get two major mood disorders (bipolar and seasonal affective) followed with an anxiety disorder (OCD). What's up with that? I've worked hard to combat my OCD and have improved in some regards. Mainly, I'm getting out of the house by myself, and I don't need my friends to check the stove for me when I go out with them anymore. This is trivial for most people but is a victory of sorts for someone with OCD.

My OCD drives Elli crazy too. For the most part, she's quite understanding about it all. One time, I came into the house all pissed off.

"God damn it! God damn, fucking OCD!" I yelled.

Elli said, "What's wrong?"

I said, "Fucking OCD — I checked the tire pressure on my car so many times that now the tire is totally flat!"

I have heard this illness called "The OCD devil," and I can relate to that for sure.

For thirteen years, OCD has been a real problem for me. It even affects my reading and writing. When I'm reading, I get "stuck" a lot and read the same words and/or sentences over and over again several times before I can move on. Because of this, it can take me a long time to read something. Writing is a real challenge as well. It involves reading and writing simultaneously, which means I am constantly checking everything I write down. It is a slow and arduous task. I have put an incredible amount of time and effort into writing my book over the last twelve years. In the earlier stages, I was kind of writing on and off, taking breaks here and there. In the last two years, I have written almost every day. I usually write for 1½ to 2½ hours a day in the afternoons or early evenings. In the last couple of years, I have been averaging ¾ of a page every day. This might not sound like much, but it really adds up when you stick with it. I write everything with paper and pen, as my computer skills are not up to par. Just in the last two years, I have written approximately 450 pages. In total, I have written at least eight hundred pages, which is enough material for two books.

As bad as my OCD is, it still pales in comparison to what I've been through with my bipolar disorder. I have never been committed to a psychiatric ward because of OCD, so that's a bonus.

CHAPTER 26
2008-2009
MOM DIED

The year 2008 was going pretty good for me until the end of November when Mom had an accident. It was Grey Cup Sunday, a week before the end of November, and Mom was at home watching the game. I was at home doing the same thing. As usual, I had already talked with her on the phone a couple of times that day, and everything was fine. I called her again in the evening, and she still seemed fine.

I went over to her place the next morning around 11 a.m. for a coffee. We sat at the kitchen table, and I noticed she was wearing long sleeves. I didn't think anything of it and stayed for about an hour. I didn't notice anything unusual, and nothing seemed out of the ordinary for the rest of the day.

I talked with her several times over the phone on Tuesday and Wednesday and was led to believe everything was OK, but I was woken by the phone at 7 a.m. Thursday morning. It was my brother, Rick. He had been at my mom's house Wednesday night, and he told me that when they were watching TV he saw something on her left arm. He had a closer look and lifted her sleeve to see her arm was badly burned. He checked further and saw that a large area of her upper body was also severely burned. I don't know why Rick didn't get mom to the hospital right then and there. She likely refused — she could be extremely stubborn. Rick said Mom had had an accident with the stove. Somehow, her shirt caught on fire when it came in contact with one of the elements. I raced over there as fast as I could.

Mom was reluctant to show me her burns at first, but eventually she revealed them. She had concealed this from me with her clothing when I was with her on Monday morning. I was shocked at what I saw, and it broke my heart at the same time. I had never seen anyone burned so badly. The majority of the burns were on her left side — her left arm, armpit and parts of her chest and stomach were badly burned. They were all third degree burns. Luckily, Mom's face, head and neck didn't get burned. The doctors said that fifteen percent of her body had been burned, but it seemed like more than that to me.

Mom showed me the shirt she had been wearing when she had her accident. It was all burnt and wet. She managed to take it off when it caught on fire. Then she put it in the kitchen sink and soaked it with water. It was a grim sight. I don't know how she took it off without burning her head and face. I felt so bad for her. She must have been terrified, and the pain must have been excruciating. It was a bad situation. Mom's burns could have been a lot worse, and the house could have burned down with her as well.

Despite all of this, Mom still didn't want to go to the hospital. She was so stubborn! I convinced her that she had to go and there was no other choice. She didn't want an ambulance to come and pick her up, so Rick and I drove her to the Kelowna General Hospital right away. We were able to get her into the emergency ward without having to wait, and they treated her immediately. One of the nurses told me she had never seen anyone burned so badly without receiving treatment for that length of time. It had been four days since her accident. I knew my mom was a very strong lady, but this was ridiculous. The emergency ward staff at KGH did their best to help Mom, but her burns were too severe to be treated properly there. After a one-night stay, they sent her by air ambulance to Vancouver where she was admitted into the specialized burn unit at the Vancouver General Hospital.

The doctors and nurses at the burn unit were fantastic. Treating burns was their specialty, and they were very good at it. The nurses were kind, caring and compassionate. They kept Mom as comfortable as possible and gave her pain medication that was more powerful than morphine or Demerol.

At least one of her kids was with her the whole time, and sometimes all five of us were there. Elli and I flew from Kelowna, but after several days we had to go home. A couple of weeks later, I flew out there again by myself as Elli had to stay home and go to work. We all stayed at a hotel a few blocks from the Vancouver General Hospital. Mom was in there for the whole month of December. It was colder and snowed more than usual for Vancouver that year. We walked through the snow and cold, back and forth between the hotel and hospital countless times.

One of the most important things was to try and prevent Mom from getting an infection. We had to put on clean hospital gowns and gloves every time we went into her room. We also had to wash our hands every time we entered and exited the burn unit itself.

I thought I would see a lot of gruesome burns when I was there, but I didn't. They kept the patients in there very private. The curtains and doors to the patients' rooms were closed, so you really couldn't see much.

Mom went through a great deal in there. Despite the precautions, she still got some infections, as well as fluid in her lungs and pneumonia. She had two operations for skin grafts, and to top it off, she had a heart attack. If all this wasn't enough, she also suffered from smoking and alcohol withdrawal. She was a heavy smoker and drank every day. Being confined to her room in the burn unit, she couldn't go outside for a cigarette. They put a nicotine patch on her, which may have helped a bit, but it's not quite like the real thing.

In the end, all this was too much for her. On January 3, 2009, my brother Jim called me at 6:30 a.m. to tell me that Mom had passed away in her sleep. I think her heart gave out on her.

My biggest breakdown was about two weeks before she died. I was outside the hospital with my brothers, and it hit me really hard that Mom might not make it. I started to cry, then began weeping and sobbing uncontrollably. It was by far the hardest I have ever cried in my life. This lasted for quite a while. I loved my mom so much and was concerned that I might go into a severe and very lengthy "chemical imbalance" type of depression when she died. Thankfully, this didn't happen. Of course, I was depressed, but it was a "normal" kind of depression a person experiences after losing a loved one. My mom was seventy-eight years old when she passed away.

CHAPTER 27
2010-2019
STAYING HEALTHY

My life isn't as exciting as it was when I was younger, but I'm not complaining. Taking into consideration my history with manic depression, I am content. As of May 2019, I have been well for over nineteen years. I still have OCD and SAD, but I don't suffer as much from mental illness as I did with manic depression. After going through hell the first ten years with this chemical imbalance, it seems like a miracle to have been balanced and well ever since. I don't miss the highs and lows of this mood disorder. Not having gone manic or gotten severely depressed in all these years encourages me to think my future looks bright.

I do have what I call "minor" depression quite often, which I hate but at least it's not 24/7, and it's not nearly as severe as it used to be. My "chemistry" is the culprit for this. Now I always get through it okay. Two of my psychiatrists told me on several occasions that I had the most severe case of bipolar disorder they had ever seen. If my illness could be treated, balanced and ultimately have a happy ending, I think the same thing could happen for anyone with bipolar disorder.

In becoming "balanced," the two most important things for me are the right psychiatric medications and the right environment. This includes keeping my stress to a minimum. I have been taking the same psychiatric medications every day since 2000 and have been well this whole time. Everyone's chemistry is different. When it comes to psych meds, what works for one might not work for another. Sometimes people get put on the right combination right away, but I wasn't so lucky.

MEDICATION COMPLIANCE!

I didn't take my illness seriously between 1989 and 1995. I regarded my manic and depressed states as something that "happened to me," then I carried on with my life as if these things didn't happen in the first place! During those first six years, I should have accepted the fact that I had a mental illness, that it is a part of me, and that I would live with it for the rest of my life. Instead, I did it the hard way; I didn't manage my illness properly. The only times I took psychiatric medications during this era was when I was hospitalized in psych wards during manic episodes. Each time I was discharged, I would stop taking my medication. To make matters worse, I was still drinking a lot and was smoking pot and hash. I loved to party, which wasn't good for my chemical imbalance. If I had managed my illness properly from the start, things may have been a little easier for me.

From 1995 to present day, I have been totally compliant with taking my psych meds. Even when the meds weren't working for me, I still took them as directed by my psychiatrists. After lengthy periods of depression, I would give up hope of getting better, but I would always take my meds. A lot of people stop taking their psychiatric medications when they start feeling better. Then they relapse. This often results in another trip to the psych ward. These individuals must realize that they felt well because they were taking their meds. To stay well, they must continue to take their meds. This is essential. Compliance is a must!

I take other medications as well, such as Metformin and Invokana for my diabetes. Most of my medications, including my psych meds, come in a blister pack I get from Dyck's Pharmacy in Kelowna. They give me a two-week supply at a time and deliver them right to my home every second Friday. Their delivery service is free! The blister packs are very convenient. It reminds me when I need to take my meds and shows whether I have already taken them. They're marked morning, noon, evening and bedtime.

I get my blood work done once a month to check my Clozapine level because it can become toxic if it's too high, and they won't give me more Clozapine until they have seen the results of my tests. I have been doing this for twenty years, and there has never been a problem. Dr. Diaz also keeps a close eye on my Clozapine levels.

THE RIGHT ENVIRONMENT

It took me a long time, but I finally realized how important it is for me to live in the right environment. Again, the main thing is stress. Simply put, I have to try and keep my stress to a minimum because too much could trigger a relapse, which is the last thing I want to happen.

There are five main categories relating to an individual's "environment":
1. Home life (spouse, family, etc.)
2. School/education
3. Work
4. Friends (social life)
5. Extracurricular activities (sports, etc.)

Because I spend ninety percent of my time at home, my "home life" environment is the most important one for me. Elli and I have been living together for twenty years, and my manic depression has been stable for all of these years! Since Elli and I have been a couple, I haven't gone manic and haven't had any serious depression. I haven't been a patient in a psych ward this whole time. This is no coincidence.

I attribute my wellness to many things, but the two main reasons are the right psych meds and having Elli as my wife. Elli means everything to me. Most importantly, she's my best friend. We have a lot in common, and we get along amazingly well. We haven't had one single argument in the twenty-three years we've known each other. Sometimes, not often, we get pissed off at one another, but we always get over it very quickly. It also helps that we can agree to disagree. Elli is also my wife and partner. She's my lover. She's my rock. She's a completely honest person, and I trust her 100%. I have more respect for Elli than any other person in my life. She understands me better than anyone else. I hate being misunderstood, and this doesn't happen with Elli. We're almost always on the same page. She is extremely intelligent and has a great sense of humor. She makes me laugh a lot. She is extremely kind, caring and very generous. Elli is also very thoughtful and considerate towards others. She has a lot of compassion and empathy. On top of all of this, she's good looking too! I feel like the luckiest guy in the world. I love Elli so much!

My home environment couldn't be any better for me. We both like being at home, and we really enjoy each other's company. We never get tired of each other. We just like hanging out together. Elli is also creative and spends every spare moment she has on visual arts, painting and drawing. We easily go off into our own worlds. Between my writing and her art projects the days pass quickly. Our home is full of peace, love, joy and laughter. It's the perfect environment for me. It's a good thing my home life is so enjoyable because it's the main part of my lifestyle, which has become more of a comfortable daily routine.

One of the reasons we stay in a lot is because it costs money to go out and do things. One of my goals is to advocate for people with a mental illness who are living on CPP Disability by trying to get the government to increase the amount of money they receive. I would like to see these "policy makers" try to live on $700/month for a year or two to get a real sense of what it's like. Obviously, I couldn't afford to get my own place. If it wasn't for Elli, I might have to live in some kind of group home. Even worse, I may have ended up living on the streets like a lot of people with mental illness do. Thanks to Elli, I have a roof over my head. I live in a warm, cozy home and have shelter from the cold. We have plenty of food to eat. I'm not suffering. Elli pays all the household bills, including the mortgage on our mobile home, and the monthly "pad rent." My $700 goes towards paying bills and buying groceries. It goes fast, and I wish I could help out more than I do. Because of my low income, I have to be very frugal with my money. During 2016, I only spent approximately $60 at restaurants. This was the only money I spent on any kind of "entertainment" for the year. I spend less than $100/year on average in this regard.

When Elli's not working, she's at home almost all the time. As a couple, we very rarely eat out, and we hardly ever spend money on any other kinds of entertainment. We haven't been able to go on one single vacation during the twenty years we've been together. The amazing thing is that I've never heard Elli complain about any of this. Not even once! I'm not complaining either — you have to live within your means.

My life isn't nearly as exciting as it was when I was in my 20s and they called me "The Rock Star," but I'm in my 50s now, and I think we all slow down when we get older. The party days were fun when I was younger, but I don't miss them at all. I haven't played golf since 2012. I played so infrequently over the previous twenty years that my game really deteriorated. When I did play, my bad back always bothered me. I don't know if I will ever try and get back into it.

I've been writing for several years and it has become like a job. I've spent several thousands of hours writing and editing this book. It's a lot of hard work, but I remind myself that I really have become a "writer," which is a job I can do while remaining healthy!

I have had the same daily routine for many years, and it plays a big part in keeping me balanced and well. Most importantly, there is very little stress in my life. The stress I suffer from is mostly because of OCD, which is minor compared to the stress I went through when I was manic and severely depressed. I am a creature of habit. I wake up around the same time every morning, take my morning medication, get a cup of coffee and have breakfast at the kitchen table. During the winter months, I turn on my SAD light — the special light that helps me avoid getting winter depression — for twenty minutes while I eat. After breakfast and before taking our dog for a walk, I go through my OCD ritual of checking everything, which takes about twenty minutes. We currently have our third Bernese Mountain dog, and her name is Stella; she's seven years old. We call Stella "our daughter," and our walk does us both good. After our walk I do dishes and some household chores. Between walking Stella every day and a change with my diabetic medication (Invokana), I have lost forty pounds.

I've had an afternoon nap after lunch every day for the past twenty-five years. Elli didn't used to, but soon after we started living together, she started to have naps with me. It quickly became her favorite part of the day! We shut everything down at nap time. No TV or radio, and our telephone is off the hook. Total peace and quiet. We usually have a good chat at this time. We always seem to have something to share or talk about, and our naps rejuvenate us for the rest of the day. Elli, Stella and I each get our own small snack bowl of mixed nuts to eat in bed at nap time. I think this has also become Stella's favorite time of the day.

I schedule my writing hours around Elli's work hours. When she's working, I try to write from 1:30-3:30 p.m. After our nap and before we have dinner, I usually write for another thirty minutes. On her days off, I write from 4:30-6:30 p.m. Sticking to this daily routine has worked well for me, and I've been amazed to see the pages add up by writing for a couple of hours every day.

We usually have dinner around 7 p.m. Elli's a good cook and makes a wide variety of healthy meals for us. After dinner, we do our "chores." Elli does the dishes, and I make our tea. Elli has chamomile tea, and we both have Bekunis Herbal tea, a herbal laxative. We call it "poop tea." It keeps us regular, and we have it every night. It works great! Way better than anything else we have ever tried. It's a tried and true remedy from Elli's mom. We've recommended this tea to several others, and it really works well for them too! Some medications can be very constipating, and it's great to have an effective product!

I take my evening medications with my tea around 8 p.m. About 9 p.m., I take my Clozapine just before bedtime, as it makes me very sleepy and groggy. Normally, I don't watch TV during the day. We relax and watch TV from around 8 p.m.-9:30 p.m. I used to relax and watch NFL football or golf on Sundays, and it was the only day I didn't write. For the last couple of years, I've been writing on Sundays as well. I still watch a little football and golf, but not for the whole day like I used to. We go to bed by 10 p.m. and read for about ½ an hour before we go to sleep. I get ten hours of sleep every night (10:30 p.m.-8:30 a.m.).

I am sound asleep this whole time. A lot of guys get up in the middle of the night once or twice to pee, but luckily this doesn't happen to me. My Clozapine takes awhile to kick in, but when it does, it knocks me right out. You could drive a freight train through our bedroom and I wouldn't wake up, which was a problem for a while. Because I was in such a deep sleep, I often used to pee the bed at night, so Elli was constantly washing the bed sheets. Finally, she'd had enough and told me to wear adult diapers to bed. I wasn't sure what to think of this at first, but I didn't have to think twice — it was a no brainer. Wearing adult diapers was a practical solution to my bed-wetting problem, and I got used to wearing them right away. It's not an issue for me, and they work great! It also saves Elli a lot of laundry work. A lot of men refuse to wear adult diapers because they are too "manly," but then their wives clean up after them. It's not a big deal, guys. Give your wife a break! If you're wetting the bed or have incontinence, wear some diapers! I think you will get used to them quickly and will be glad you did.

I never have a problem occupying my time. I'm always busy doing something. I like to cut the grass, do yardwork and shovel the snow from the driveway. My routine works well for me. I keep busy, but not "too busy." I go at my own pace. I don't have a lot of stress in my life, which is a key component regarding my health and well-being.

FISHING TRIP OF A LIFETIME!

In the summer of 2011, Dave Lambert took me with him and his friend, Wayne Battle (from Edmonton), on a fishing trip of a lifetime! We went to Haida Gwaii, which used to be called The Queen Charlotte Islands. Haida Gwaii is in British Columbia and is located northwest of Vancouver Island. This region is well-known to have some of the best fishing in the world.

I flew from Kelowna to Vancouver where I met up with Dave and Wayne. We stayed at a hotel near the Vancouver Airport that first night of our trip. Dave and I shared a room. The next morning, we took the two-hour flight from Vancouver to Haida Gwaii in a mid-size plane. The airport terminal was the smallest one I have ever seen, but it was really busy. It appeared that most of the people were doing the same thing we were: going fishing!

When I left Kelowna, it was hot, but the temperature at Haida Gwaii was much colder. Fishing outside on our boat in the middle of the Pacific Ocean, it became even cooler. Luckily, Dave had made this trip before and knew what to expect. I took his advice when he told me to bring a lot of warm clothes. I was sure glad I did! When we were fishing, I wore my winter jacket, heavy sweater, lined fleece jeans and boots.

The captain of our boat, Ron, picked us up at the airport. We stopped for supplies and went straight to Ron's boat, our fishing vessel. About an hour earlier, I had taken some Dramamine to help prevent seasickness. Before we got to Haida Gwaii, Dave, Wayne and I made individual lists of what we wanted to eat and drink during our trip, which Dave sent to Ron. Ron's wife got all our groceries, then stocked the boat with them. We were all set!

We would be fishing for four full days. Dave had made this trip with some of his other friends and Captain Ron previously. I thought we might be staying on a fancy yacht or something. Wishful thinking. Instead, we would be staying on an old, large, commercial fishing boat. This boat was anything but fancy, but it was sufficient. We fished off the back of the boat. On the inside, there was a table to sit at and a bit of a kitchen area. There was a fridge, stove and sink. It was always nice and warm inside the cabin. Down below were two sets of bunk beds in a very confined area. This is where Dave, Wayne and I slept. Captain Ron slept on the floor upstairs.

Ten minutes after we left the marina, I started to get seasick. I should have taken the Dramamine much earlier than I did. I went down below and laid on one of the bottom bunk beds. After laying there for about fifteen minutes, it just kept getting worse and worse. I felt like I was going to throw up, so I went to the toilet. I was down on my hands and knees, dry heaving for quite some time. I was so sick! I was literally praying for the good Lord to come and take me with him. I couldn't tolerate this anymore. Dave came and checked on me, to make sure that I was going to be OK. My whole body felt out of whack. I started to worry about my blood sugar levels and my diabetes. I thought that Captain Ron might have to rush me back to shore and get me to a hospital. It was brutal. I just wanted to die right then and there. At the same time, I was really hoping I didn't have to go back to shore because I didn't want to spoil everyone's fishing excursion — especially on the first day! After about forty-five minutes at that toilet, I managed to go up top and sit at the table. I was still extremely nauseated. Captain Ron stuck something behind one of my ears to help alleviate my sea sickness, which worked like a miracle. It was some kind of patch. Within an hour or so, I felt much better. It was such a relief! I kept the patch on that night and the following three days and felt fine for the rest of our trip.

Feeling much better that first night, I turned into a bit of an entertainer. I was telling some stories and was just being my goofy self. I had Dave and Wayne laughing their heads off. I was on a roll for quite a long time. We were all in tears laughing, and we really had a great time together. We stayed up until past midnight.

Wayne and I had never met each other before this trip, so when Dave invited me, he told me a little bit about Wayne and said the three of us would be "a good fit." He was right. Wayne and I got along well right from the start, and the three of us jelled perfectly. Wayne was just a few years older than Dave and I. Captain Ron was a decent guy too. When four men are together in the small confines of a boat twenty-four hours a day for four consecutive days, you all better get along or those four days will seem like four months!

We did some serious fishing. On the second and third day of our trip, Dave and Wayne fished from 6 a.m.-8 p.m. — fourteen hours of fishing. I fished from 7 a.m.-8 p.m. but took a nap in the afternoons. I still fished for about eleven hours a day, which was a marathon for me. We caught a ton of fish, the majority of which were chinook salmon. We also caught quite a number of halibut, ling cod and red snapper. Many of our salmon were over twenty pounds, and I caught the biggest chinook: twenty-eight pounds!

Halibut can weigh several hundreds of pounds, but the ones we caught were much smaller — about 15-25 pounds. The ling cod were approximately 10-20 pounds, and our largest red snapper was about 15-20 pounds. All these fish put up quite a fight, and I found the salmon and halibut gave me the biggest struggle. Trying to reel in a salmon that is over twenty pounds was incredibly exciting. Fishing like this was a real thrill for me!

The worst part for me was that there weren't any chairs or anything to sit down on while we were fishing for all those hours. We had to stand up the whole time, which was really hard on my back. It hurt like hell, and after four days my back was fried.

At one spot, Ron pulled up some crab traps full of pretty large crabs. He took some out and cooked them up for our dinner. Then he made crab soup with the rest. It was delicious!

We were fishing pretty far north. At one point, we were only about forty miles from the Alaska border. The weather was chilly, but we were all dressed for it, and it didn't rain during our trip. Overall, the conditions were pretty good. We didn't have to endure any rough waters, and I didn't get seasick again.

One evening, Dave was going to BBQ some steaks on the back deck. When he started the BBQ there was a loud "hissing" noise — a major propane leak! It scared the shit out of me! I thought we were all going to get blown to pieces. "What a way to die!" I thought. Luckily, Dave was right on the ball. He turned off the propane tank immediately, and the hissing noise stopped. I felt like he had saved the day. Obviously, there was a significant hole in the apparatus that connected the propane tank to the barbeque, so if a flame from the barbeque had ignited that leaking propane, it could have been a disaster. Instead, Dave calmly took the steaks inside and cooked them in a frying pan on the stove. These steaks were massive — they were like Fred Flintstone steaks! They were high quality, and Dave cooked them perfectly. We had all the trimmings to go with it — quite a feast.

We stayed up until about midnight talking and telling stories and jokes for the first three nights. Dave and Wayne had a few beers, and I drank my non-alcohol beers. Mainly, we just socialized, with Captain Ron always nearby. He would have a beer or two, but he didn't drink very much. He had the responsibility of managing his fifty-foot boat and was responsible for our safety as well.

On our final day, we fished until about 6 p.m. and then headed back to Haida Gwaii. It was another thrilling and very successful day of fishing. Another good thing was that Ron cleaned all the fish we caught. The fish were kept on ice in a big cooler on the back deck of the boat.

We stayed in a motel that night with Dave and I sharing a room again. Our room had a beautiful view overlooking the ocean. It felt great to have a shower and to sleep in a normal bed. The next morning after breakfast, Ron picked us up at the motel and drove us to the marina where his boat was. We took some good pictures of each other holding some of the fish we caught. The salmon was very impressive. (I also recorded some of our fishing with a video camera from the boat.) We flew from Haida Gwaii back to Vancouver. From there, Dave flew to Anchorage, Alaska, where he did some more fishing. Wayne flew back to Edmonton, and I flew back to Kelowna. I slept a lot the next four days. I was totally wasted after this trip. I simply wasn't used to going at that kind of pace. I was exhausted, but I'm sure glad I went.

Ron made arrangements to leave all of our fish in Haida Gwaii at a fish processing plant, and we had our salmon filleted, smoked and canned. The halibut, ling cod and red snapper were filleted. Our fish was flash frozen and delivered in coolers by courier directly to our homes about three weeks later. We each received one hundred pounds of fish. Elli and I don't have a deep freeze, so we kept our fish in a friend's deep freeze (John and Thao Kenny) who live close to us. We gladly shared some of our fish with them and with some other friends and neighbors. Elli and I appreciated having this fresh/frozen supply of fish immensely! It was absolutely delicious! Even after sharing some of it, we still had about a one-year supply.

It was really good of Dave to bring me on this trip with him and Wayne. And very generous. Dave paid for my expenses. I don't know what the total costs were, but I have a rough idea, and I know it wasn't cheap. There is no way I could have done this without his help. I really hope that someday I will be able to do something very special for him. It really was a fishing trip of a lifetime!

CHAPTER 28
2020
TODAY

I have been well for twenty years, which amazes me. The time has gone by so fast! When I was depressed, I had no hope of getting better, and each day seemed like a year. I don't miss the mania either. Being picked up by the police, committed and locked up in psych wards, and administered harsh psych meds to bring me down from being manic are things of the past. I have been balanced for a long time, and my future looks very promising.

If I can overcome this mental illness, anyone can. More than anything, I want my story to give hope to others, especially to those who have bipolar disorder, but also to their families, friends and loved ones. I also hope my story will educate others, and that it will help erase some of the stigma attached to bipolar disorder and depression.

I have overcome some major obstacles in my life. I beat alcoholism, I quit smoking after twenty-five years, and, of course, it appears I have conquered severe mental illness. Overcoming these obstacles wasn't easy, but I'm sure glad I did it! I have learned some very important life lessons — mostly the hard way. I hope that sharing my mistakes helps others make better decisions. This applies to everyone, not just to those with mental illness.

When I was younger, I believed in "love at first sight." I don't anymore. I think it's more like "lust at first sight." Lust happens very quickly, but love takes time to build and grow. To be in a relationship with someone, my top priority was that they had to be extremely good looking, which was very superficial. I didn't know what true love was until I met Elli. As of 2020, we have been together for twenty years. Elli is very attractive, but above all we remain best friends. In building our relationship, Elli has seen me totally manic and severely depressed. She knew what she was getting into when she became my partner, and I know she won't leave me if I get depressed or manic again. Love will stick with you through the bad times as well as the good ones. Lust isn't nearly as reliable.

A lesson of equal importance is to be honest with yourself and don't go into denial about behaviors that are harming you. The three main poor behaviors I had were drinking alcohol, smoking cigarettes and not looking after my mental health properly. I knew I was drinking too much. It started when I was a teenager and went on until I quit at twenty-nine. I don't think alcohol caused my mental illness, but I know it sure didn't help. My drinking got me into trouble and caused me a lot more harm than good. Quitting was in my best interest and may have been the smartest thing I've ever done. I'm proud to say I have been a "sober alcoholic" since 1994. I stopped smoking pot and hash shortly after.

I quit smoking after twenty-five years. I loved smoking and had no intention of quitting, but I had a bad "smoker's cough" and decided it was time to stop. I'm glad I did. It made other people happy too, particularly Elli, my niece, Keely, and my nephew, Roan. The kids had been encouraging me to quit for a long time. My smoker's cough is long gone. My advice is don't start smoking in the first place. It is very addictive and difficult to quit. Obviously, it's not good for your health. For one thing, it can cause cancer. It's also a very expensive, bad habit.

In the beginning, I was in denial about my diagnosis with manic depression. I didn't take it seriously. Neither did my family. After my fourth manic episode (and fourth trip to the psych ward) in 1995, I finally realized I should start taking this matter very seriously. I hadn't seen a psychiatrist or taken psychiatric medications on a regular basis. I was finally put on the right combination of psych meds in 2000 and have been well ever since. I am totally compliant with taking my medication.

I have learned the importance of keeping my stress factors to a minimum. My lifestyle and living environment is conducive to my wellness and my mental health. In large part, I have taken the responsibility of taking good care of myself.

Because of my mental-health issues, I can't work at a "normal" job. But, thankfully, I am able to write, as long as I can go at my own pace without being pressured by anyone.

WHAT ABOUT THE "SPIRIT WORLD"?

As humans, we identify ourselves in a physical sense. Many people (including me) believe we originate from heaven. It makes sense to me that in heaven (or the spirit world in general), spirits/souls identify each other as such and get to know each other. We are mind, body, spirit/soul, psyche and consciousness. We have the ability to sense (and communicate) with other spirits. This includes spirits that are residing in the spiritual realm and ones that are incarnated into a physical/human person. I believe in reincarnation, and that most of us have lived many lifetimes on Earth but don't remember them. Between lifetimes we go back to heaven. We have one soul for eternity.

Most of our souls have resided in heaven or the spiritual realm for a lot longer than we've been humans.

While I was in a state of mania, my inner core (spirit) sensed the presence of God, the devil or "regular" spirits residing in the spiritual realm and through other human beings living in the earthly realm. It's not about "Don Walin," it's about "spirit sensing spirit." Several symptoms of mania put me in a state of consciousness whereby I thought I was God and Jesus. At the same time, I always knew I was still Don Walin. (My psychiatrist said this is very important.)

Most people haven't had the types of "spiritual experiences" I've had. Many are simply non-believers or skeptics to begin with. One percent of the population is bipolar. Two percent of those people have thought they were Jesus Christ, and less than one percent of those have thought they were God. The fact that I have thought I was both God and Jesus is even more rare. I believe I reached a state of enlightenment. Because of my spiritual experiences, I became very interested in this phenomenon. Over the last twenty years, I have gained insight and knowledge in this regard, mainly by reading many spiritual books. I have combined my spiritual knowledge with my extensive personal experience with mania and spirituality and formed my own theory as to how these things are all interconnected. I have always believed that my spiritual encounters were genuine and authentic. At the same time, I was diagnosed as being delusional and psychotic by many psychiatrists over a ten-year period.

I was close to finishing writing this book when something important happened to me. I will never forget the date: July 16, 2018. Dr. Diaz and I talked for over an hour. We've had many great conversations over the years and have talked quite extensively about my spiritual experiences. I often write down several notes and questions for him for our meetings. I had five pages of notes prepared for this particular day. During our conversation, I articulated my experiences better than I ever had with him. I told him I thought the same reasons applied to other people who are bipolar and thinking they are God and/or Jesus. I explained my "Mania Spirit Theory" to Dr. Diaz.

MY "MANIA SPIRIT THEORY" SYMPTOMS OF MANIA

- Increased energy (physically, emotionally, mentally and psychically).
- Enhancement of one's senses (including our sixth/psychic sense, sensing energy).
- Heightened awareness.
- Increased perception.

- Elevated state of consciousness (sensing the spiritual realm, becoming one with God and Jesus).
- Mental telepathy (communicating with spirit).

Several symptoms of my mania enabled me to get into a state of consciousness whereby I could sense the presence of other spirits/entities. These same symptoms of mania put me in a state of consciousness whereby I thought I was God and Jesus.

SPIRITUAL BELIEFS

Every book I've read about spirituality has been very consistent with regard to people's beliefs towards this subject. The following list includes some of the main beliefs.

- There is a universal collective consciousness.
- We are mind, body, spirit/soul, psyche and consciousness.
- Everything in the universe is energy.
- God is the creator and is in every living thing.
- God and Jesus are in all of us.
- The Trinity exists (The Father, Son and Holy Spirit).
- We are all part of one.
- God is love.
- In a sense, we are God.
- Christ Consciousness means becoming one with the Christ within us.

I agree with all of these beliefs, which helps explain why I (and others) thought we were God and Jesus when in a state of mania. Our consciousness became a part of one with them.

As I was explaining my theory to Dr. Diaz, he was extremely interested and appeared somewhat fascinated. When I finished talking, he said to me, "I don't think you are delusional." That meant a lot to me. It validated my beliefs and gave me some reassurance. And it felt great! Maybe I'm not so crazy after all?!

Dr. Diaz has been my psychiatrist for almost twenty years. We have a good relationship, and I like him. I only see him twice a year now and have never really needed any psychological advice from him. Mainly, he makes sure I'm doing okay and monitors my Clozapine level. We usually talk for close to an hour, and I think we both enjoy our conversations. Dr. Diaz is extremely intelligent and is humble. He has compassion and is a nice man. What I like most about him is his open mindedness and willingness to discuss spiritual matters with me. He is quite knowledgeable about this topic, and it helps me to be able to talk with someone who has an understanding of my spiritual encounters. I think Dr. Diaz is a good psychiatrist, and I always look forward to seeing him. He's never had to treat me when I've been in a state of mania or severely depressed, but I think I would be in good hands under his care if I ever happen to go down that road again.

Through my mania and depression, it has felt like my brain has been twisted, bent and stretched to the outer limits. My mind has been tormented a great deal. I have endured the pain and suffering that manic depression has put me through. I have been through the depths of hell and have experienced a taste of heaven.

How to Treat People with a Mental Illness

People understand and have compassion when someone's heart, lungs or liver are failing them. What about the brain? Why don't they perceive someone with a chemical imbalance, such as bipolar disorder, the same way? People are quick to have compassion towards others who have a physical injury or ailment like a broken leg or cancer. We identify with this readily. We automatically feel sorry for them and are sympathetic towards them. This is what should happen with mental illness as well.

Why is it so different with mental health? Far too often, there are negative aspects associated with mental illness that aren't accurate or are just completely false. People can be very ignorant, and the general public needs to be educated regarding this matter. There is way too much stigma associated with mental illness. People who have a mental illness shouldn't be criticized or blamed by anyone else. And we shouldn't feel embarrassed, ashamed or disgraced because we have this illness. We didn't ask to get our mental illness, just like others didn't ask to get that broken leg or cancer. Someone with a mental illness should be treated like any other decent human being on Earth: with dignity and respect. Having some empathy and compassion for them would be nice.

CHAPTER 29
THANK YOU FOR RIDING ALONG WITH ME!

I feel like my life has been one very long emotional roller coaster ride. I've had so many ups and downs, twists and turns. A lot of times I was just hanging on for dear life! I'm grateful I had the perseverance to get through the difficult times, and that I've made it this far.

It has taken me approximately ten years to write this book, with the majority of it written in the last two years. Besides beating severe manic depression, bringing this book to fruition is by far the most difficult thing I've ever done. My desire, determination and dedication toward this project are key elements I needed to accomplish my goal of becoming an author. Over the course of writing my book, I have gained a new appreciation towards authors — this isn't easy! Writing a book can take several years and be very challenging, and it would be quite difficult for the average person to write a book. Writing my book while having to deal with three mental illnesses has been very difficult, so I'm glad I was able to hang in there and complete this task.

Thank you so much for buying my book and for taking the time to read it. I hope you enjoyed it. This is a tremendous honor for me. I have an immense appreciation for your interest in my writing and toward my life story, including my battle with mental illness. I hope I was able to give you some insight as to what it's like living with manic depression (bipolar disorder), obsessive-compulsive disorder (OCD) and seasonal affective disorder (SAD). Hopefully, my story has enlightened you and has answered some questions you may have had.

As you should know by now, I love humor. I hope I've been able to make you laugh and/or smile a few times along the way. I believe things happen for a reason, especially the major events in our lives. In short, I believe my fate and destiny were pre-determined, and that my life has happened the way it was meant to. Writing this book and sharing my story with you is a major factor in my life journey.

Being a writer is a lot different than being a golf pro. Working at golf courses, I would interact with up to two hundred people a day. It was a very social job and brought out the extrovert in me. It was an exciting atmosphere to work in and was a lot of fun. As an instructor, it was rewarding to help people improve their golf game. I loved playing golf and competing in tournaments.

I write in solitude. Just me, a pen and a notebook. My state of mind becomes very much introverted. I don't talk with anyone else when I'm writing. I get focused and get into my own little world. I lose track of time when I'm writing. I wish I could say that writing is fun, but it's not. At least not for me. It's hard work and takes my full focus and concentration. And it takes a tremendous amount of thought. I think very carefully about almost every word I write down. Because of this, it's very time consuming. It boils down to a lot of time and effort!

My reward for writing this book is to help others. My number one goal is to give hope and inspiration to as many people as possible. I want to encourage everyone to realize that if "The Crazy Golf Pro" can conquer manic depression, anyone can.

A few tips from a "pro"!

The End.

A LOT OF NICE GOLF PROS

I loved my occupation as a CPGA Golf Professional. It was kind of like a dream job for me. But if you have read my story, you will realize that I had some bad luck when it came to working for and with other pros. A lot of this came down to "personality conflicts." This was very stressful for me and contributed towards my mental illness.

Working as a golf professional is like any other occupation. Working for and with the right people can make your job a very enjoyable experience. The wrong ones can turn a dream job into a nightmare. I just wish I would have worked with the type of golf pros whom I liked and got along well with. My advice is that when you are seeking employment, know who you are getting involved with and choose carefully.

Despite my work experiences, I have gotten to know several golf pros I liked a lot. There are over 3,700 CPGA Golf Professionals in Canada and close to 30,000 PGA Golf Professionals in the United States. There are many other professional golf associations around the world.

In fairness, a large number of these golf pros would be nice people.

INDEX

delusional x, xi, 9, 12, 133, 143, 181,
    182, 199, 204, 206, 208, 225,
    240, 244, 249, 274, 275
delusions of grandeur 7
denial 15, 134, 187, 272, 273
Denny Andrews Nightclub 76, 141
depressed xi, 33, 101, 102, 103, 104,
    106, 130, 133, 135, 137, 147,
    161, 187, 202, 216, 217, 218,
    220, 221, 222, 223, 224, 227,
    228, 232, 242, 262, 263, 266,
    272, 276
depression ix, x, xi, 14, 15, 99, 101,
    102, 103, 104, 133, 134, 135,
    136, 137, 139, 140, 143, 147,
    148, 160, 182, 187, 188, 202,
    206, 215, 221, 222, 223, 224,
    227, 228, 241, 242, 243, 253,
    255, 262, 263, 264, 265, 266,
    272, 273, 276, 277, 278
Derrick Golf & Winter Club 46
Desert Hills Golf Club 72, 73
Desipramine 242, 243
Devil x, xi, 180, 181, 182, 183, 196,
    197, 198, 202, 203, 208, 214,
    215, 218, 219, 226, 227, 249,
    258, 274
diabetes 264, 269
Dial-A-Bottle 88, 89
Diaz, Dr. Fernando 290
Dickson, Scott 7, 92, 93
Dougherty, Tim 143
Dragon 198, 230
Dramamine 268, 269
Drayton Valley, Alberta 27, 35, 36
DUI (driving under the influence) 61,
    70, 71
Dzaman, Lance 51

E

Eastcott, Bruce 48
ECT (Electro Convulsive Therapy)
    227, 228
ECT treatments 228

Edmonton Country Club 24, 89, 141,
    142, 143
Edmonton Fire Department 117, 118, 176
Edmonton Oilers ix, 28, 45, 46, 68,
    125, 141
ego 111, 127, 190
electromagnetic 204
elevated state of consciousness 275
Elk Island Golf Course 86
Encinitas, California 61, 66, 67, 68,
    69, 170
energy x, 9, 134, 141, 143, 147, 181,
    195, 204, 211, 222, 225, 226,
    242, 274, 275
enhanced "psychic" awareness 204
Eric Martin Pavilion 14, 15, 102
Escondido, California 55, 56
euphoric 7, 8, 104, 145
evil 8, 9, 197, 204, 226

F

Fairbanks Ranch Country Club 61
Fipke, Chuck 254
Flett, Bill (Cowboy) 45, 46
flight of ideas 12
Flockhart, Ron 48
Fonteyne, Cathy 30, 32
Fonteyne, Dean 32
Fonteyne, Val 32
Fort McMurray, Alberta 107, 116, 117,
    120, 121, 122, 123, 125, 126,
    127, 130, 132
Fox, Michael J. 47, 64
Fuhr, Grant 47, 140, 141, 142, 143

G

Gemini 18, 34, 198, 230
genius 12, 47, 144
Geopfrich, Jack 52, 64
Gibson, Rick 3
Glen Meadows Golf & Country Club
    1, 12, 14, 89, 91, 171, 172

Kelowna General Hospital (KGH)
203, 205, 207, 226, 228, 229, 261
Kenny, John 178
Kenny, Thao 271, 289
Knickerson, Doc 127
Koral, Linda 79
Kurri, Jari 47

L

Labatt's Pro-Am 46
Lacombe Golf & Country Club 22, 27
La Costa Golf Resort 62
La Jolla, California 56, 64
Lake Okanagan 243, 245, 249, 251, 252
Lake Okanagan Resort 245, 249
Lambert, Alec 35, 37
Lambert, Bernice 37
Lambert, Dave 14, 35, 56, 74, 150
Lambert, Ralph 36, 37
Latimer, Dr. Paul 229
Leach, Kevin 6
Lecuyer, Doug 2
Lecuyer, Gary 46
Letterman, David 207
Leucadia, California 57, 58
Licensed Practical Nurse (LPN) 220, 243
Lindley, Roxanne 251
lithium 225
Loewen, Dr. Linda 219
Lord Beaverbrook High School 33,
34, 167
Lowe, Kevin 100, 101, 234
Lucifer x, 226

M

MacDonald, B.J. (Blair) 28
MacDonald Island Recreational
Facility 107
MacDonald, Ken 212
MacKay, John 248
MacLeod, Ron 82, 105
Macleod Trail 145, 146
magic mushrooms 36
magnets 212, 213, 215

Mahovlic, Doug 3, 89
Mandell, Howie 256
mania x, xi, 4, 7, 8, 9, 12, 101, 137, 140,
144, 145, 146, 147, 186, 187, 204,
213, 215, 227, 236, 240, 242, 250,
255, 272, 274, 275, 276
Mania Spirit Theory (My) 240, 274
manic ix, x, xi, 2, 3, 4, 5, 6, 7, 9, 12, 14,
15, 16, 38, 97, 99, 102, 103, 104,
106, 123, 134, 137, 139, 140,
141, 142, 143, 144, 145, 147,
148, 157, 160, 161, 181, 182,
184, 186, 187, 191, 193, 195,
197, 198, 199, 202, 203, 205,
206, 207, 208, 211, 213, 214,
216, 218, 219, 220, 221, 222,
225, 227, 229, 230, 231, 232,
234, 235, 237, 238, 239, 240,
241, 242, 244, 247, 249, 250,
253, 263, 264, 265, 266, 272,
273, 276, 277, 278
manic depression ix, x, xi, 14, 15, 99,
102, 104, 134, 139, 140, 143,
160, 182, 206, 241, 253, 263,
265, 273, 276, 277, 278
manic episode x, xi, 4, 7, 38, 103, 106,
123, 139, 140, 142, 145, 147,
148, 186, 187, 193, 197, 199,
202, 203, 221, 242, 264, 273
manic grandiosity 12
manic promiscuity 5, 232
manic spending spree 16, 203
marijuana 33
Mayes, Dave 158
McCulloch Orchard Greens
Golf Club 194
McDonald, Darrell 42, 48, 55, 116
McKercher, Dr. Catherine 208
McNair Unit 203, 206, 207, 217, 219,
224, 229
McSorley, Marty 47
Meeker, Howie 128
mental health xi, 188, 200, 232, 233,
239, 245, 272, 273, 276

mental-health advocate lawyer 232, 233, 239
mental illness iv, ix, x, xi, 3, 30, 37, 97, 99, 104, 116, 137, 150, 152, 158, 187, 193, 195, 200, 216, 220, 221, 222, 230, 231, 234, 240, 243, 253, 263, 265, 272, 273, 276, 277, 279
mental institution 183
mentally ill 14, 97, 99, 143, 145, 146, 183, 184, 188, 196, 200, 205, 206, 218, 230, 238, 241
mental telepathy 211, 275
Mercer, Lilli 289
Merlin's Nightclub 5, 97, 98
Messier, Mark ix, 47, 49, 64, 99, 100
metaphysics 208
Metformin 264
Meyers, Gary 49, 82
Michaelbrook Ranch Golf Club 193
Mickelson, Phil 51, 52
Midnapore 34, 35, 145
Mid-Niter Drug Store 41, 49
Millwoods Golf Course 116, 117, 144, 149
Miskanaw Golf & Country Club 107, 116, 121, 128
Mitchell, Kim 150
Mohler, Mike ix, 129
Montreal Canadiens 17, 64, 65, 66, 127
mood disorder x, 103, 104, 137, 258, 263
mood stabilizer 225, 242
Morinville, Alberta 183, 199
Morris, Johnny 117, 176, 290
Mowatt, Johnny 143
Murray, Kelly 1, 2, 123
music 58, 63, 67, 85, 109, 125, 144, 147, 160, 161, 191, 196, 224, 237

N

Nakamura, Ken 251
National Aeronautics and Space Administration (NASA) 210
Nelford, Jim 94

New Orleans, Louisiana 160
New York Rangers 101
Nicklaus, Jack 3, 62, 63, 97, 98, 99, 172, 203, 204
Nicklaus, Jack Jr. 97, 98
Noel, Robert 53, 63
Norman, Greg 62, 75
Norman, Ron 30
Novis, Joe 53, 55, 170

O

obsessive-compulsive disorder (OCD) ix, 234, 256, 277
O'Doul's non-alcohol beer 48
Okanagan Golf Club 249
Okanagan Lake 190, 220, 224, 225
Okanagan Valley 105, 108, 110, 115, 221
Oprah 47
Otto, Dr. William 144
ouzo 36, 49, 66, 100

P

Palm Springs, California 68
paranoid delusions 145, 230
paranormal 181, 197
Parker, Steve 96, 97, 175
Penn Hall 235, 236
Penny, Bill 143
Pepsi Juvenile Golf Championship 23
Peptalk 216, 217, 218
PGA Assistant Golf Professional 78, 97
PGA Head Golf Professional 209
PGA Tour 6, 25, 44, 51, 52, 62, 75, 80, 96, 123, 149
phenomena 72
Phillips, Rod 28
physical senses 9
physics 22, 204, 208
physiotherapist 10
Pifer, Joyce 196, 197
police 11, 12, 15, 16, 30, 61, 70, 71, 145, 146, 147, 182, 183, 184, 185, 197, 198, 199, 202, 218, 238, 272

possessed 94, 258

pot 33, 36, 45, 49, 57, 109, 264, 273

practice 3, 21, 22, 45, 66, 96, 111, 125,
131, 190, 209, 216, 227, 244, 248

Prince, Jerry 180

professional golfer 2, 80, 96, 99, 122,
141, 149

promiscuous 148, 232

Provost, Keith 41

Provost, Leone 41

psychiatric institution 199

psychiatric medications (psych meds)
4, 15, 102, 145, 161, 186, 199,
213, 221, 222, 227, 238, 243,
258, 263, 264, 273

psychiatric nurse (psych nurse) 13

psychiatric ward (psych ward) x, 14,
38, 144, 146, 196, 201, 203, 206,
207, 215, 216, 222, 229, 232,
238, 259

psychiatrist xi, 9, 13, 14, 102, 144, 161,
183, 186, 187, 204, 208, 217,
219, 222, 226, 227, 229, 231,
232, 233, 239, 240, 241, 242,
256, 263, 264, 273, 274, 275

psychiatry 219, 229

psychic 9, 204, 274

psychic realm 9

psychological 22, 104, 134, 137, 221,
222, 275

psychologist 102

psychosis x, 143, 181, 182, 199, 204, 240

psychotic x, 204, 234, 240, 274

putting 6, 20, 21, 24, 34, 44, 45, 46, 53,
54, 80, 82, 135, 149, 234, 239,
248, 258

Q

quantum physics 204, 208

Queen Charlotte Islands 268

R

racing thoughts 12

Rancho Bernardo Golf Resort 63, 65

Rancho Santa Fe, California 51

Rancho Santa Fe Golf Club 69

Registered Practical Nurse (RPN) 243

Reinmuth, Dean 52

relapse 231, 250, 253, 264

review panel form 232, 233

review panel hearing 233, 239

Riggin, Pat 79

Risperdal xi, 186, 227, 242

ritual 257, 266

Riverside Golf Club 23, 78

Riverview Psychiatric Hospital 229,
230, 238

Rocking Horse Saloon 158

Rock Star ix, 48, 49, 168, 192, 236, 266

Rodman, Dennis 204

Rose's Pub 203, 205

Rotary Beach Park 220, 224, 225

Rotary Classic Golf Classic 121, 122

Royal Canadian Mounted Police
(RCMP) 30, 125, 183

Royal Jubilee Hospital 14

Rudolph, Dick 62

Ruff, Lindy 28

Rusty Pelican 64, 65

Rutledge, Jim 94, 95

S

SAD light (seasonal affective disorder)
221, 266

San Diego, California 50

San Diego Golf Academy (SDGA) ix,
50, 51, 54, 72, 78, 170, 171

Satan x, 181, 197, 198, 202

schizophrenia 200, 208, 234

Scott, Dr. 233, 239, 240

seasonal affective disorder (SAD) ix, 277

security guards 12, 144, 230

sedated 4, 15, 116, 144, 186

sedative 13, 145, 227, 242

Segal, Dr. Ben 187

Semenko, Dave ix, 46, 47

sensation 51, 181, 195, 204, 208, 214,
218, 225, 228

ACKNOWLEDGEMENTS

In order to get my book published, I am most grateful for the help of my wife, Elli. My book project wouldn't have come to fruition without her. I wrote my book the old fashioned way: with a pen and a notebook. I'm also not very savvy with the computer. Elli did a lot of typing, and she formatted my writing into a manuscript that could be presented to publishers. She did a very professional job of this.

Elli's sister, Lilli Mercer, typed up the majority of my manuscript. She did a great job and was a huge help. Elli and Lilli have been my two biggest supporters throughout this whole process.

I had my book self-published, and we didn't have the money to pay for this. I wouldn't have been able to complete this project without the generous offer to pay for the publishing costs from my good friend Dave Lambert, of Aspen Creek Investments Ltd., whom I've known since 1980. I'm grateful for his help and for his team members June Yan, Matt Enns and Eyun Soon. Dave has played a huge role in helping me accomplish my dream of becoming a published author. His financial help was crucial in all of this, but Dave has also been a great moral support every step of the way. He's been steadfast with his encouragement and support.

When I finished writing my manuscript, I realized I had twice as much material as I needed (and wanted). The editing process involved cutting out a lot of words. I would have liked to have written a lot more about several of my friends, but this just wasn't possible. I didn't realize until I started editing my manuscript that I wrote very little about some of my friends, and even worse, that I had left out others altogether. For those people who fall into this category, I sincerely apologize to you. I will try to make amends by including your name in this section of my book! I would like to give a very special thank you to John and Thao Kenny. We met in 2008 and became very close friends. John moved to Canada from Ireland, and Thao moved here from Vietnam. Neither one of them have family close by, and when their son, Leo, was born, Elli and I became Oma and Opa, one set of substitute grandparents for Leo. Leo also has a second set of substitute grandparents, Richard and Cathy Nygren, known as Grampa and Nana. Leo is already eight years old, and we're proud to have him as our grandson. John and Thao are kind, caring, thoughtful and generous people. The Kennys have been very supportive towards my book project. John was good enough to accompany me to Victoria when I met some of the Tellwell team (my publishers) in August 2019. This was a very important time, and it was a big help to have my buddy right there with me for support through the process. That three-day trip was very memorable and enjoyable.

There have only been a few people outside of my family who have stuck with me throughout the years I have been battling mental illness. Johnny Morris, Jack Thomson, and Norm and Lisa Claffey always stayed in touch with me and never gave up on me. They saw me when I was very ill, but their friendship never wavered. Johnny is a retired captain of the Edmonton Fire Department. He's a great guy and has the best sense of humor of anyone I know. Jack is a former roommate and, sadly, passed away in January 2020 after losing his battle with cancer. Norm was a roommate while attending the San Diego Golf Academy. They are all from Edmonton.

Other special friends include Alex Kalinowski (a financial consultant) from Edmonton and Larry Webb. Larry is a consultant in the oil industry. He lives in Costa Rica and has been working in Saudi Arabia for several years. I have known all of these people for over thirty years.

Another person I have had the pleasure to get to know in more recent years is Jack McCarty, who lives in Red Deer, Alberta. Jack's another great guy and has been one of my biggest supporters towards getting my book published.

There are many others who are important to me including Linda Clark, John Copeland, Kathy McNeil, Mary Morris, Jeanette Moser and Steve (Tex) Parker. I apologize for not keeping in touch with most of you better over the years, but all of you have been good friends to me, which I really appreciate.

I would like to thank my doctors. First, I want to thank my psychiatrist, Dr. Fernando Diaz. I've been one of his patients for almost twenty years. I like Dr. Diaz, and we have formed a good relationship. He has never seen me mentally ill, neither manic or severely depressed. If this ever happened, I would be in good hands under his care.

I would also like to give a shout out to my former GP, Dr. Ronald Mark Corbett, who was my family doctor for many years before he retired. Dr. Corbett was an excellent doctor, and we got along very well. He even came to see me every time I ended up in the McNair Unit (psych ward) at the Kelowna General Hospital. I missed him when he retired.

After Dr. Corbett, my current GP is Dr. Florin Covaser. He had big shoes to fill. I've been one of his patients for over ten years now. Thanks Dr. Covaser.

FAMILY

I would like to express my gratitude towards Elli's immediate and extended family members. Thank you for accepting me and allowing me to become a part of your family. All of you have been very good to me. I was never an "I Love You" guy until I learned how to be from Elli and you guys. You are a very "loving" family.

Thank you to Elli's brothers, Erich and Walter Bachmann. Also, to my nephews Dale Mercer and Darrell Bachmann (Lilli's sons). I have become close with Darrell's family. This includes his wife, Colleen, and their four children (my great nieces and nephews), Baylee Bonnell, Mason, Keely and Roan Bachmann. I've also gotten to know Colleen's parents well (Vic and Margaret Ann Fast). Margaret Ann has been interested in my book project for a long time and has always encouraged me. Thank you for your support.

Darrell is an avid golfer and good player. He has a good understanding of the game, and I enjoy "talking golf" with him. Several years ago, he invented an excellent product called "Kickspike," a retractable metal spike device that is attached onto the bottom sole of various types of footwear, such as work boots, in order for the user to get better traction on slippery surfaces such as snow and ice. It works great! I've never seen anyone work as hard as Darrell in order to make his dream a success. Check out his website, www.kickspike.com, to learn more.

A special thank you to Darrell's business partner, Sab Ravalli. Sab most generously offered to purchase 140 copies of my book to put into gift bags for all the golfers playing in his company's golf tournament in Toronto, Ontario.

Andrea and Desni Bachmann and Tyler Kraft have always been good to me as well. Thanks guys.

THE WALIN BROTHERS

I want to take this opportunity to thank my four brothers. My oldest brother, Doug, second oldest Jim, followed by the twins Gary and Rick. You guys have always been there for me, especially during my most difficult times. Every time I ended up in the psych ward, you guys were right there in a heartbeat. No hesitation whatsoever. Nothing like the Walin brothers having your back! I think the relationships between all five of us are the epitome of unconditional love. I certainly love all of you and feel extremely lucky to have you as my brothers!

<u>Tellwell Publishing</u>

Thank you to the whole Tellwell team. Publishing my book is a dream come true for me! I really enjoyed working with Publishing Consultant Scott Lunn. I found him to be a real expert in the publishing business. He was extremely helpful, friendly, personable and a great communicator. He was also very generous with his time. Thanks to my project manager, Simon Page, and a special thanks to my editor, Darin Steinkey.